IMAGES
of America

AFRICAN AMERICANS OF LOWER RICHLAND COUNTY

On the Cover: The new Hopkins High School in 1954 was the first consolidated school for the Lower Richland African American students. (Barber family collection.)

IMAGES
of America

AFRICAN AMERICANS OF LOWER RICHLAND COUNTY

Marie Barber Adams and
Deborah Scott Brooks

ARCADIA
PUBLISHING

ISBN 978-0-7385-8665-6

Published by Arcadia Publishing
Charleston, South Carolina

Printed in the United States of America

Library of Congress Control Number: 2010927343

For all general information contact Arcadia Publishing at:
Telephone 843-853-2070
Fax 843-853-0044
E-mail sales@arcadiapublishing.com
For customer service and orders:
Toll-Free 1-888-313-2665

Visit us on the Internet at www.arcadiapublishing.com

We proudly dedicate this book to our parents, grandparents, and other ancestors, whose spirits have shaped and guided us on this historical journey.

Contents

Acknowledgments

The following publications provided us with most of the information we needed to organize our content so that it flowed in the same direction as the settlements in the Lower Richland area: *Lower Richland County Historical and Architectural Inventory*, a 1993 survey report for the Historic Columbia Foundation and the Sunrise Foundation and *Columbia and Richland County: A South Carolina Community, 1740–1990*, by John Hammond Moore. Dr. Robert Weyeneth and students in his Public History Program at the University of South Carolina created a community-based public history research publication entitled *Prized Pieces of Land: The Impact of Reconstruction on African American Land Ownership in Lower Richland County, South Carolina*.

John Middleton provided information about families and churches in the Lower Richland community in his research entitled *Lower Richland Black Heritage*. Brenda Clarkson Turpeau wrote a pioneering and fact-filled inspiration entitled *Almost Forgotten*. From the Mount Olive Baptist Church in Kingville, we thank George Wilson, Ada Hopkins, Portia Seymore Richardson, and other members. From Gadsden, Herbert Sims, Zack and Levola Taylor, Margaret Sims Goodwin, and Deacon Doctor Adams were generous with their family pictures. Blanch McRant McFadden and Wayne and Hazel Adams gave us pictures of their families. In Hopkins, we have a significant number of individuals to thank: Ernestine Alston, Rosa Lee James Alston, John B. Barber Jr., Jocelyn Clarkson, Caroline Forney, Eugenia Middleton Griffin, Thomas Gunter, E. Marie Jones, Ruby Robinson, and Joann L. Washington. The contributions for the Eastover chapter came from Bernice Scott, Billie Woodard, Mary Butler Walker, Allen House, and Levola Taylor. Dr. Bobby Donaldson, associate professor of history and African American studies, counseled us, provided facts, and publicly championed our projects. Our children and grandchildren provided the inspiration for us to leave a lasting legacy for them to share with future generations from Lower Richland. Our large extended families collectively accounted for a large portion of the book. Without "Uncle Johnny" Barber's phenomenal computer skills and photographic memory at age 89, we would not have been able to capture the essence of the Lower Richland community with accuracy and colorfulness. He was our tireless cheerleader! The contributions from all of these individuals made it possible for us to show the connectivity of the families in the Lower Richland Heritage Corridor.

Introduction

It is impossible to tell the whole story about the Lower Richland community and its rich history in the limitations of this book, but the following pages attempt to paint a realistic picture of the African American families intertwined and linked together like an endless stretch of railroad tracks. The book will trace the lives of families who remained on plantation lands in this area or moved to other Lower Richland villages when jobs and land became available to them during the years of Reconstruction. Families made sacrifices to secure educational opportunities for their sons and daughters after being denied the rights granted to them by the Constitution of the United States of America. Enduring slavery, discrimination, corruption, and hostility, African Americans of Lower Richland became resilient and industrious citizens and persevered!

Kingville became the largest settlement in Lower Richland around 1840, when the railroad made its way across the Wateree River into Richland County. Before the railroad was completed, goods were shipped down river to reach Charleston and other ports. Until the tracts were completed into Columbia, people who lived in the midlands of the state traveled to Kingville by horse-and-buggy, wagon, or stagecoach to pick up farm products and other goods shipped to the train depot.

As a result of the railroad construction, villages developed around each train depot and provided a stable economy in Lower Richland until the 1930s Depression years. This historic journey began in Kingville and continued to the villages of Gadsden, Weston/Congaree, Hopkins, and Eastover. What we discovered on this journey was a plethora of untold stories of unsung heroes, some disturbing and sad while others were mysterious and humorous. We are duty-bound to tell their stories through these photographs and documents, which have come from our family collections and from families and friends of the communities lovingly shared in this publication.

Many of the people we interviewed had families with roots in Kingville. A large migration occurred during the Reconstruction years, when lands formerly owned by large plantation owners were relinquished to the South Carolina Land Commission established by the legislature in 1869. South Carolina then became the only southern state to promote the redistribution of plantation land so that freed men and women could purchase plots for their own families. The majority of the former slaves were now able, for the first time in their lives, to own their land and to take advantage of this unique program. This, however, was no easy task for families who managed a living sharecropping until enough money could be saved to purchase tracts of land for farming. Gadsden, Hopkins, and Eastover became the utopia for families in Lower Richland who were seeking a place to establish a homestead. The South Carolina Land Commission offered seven tracts of property in Lower Richland County: the Adams Tract in the Old Bluff Road section of Hopkins, the Back Swamp Tract in Hopkins, the Disaker Tract in the Congaree/Weston section, the Hickory Hill Tract in Eastover, the Hopkins Tract in Hopkins, the Hunt Tract in Hopkins located within the boundaries of the Congaree National Park, and the O'Hanlon Tract in Hopkins.

Generations of families loaded up their wagons and settled on new ground, the land they purchased in lots anywhere from 6 to 108 acres each. The price per acre ranged from $3 to $13.50 for the various tracts. This was an enormous sum of money for former slaves, but family members helped each other during the planting and harvesting. Equipped with their faith in God and their physical strength, the families built homes, dug wells, planted crops, and sustained their families.

Religion played an important role in the establishment of communities throughout the area. According to the research of Rev. John Middleton, Beulah Baptist Church was the mother of all churches in Lower Richland. The church clerk recorded that two slaves were given permission to serve as deacons among the black members. When the Emancipation Proclamation ended slavery, most African American families continued to worship on alternate Sundays in the same church their former slave masters attended. This practice continued until May 14, 1866, when Shiloh Baptist Church was organized in the Weston community. For various reasons, the church became defunct, but other churches began to flourish. New Light Beulah had separated from Beulah Baptist by 1870. Zion Benevolent became established in 1871. Pilgrim Baptist Church was organized in 1873 on the Old Bluff Road. In 1872, St. John Baptist was organized near Clarkson Road alongside Cedar Creek. By 1873, Siloam was established less than half a mile from New Light Beulah. Other churches included Jerusalem and Mount Moriah, founded 1872, where again the purchasing of land became the determining factor for the establishment of each new community with a church and a school.

Churches throughout the Lower Richland Heritage Corridor provided a place of refuge and hope as well as stability for villages and communities. With almost every church building came a one- or two-room school for children of the recently freed slaves. With education came more opportunities for African Americans away from the fields and homes of former slave owners. Booker T. Washington High School, opened in 1916, was the only school in Richland County where they could complete the requirements for a diploma. Parents made the ultimate sacrifices to send their best and brightest to Columbia to attend high school and ultimately to attend Benedict College, Allen University, Morris College, and other institutions of higher learning. Others were trained to be carpenters, blacksmiths, well diggers and repairmen, truckers, midwives, nurses, veterinarians, railroad workers, barbers, cooks, and business owners with cotton gins, syrup mills, sawmills, gristmills, and general or variety goods stores.

From the glory days of Kingville, the villages of Gadsden, Weston/Congaree, Hopkins, and Eastover sprang up around train depots. Along the train tracks, families found a sense of community and anchorage in a way of life that sustained them. The railroad brought jobs to the area after a period of helplessness and hopelessness during the Civil War years and the aftermath. What a remarkable story of survival to pass on to countless generations that will follow us! While many other families are part of the dynamics of each of these Lower Richland communities, it would be a tremendous and ambitious undertaking to include all the great contributors to this heritage corridor. We hope that we have some representation of a family connection that each reader will be able to relish and cherish in this labor of love!

One

Kingville

The town of Kingville remains a mystery today, but it has a glorious past with a rich history of African American families who farmed the land, worked on the railroad, and toiled in various jobs to make it possible for future generations to get an education and make a better life for their families. When the Southern Railway Company began the monumental task of creating a railroad from Charleston to Columbia, the village of Kingville would become the birthplace of the rail system in Richland County. According to some stories passed down from local families, Kingville was a vibrant town with taverns, hotels, businesses, and homes surrounded by small and large farms.

The Kingville train depot was located 23 miles southeast of Columbia. However, the Louisville, Cincinnati, and Charleston Railroad had reached Lower Richland across the Wateree River by 1841. The Kingville station was the first to receive service in Richland County. According to Samuel M. Derrick, Kingville grew in importance as a transportation hub until February 1865, when Sherman's troops destroyed the facilities after they invaded the Richland District. They burned the depot and various outbuildings in Kingville, and they took rails from 3,000 feet of track, heated them in the middle, and twisted them around trees. The town recovered from this tragedy around 1880; however, many of the African American families had moved closer to Columbia or out of the state completely.

The town of Kingville made a significant contribution to the development of the county with successful agriculture, logging, and transportation markets. African American laborers were used to build dykes to help in the cultivation of cotton and other crops in the bottomland swamp and to build railroad maintenance facilities and stations every 10 miles from Kingville. Although Sherman's troops destroyed the railroad and the train depot, Kingville survived with families who remained on the land to eke out a living by farming and later by harvesting trees from the Congaree River area that now makes up a huge portion of the Congaree National Park.

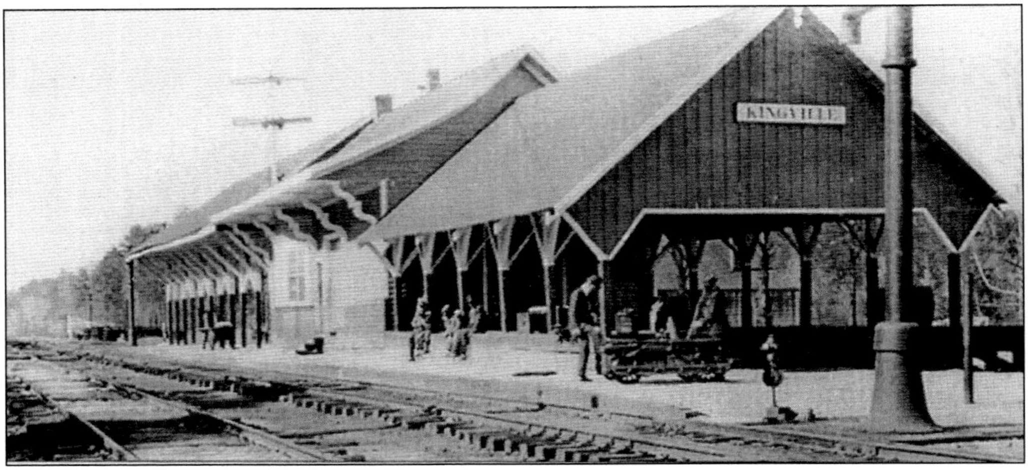

A 1917 photograph of the Kingville Train Depot was discovered recently in the *Palmetto Leader*, a South Carolina newspaper covering the colorful lives of African Americans who lived in and around the Midlands. The depot was located 23 miles southeast of Columbia and was operated by the Southern Railway Company. The Shelley Cope Store played an important role in the community in the later years. Cope, of Mount Olive Baptist Church, donated almost all of the building materials for the new church after the old sanctuary was destroyed by fire in the 1920s. (Debbie Bloom, Richland County Public Library.)

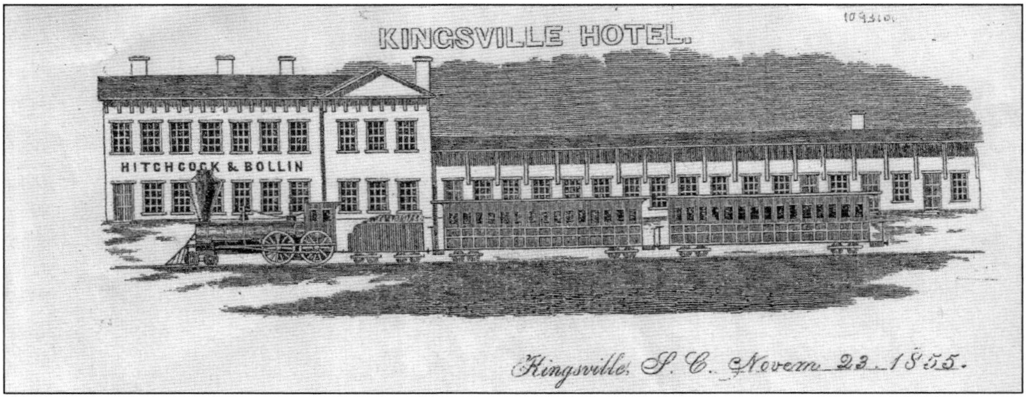

Letterhead from the Kingville Hotel provides evidence of the prosperous town of Kingville in 1855. The hotel was a resting place for passengers from various destinations along the Southern Railroad. According to a memoir written by Richard Jones, slaves built the Kingville station and the track bed for the railroad. (Debbie Bloom, Richland County Public Library.)

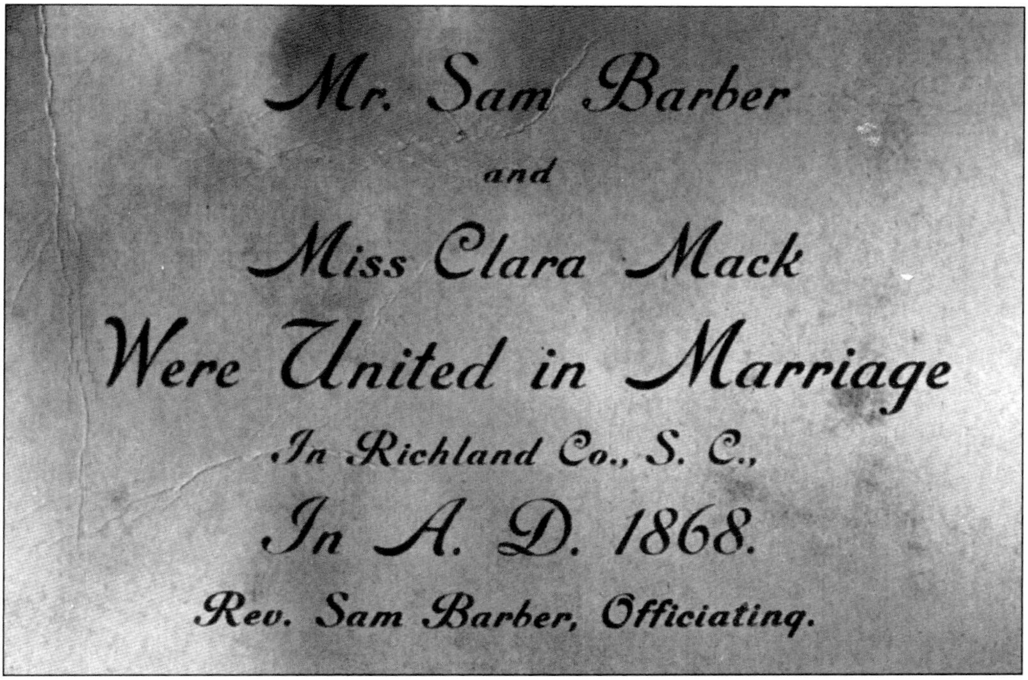

Rev. Sam Barber and his family were living in Kingville after the emancipation of slaves in this state. He officiated the marriage of his son Sam Barber and Clara (Clarissa) Mack in 1868. Sam Barber was born in Blackstone, Virginia. Sam Barber Jr. was born in 1840, but it is not known exactly where he was born. He became a well digger, learning the skill from his father. (Barber family collection.)

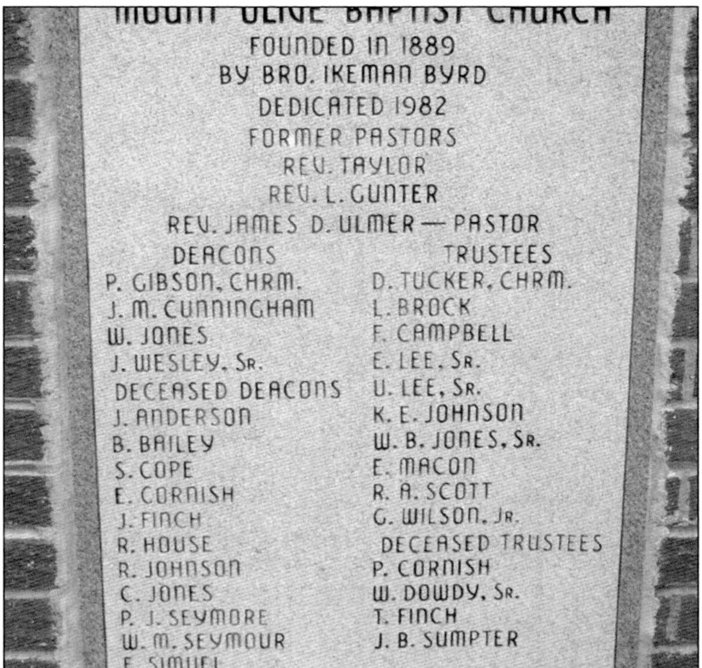

Mount Olive Baptist Church was the first church built in Kingville by members who formerly worshipped at Red Hill Baptist Church in Gadsden. The new church was first called Mount of Olives, according to the church history. Sam Taylor, Esau Simuel Jessie Reese, and Isiah Wilson were the organizers, and Ikeman Byrd was acknowledged as the founder. In August 1889, Rev. Lewis Lowman preached the first sermon. (Photograph by Deborah Scott Brooks.)

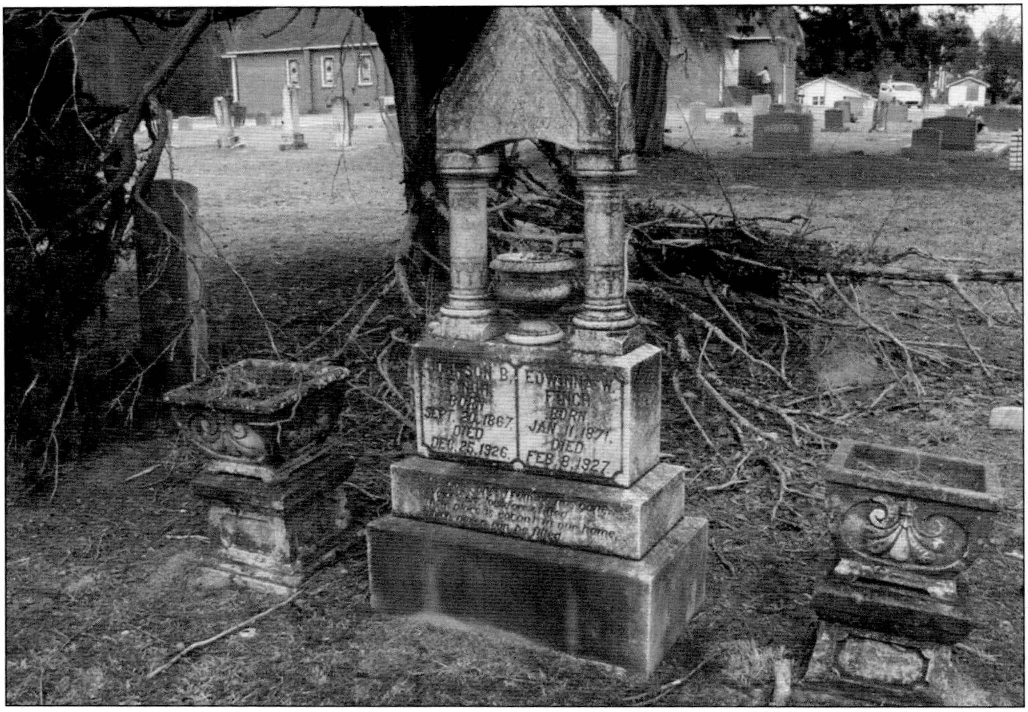

Tombstones pictured in the Mount Olive Baptist Church graveyard are those of Johnson Finch (1867–1926) and Edwinna W. Finch (1871–1927). They were the parents of Lucille Finch, born in 1893. Inspired by her aunt Amanda, she graduated from Benedict College and became a teacher at the Gadsden Graded School and later in Dillon County. During the summers, she worked in New York earning money for her family. She is fondly remembered for Christmas stockings she provided for all of the children at Mount Olive, Mount Nebo, and Pleasant Grove Churches. (Photograph by Deborah Scott Brooks.)

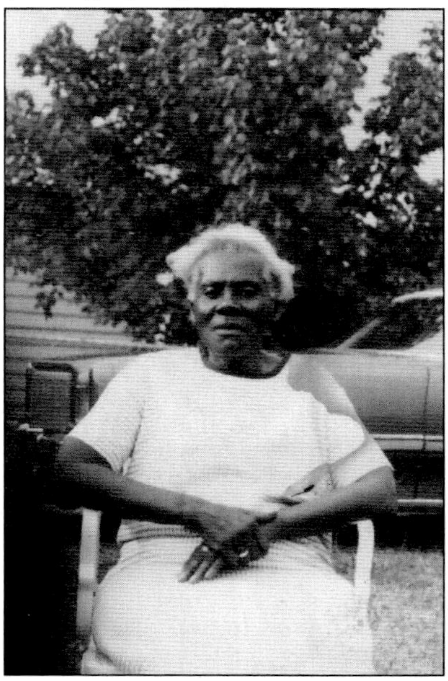

Sallie Powell Tucker was born in Richland County. She was married to Thomas Tucker, and their children were Eva, Louise, Lurline, Willie, Samuel, Ernest, and Warren. Sallie was active in the church and the community. She was a member of Mount Olive Baptist Church and the United Order of Tents of Eastover. (Cora Dowdy Scott.)

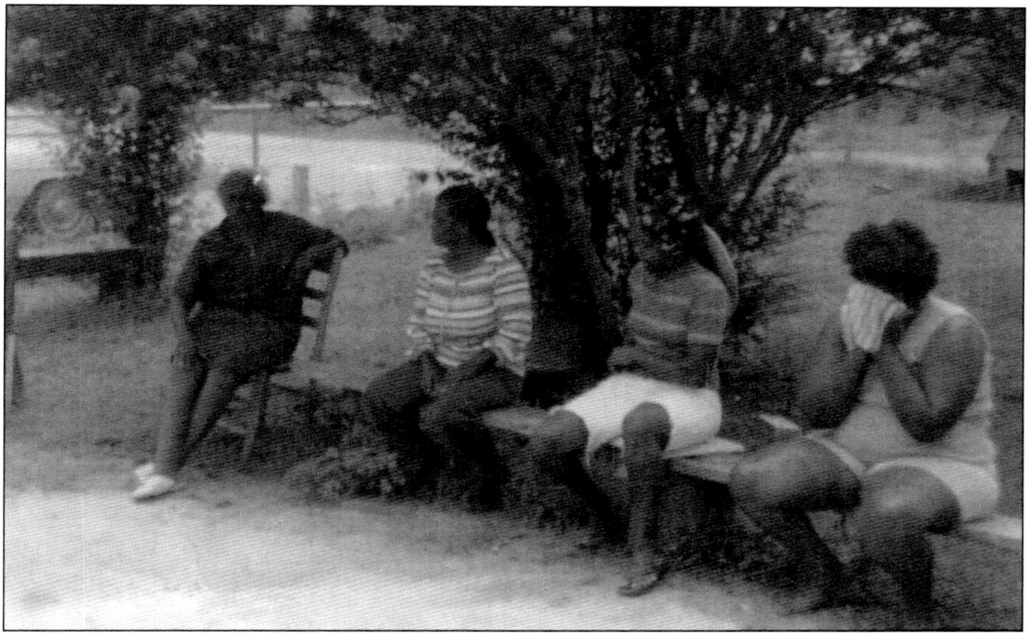

The Tucker family became active members of Mount Olive Baptist Church. A reunion of the descendants of Jimmy and Eve Ward Tucker was held in August 1997. From left to right, Sally Tucker, Rosa Lee Williams, Cora Dowdy, and Willie Mae Tucker are pictured here enjoying the peace and serenity of Kingville. (Tucker family.)

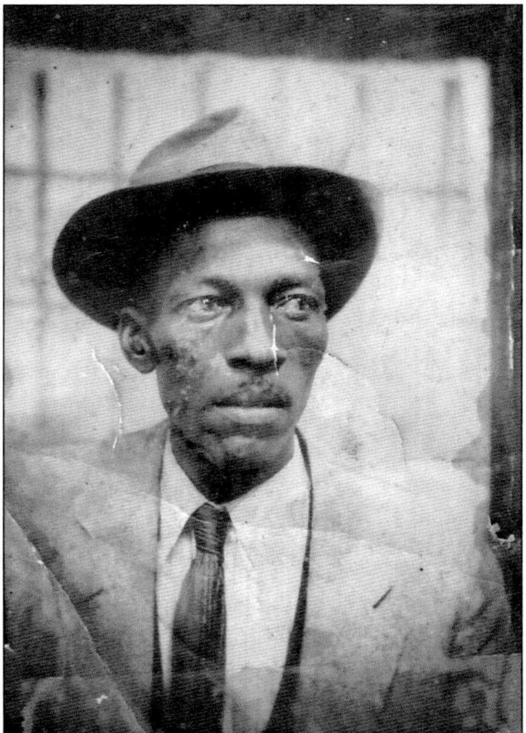

The Tucker family's roots can be traced back to James Jimmy Tucker, born 1846, and Eve Ward Tucker. They were married in 1870 and joined Red Hill Baptist Church after worshipping at Congaree Baptist Church during slavery. Their children were Hattie, Harry, Titus, Minnie, Jimmy Jr., Laura, Ben, Rebecca, and Thomas. Thomas is pictured here. (Tucker family.)

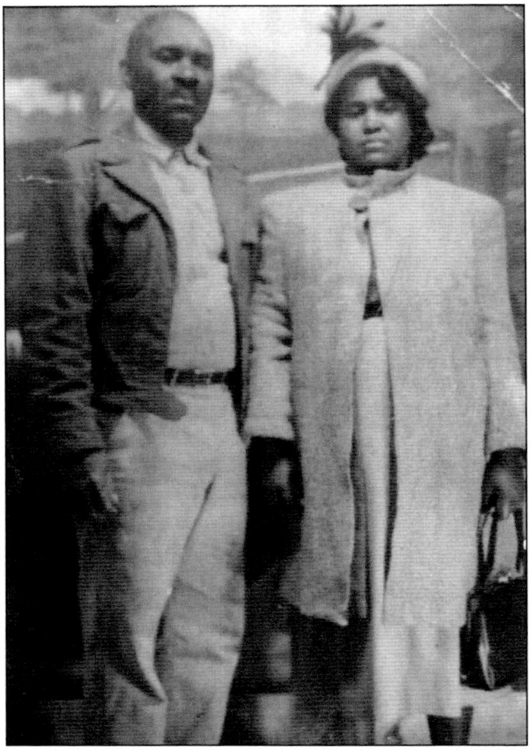

Deacon George Wilson (1901–1961) was the son of Rev. Isiah and Dina Wilson. He owned and successfully farmed hundreds of acres in the Kingville area. At Mount Olive Baptist Church, he served as superintendent of the Sunday school, deacon, and church sexton for 35 years. Married to the daughter of Wash and Louise Higgins, he was a well-respected member of the community. Their children were Joseph, Rhaney, Nathaniel, Wendell, George Jr., Thelma, Blanche, Ruby, and Lillie Mae. (S. George Wilson.)

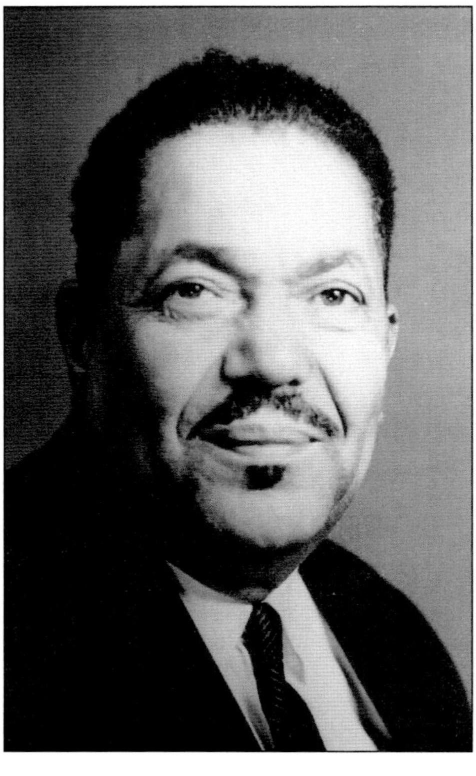

William Seymore was fondly remembered as the jovial mathematics teacher who came to the new consolidated high school in Hopkins in 1954. He had been teaching in Cross, South Carolina, and later at the Mill Creek School, located near Lykesland, before he was placed at the new school. He reared his nephew Richard, whose son Richard Jr. became a successful NFL player. (Blanch McRant McFadden.)

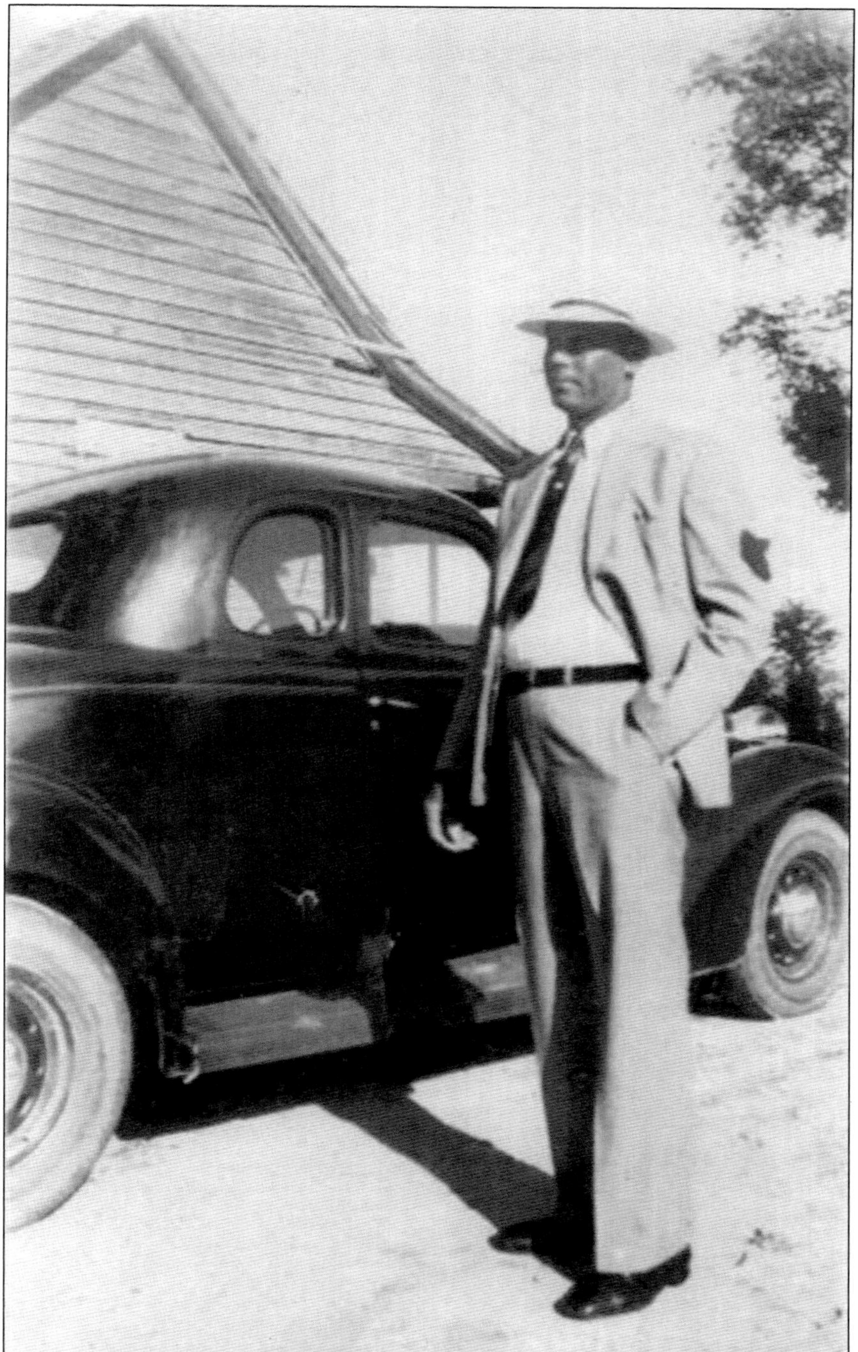

Peter James Seymore was born on November 16, 1911. He was the son of Georgianna Seymore and Richard Saxby Joyner. His brothers were Robert, Julius, Ernest, William, and Paul. Peter worked for the Southern Railroad until his retirement in 1972. He worked as a railroad foreman, and he was also a barber in the Kingville community. At his family church, Peter served as a Sunday school teacher, treasurer, and deacon. (Portia Seymore Richardson.)

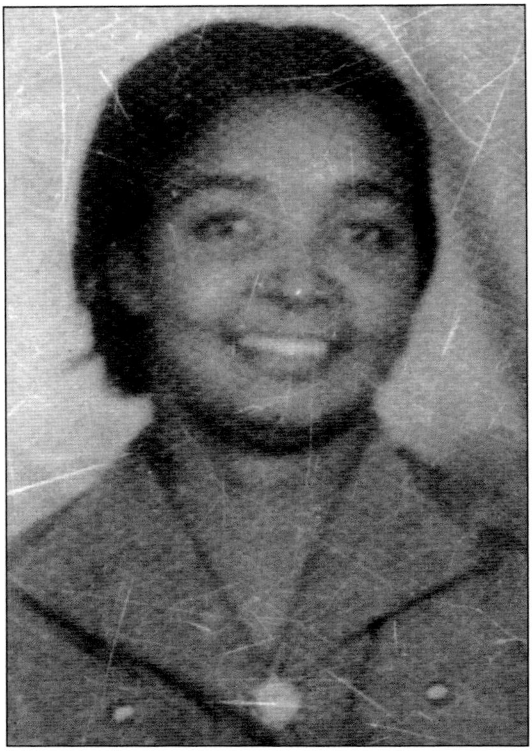

Ora Elizabeth Finch Seymore was the daughter of William Richard Finch and Tina Finch, another family firmly grounded in Kingville. Ora married Peter James Seymore, and their two daughters were Portia and Ada Ruth. (Portia Seymore Richardson.)

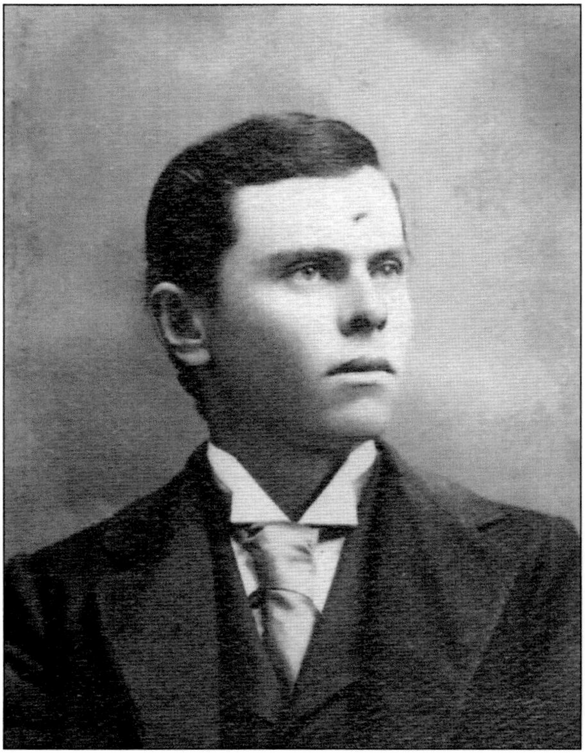

Richard Saxby Joyner (1880–1960) was a farmer who owned hundreds of acres in the Kingville community, and he also rented houses to residents of Kingville. He was the father of Peter James Seymore and five Wilson children: Blease, Cole, Gladys, Marie, and Joseph. The mother of the children was Maggie Macon Wilson. (Cole Wilson.)

Nicholas Calhoun Joyner, born in 1848, was the son of Absalom and Mary Joyner and lived in the Richland District in 1870. He served in the Confederate army during the Civil War. Nicholas married Cassandra Darrill of Charleston. They were the parents of Saxby Joyner. (Cole Wilson.)

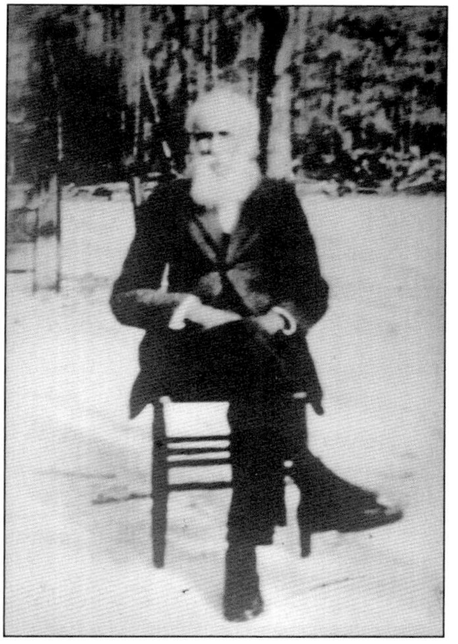

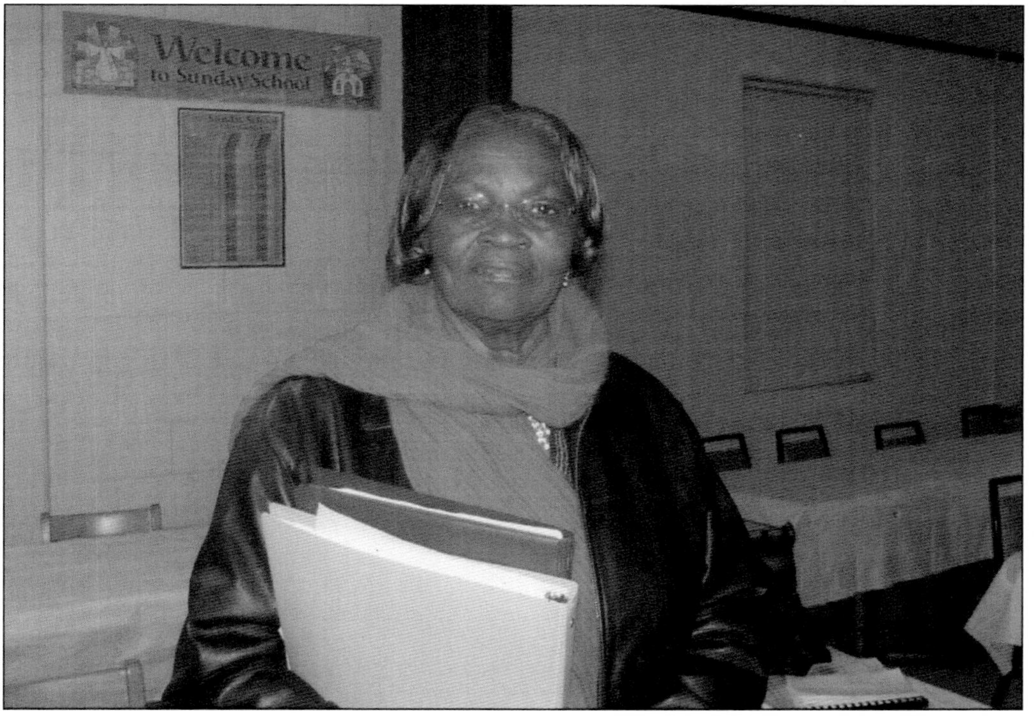

Ada Young Hopkins is the daughter of John Young Jr. and Pauline Hardy Young. Her father was a World War I veteran and railroad worker. Their children were Willis, Ethel, Ada, John, Earthaline, and Vivian. Ada attended school in Kingville and graduated from Benedict College with a degree in elementary education. While teaching in Gadsden Elementary, she was selected Teacher of the Year 1967 and District Teacher of the Year. She continues to work at age 80 in the local schools as a tutor. (Photograph by Deborah Scott Brooks.)

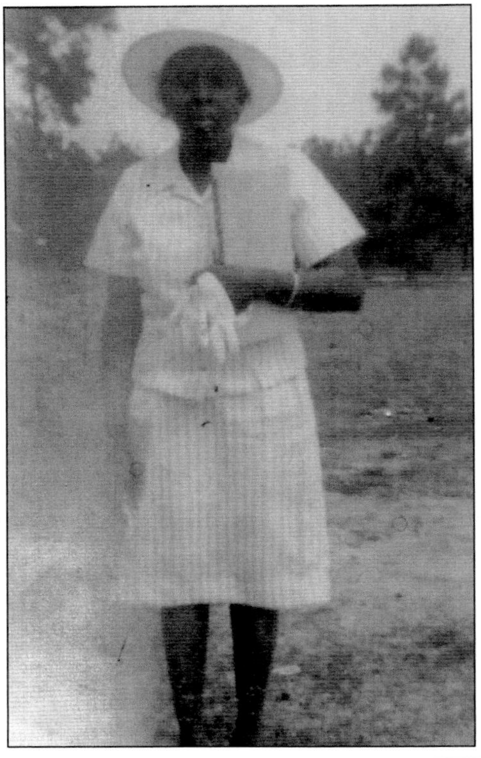

Florence Cornish Powell was fondly remembered as the midwife for most of the families in this section of Lower Richland. In fact, she was instrumental in naming many of the children she delivered. (George Wilson.)

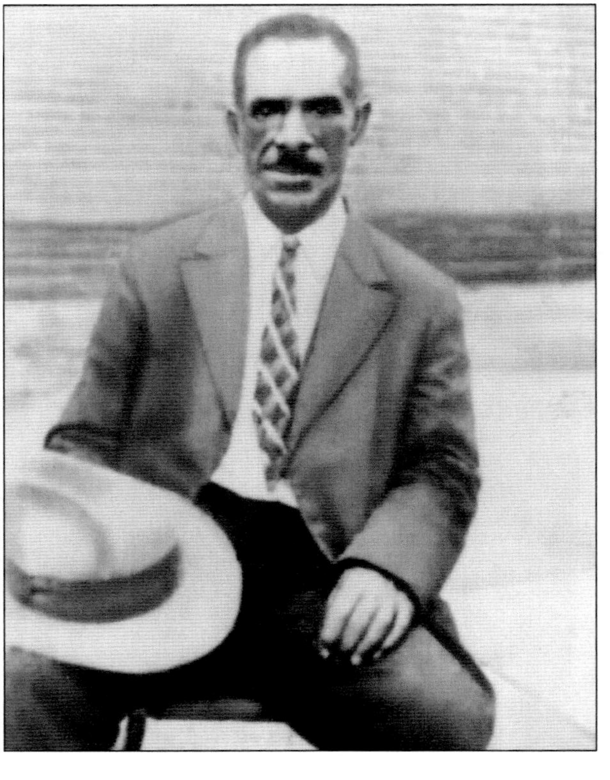

John Henry Anderson worked tirelessly for the Mount Olive Missionary Baptist Church. He served as a deacon and lived to see the burning of the mortgage long before his death in February 1943. (George Wilson.)

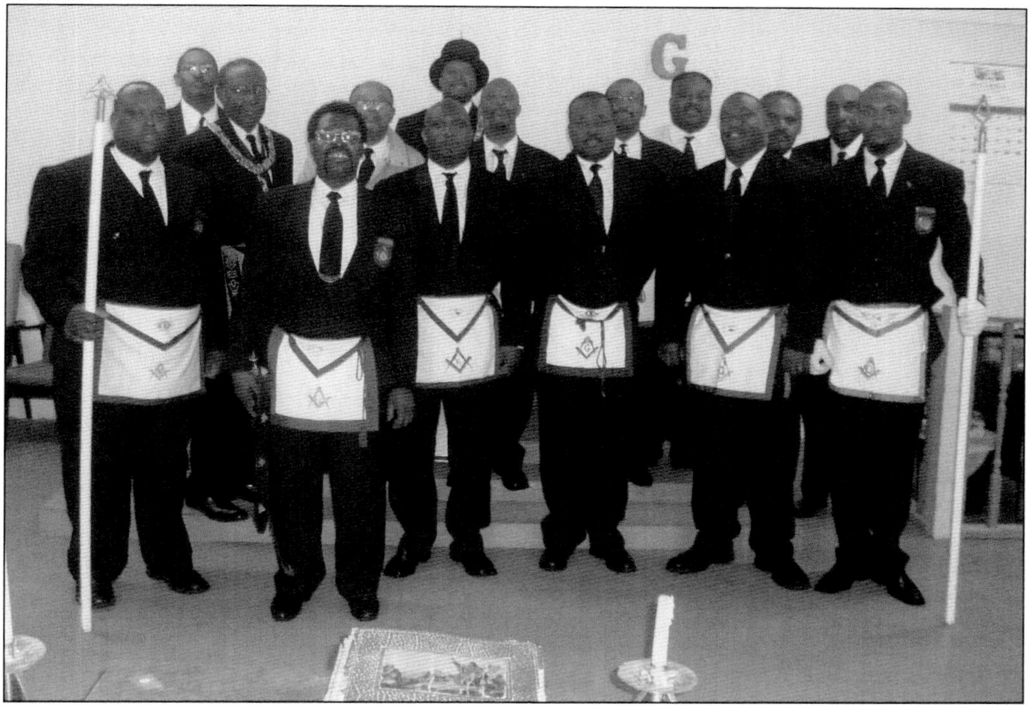

The Mount Olive Lodge No. 434 for Prince Hall Masons has a 58-year history in the Kingville area. William Seymore led the group as worshipful master for the first 29 years. In this society of fraternal members, Masonic rites are traditionally passed from one generation to the next. The group currently consists of 31 active Prince Hall Masons. (Gregory Adams.)

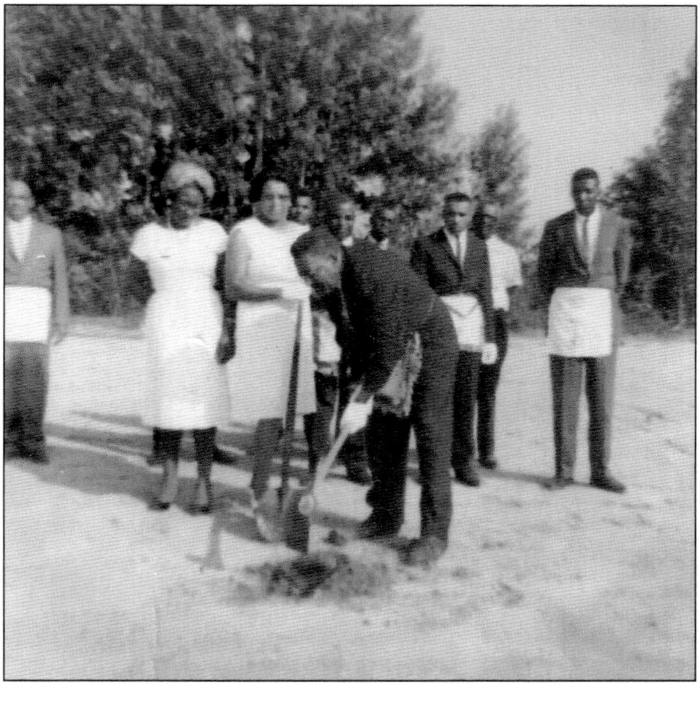

William Seymore, worshipful master and a founder of the Mount Olive Lodge No. 434 for Prince Hall Masons, is shown here at the ground-breaking in 1975. The organization was founded on November 14, 1952, with meetings held in local churches until a permanent home was built on Bluff Road in Gadsden. Founding members were William Seymore, Clem Davis, Charlies Robinson, John Sims, Doc Sims, Henry Jackson, and Doc Adams Sr. (Greg Adams.)

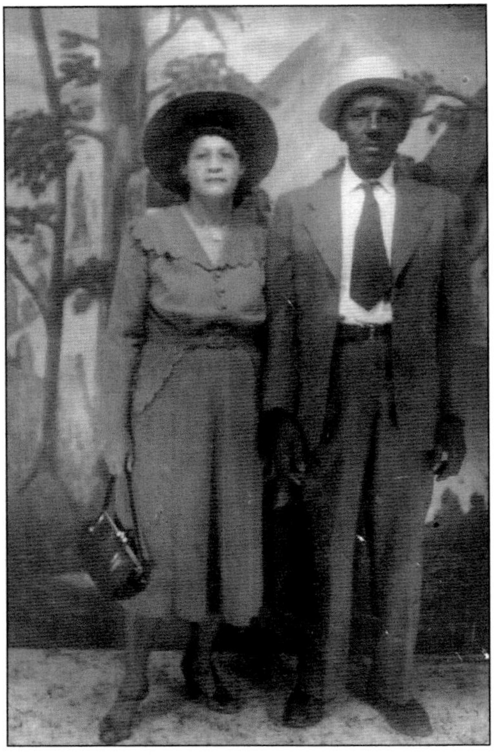

James E. Cooper was born in Stone Mountain, Georgia. He worked for Southern Railroad, which brought him through Kingville, where he met his future wife, Ruth Rivers. Ruth Rivers was born in Kingville, and she became a substitute teacher in her young adulthood. James and Ruth were joined in matrimony in 1926, and to this union, six children were born: Rutha, Earline, Jimmie, James, Walter, and Marion. (George Wilson.)

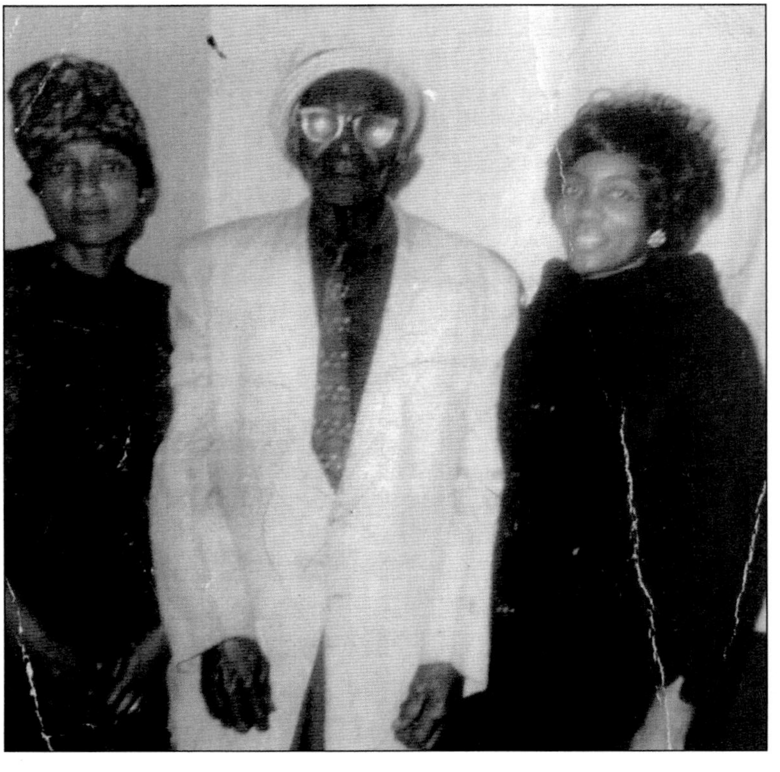

Luke and Anna Scott were residents of Kingville from the late 1940s. Luke, pictured in the center, was known as "Mr. Jay." His wife, Anna, was known as "Mrs. Child." Luke was a farmer. This picture was taken in 1967, and it also shows two of their nine children, Ruth (left) and Alice. The other children were Belton, Howard, Robert, Melvina, Luke Jr., Lillian, and Geneva. (George Wilson.)

Two

Gadsden

Gadsden was the first stop on the railroad after the train left Kingville. Just a short distance away, the village of Gadsden was thriving by the 1860s. Two of four free black farmers were Uriah Portee and Charles Frost, who accumulated substantial real estate in the area. Uriah owned a 450-acre farm with 3 horses, 3 mules, 18 cattle, and 14 swine, and he produced corn, peas, beans, sweet potatoes, and butter. Frost was even more prosperous, with 1,200 acres of land where he produced corn, cotton, hay, sweet potatoes, beans, peas, and butter. His successful farm included horses, 77 cattle, 123 swine, and 10 sheep. Three teachers were employed at a large school building in Gadsden owned by blacks. Records for the 1869–1870 school year revealed that the school had both black and white students.

The Red Hill Baptist Church was organized in 1868 after approximately 500 former slaves withdrew from the Congaree Baptist Church, located at the corner of Bluff Road and Congaree Church Road. The founding families began to worship at a nearby location on a red clay knoll on Congaree Church Road. The church was organized under the leadership of Rev. Jonas Anchrum, a former slave on the Thomas Clarkson plantation. Deacons who served during the early years were James Scott, Joseph Lowe, John J. Hoff, Simon Haynes, Benjamin Hamilton, William Shiver, Steven S. Cochran, and Lewis W. James.

Red Hill School was started in 1868 in the Red Hill Baptist Church yard. It was generally acknowledged as a Freedman's Bureau School. Children of the newly freed slaves from far and near attended school at this location on Congaree Church Road. Many of the families had worshipped in the slave gallery at the Congaree Baptist Church, which was located about 2 miles away. Pleasant Grove Baptist Church was established a short distance down the road from Red Hill Baptist.

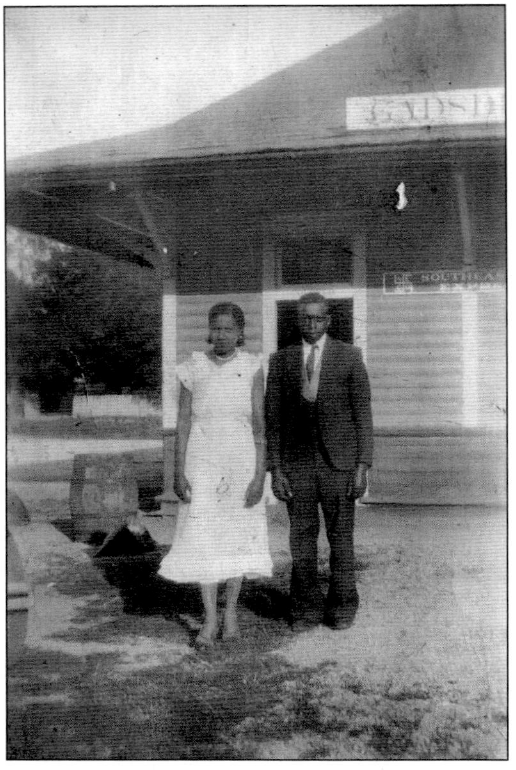

Annie Portee is pictured with a friend at the Gadsden train depot in the 1930s. The train was a major source of transportation for numerous African Americans who worked in Columbia and returned home to Gadsden on the weekends. The railroad continued to provide employment for African Americans who lived in this section of Lower Richland. In 1880, Gadsden reportedly featured three general stores, a harness shop, and a doctor. The first post office on record was operating as early as 1851. (Barber family collection.)

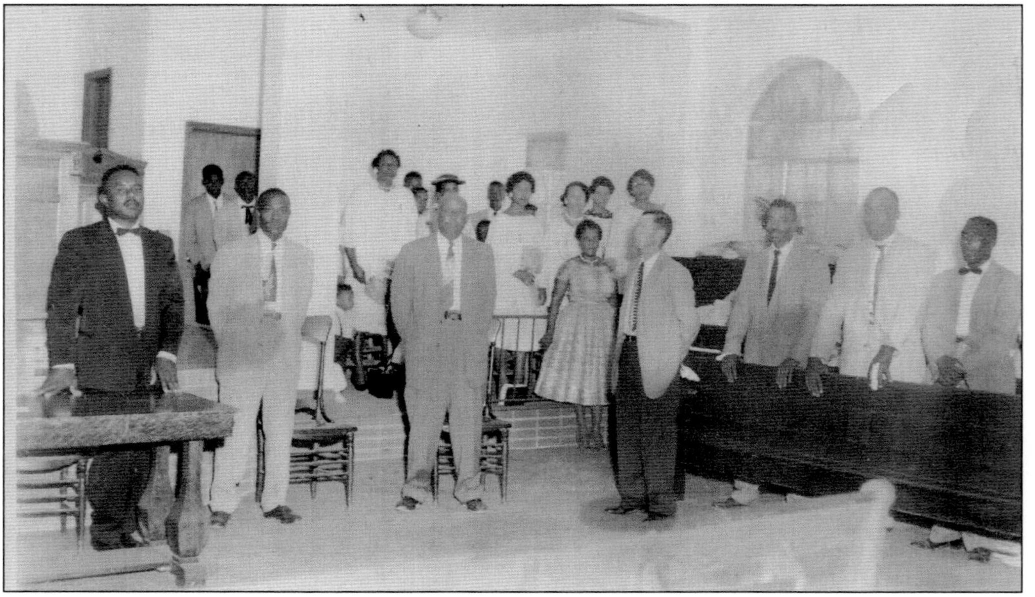

St. Mark Baptist Church was founded on January 8, 1883, in Gadsden. The founding members were former worshippers at Zion Benevolent Baptist Church in Hopkins. The first place of worship was a bush arbor located at a bluff site. The first pastor was the Reverend Daniel Boyd. The congregation had grown and needed a larger building, so the members were able to construct a small building at the current location. (Doctor Adams Jr.)

Rachel Anderson Mosley was a mulatto, the daughter of Sylvia and Townsey (Townley) Anderson of Kingville. Her father, born 1834, was a blacksmith during slavery. Rachel was a housekeeper for the Campbell family. Her husband, William Mosley, ran the cotton gin for the same family. She continued working as a laundry lady after the emancipation and saved enough money by 1917 to purchase a 26.3-acre tract of land. (Barber family collection.)

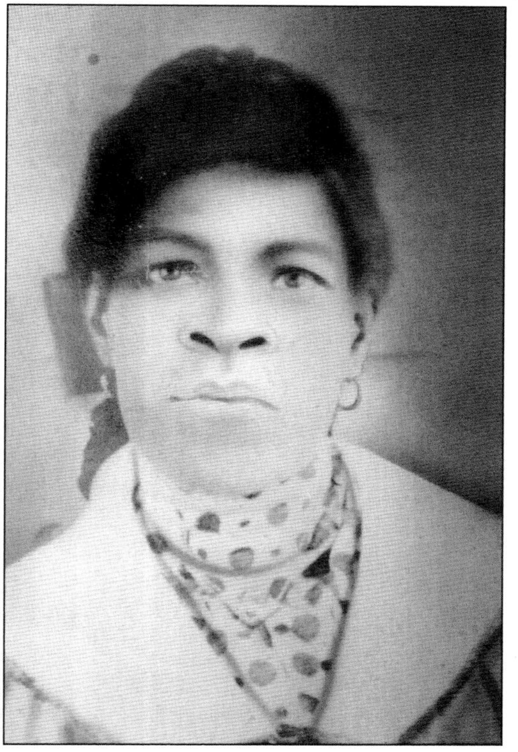

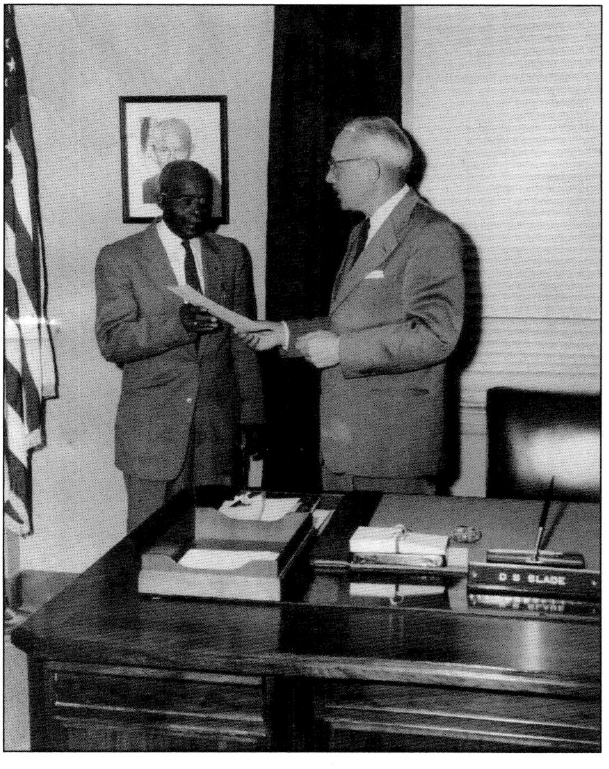

The family of Andrew Jackson can be traced back to Richard Jackson and his wife, Irena Adams Jackson. Their son, Ishmael, was born in 1857. From the union of Ishmael and Nancy Sumter, 14 children were born. Andrew was one of the sons, born in 1893. Andrew and his wife, Charlotte Green, had sons Robert, Andrew, and Joseph and daughters Essie and Mearrilease. Andrew Jr. became a bishop and founder of Bibleway Church of Atlas Road. His son Darrell became his successor and was elected to the South Carolina Senate in 1993. (Joseph L. Jackson.)

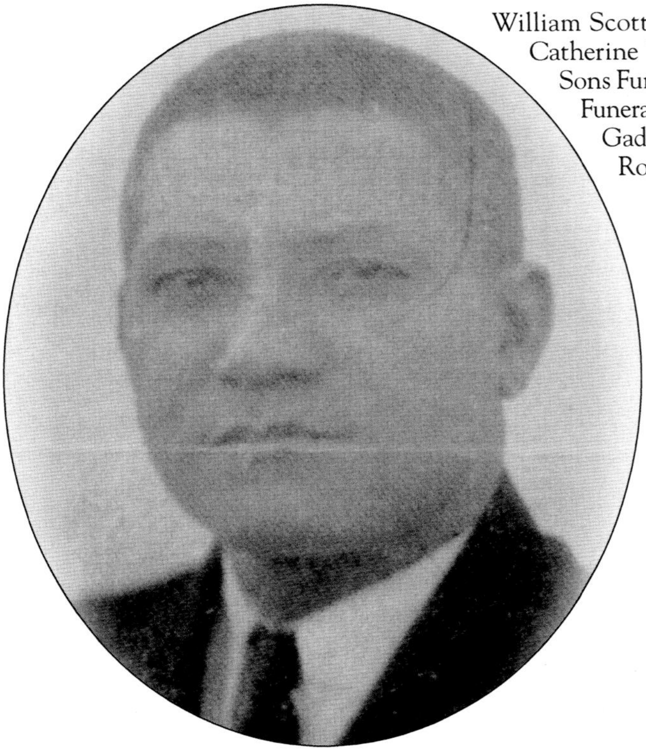

William Scott Holley (1899–1949) and his wife, Catherine Weston Holley, started Holley and Sons Funeral Home in 1917. The J. P. Holley Funeral Home had its humble beginnings in Gadsden in a one-story building on Bluff Road. (Barber family collection.)

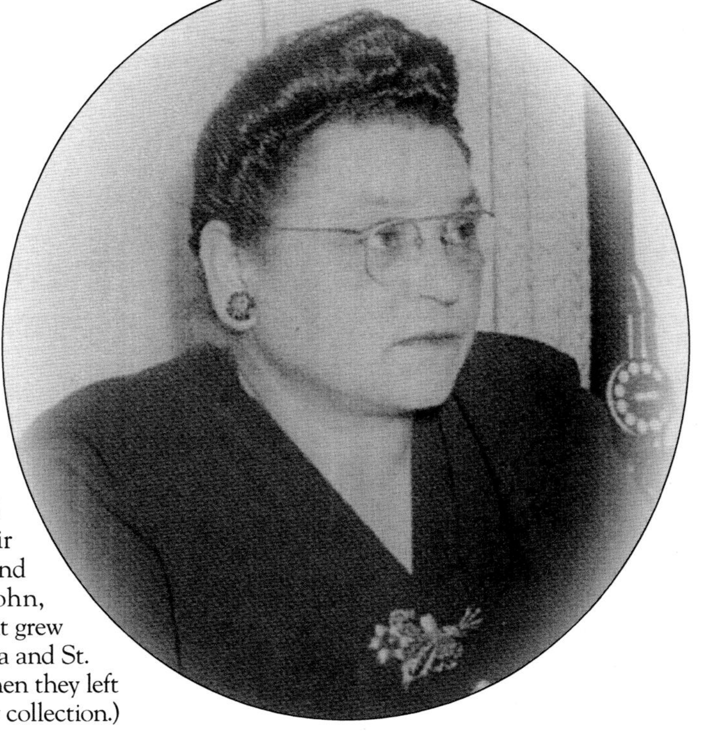

Catherine Weston Holley, born in 1886, was the daughter of Catherine Adams Weston and James H. Weston. She married William Scott Holley, and their children were Willie, Maria, and John P. William's brother, John, joined the family business, and it grew to include locations in Columbia and St. Matthews as well as Hopkins when they left the Gadsden site. (Barber family collection.)

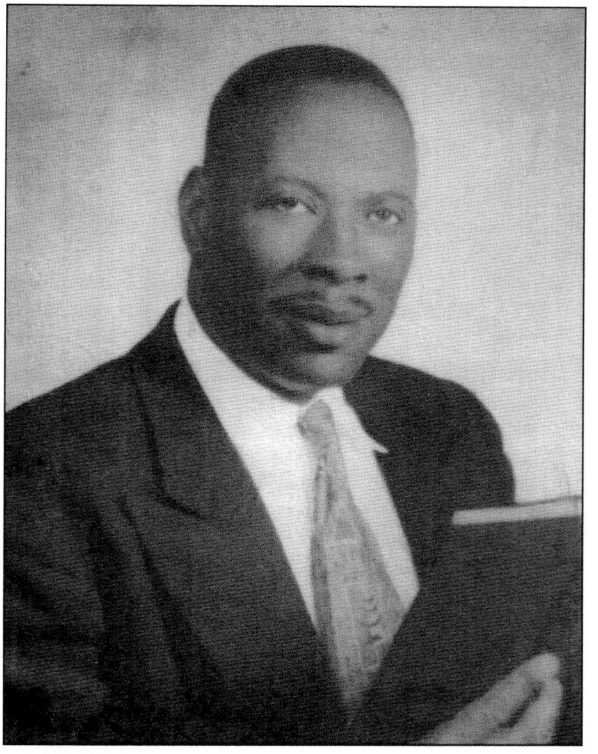

Rev. Simon Moore was the son of Esau and Clarisa Moore. He was born in Gadsden in 1905 and attended the Gregory Graded School near Red Hill Baptist Church. Moore was baptized at Pleasant Grove Baptist Church, and he inspired many with his singing talent. He served many of the churches in the community, including Daughter of St. Matthews in Eastover, St. Paul in Gadsden, Zion Pilgrim in Hopkins, Zion Benevolent in Hopkins, Friendship in Lykesland, and St. Mark in Gadsden. Rev. Simon Moore was married to the former Charlotte Goodson. (Barber family collection.)

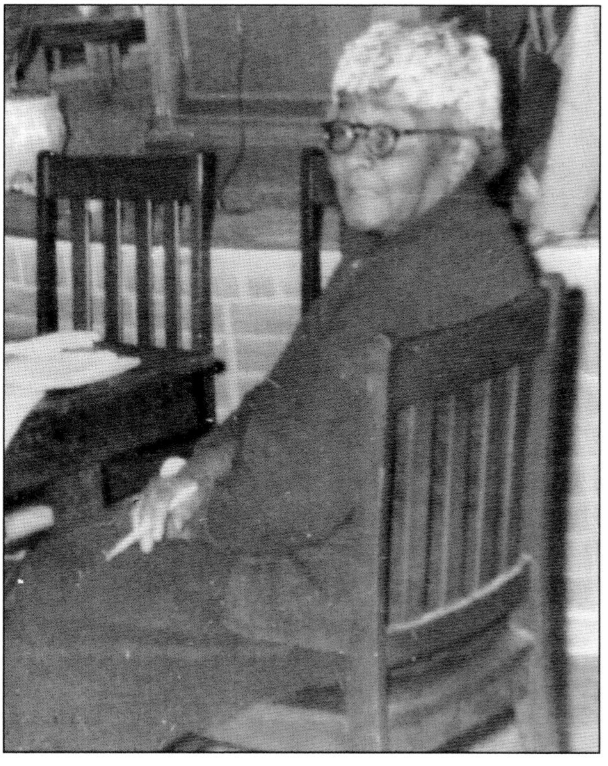

Carrie Portee Mosley was the daughter of Rachel Anderson Mosley and William Mosley. She attended school in Gadsden and later became trained as a midwife and nurse. She married Irvin Portee, and to this union, four daughters were born: Eloise, Annie, Louise, and Lessie. She was a Sunday school teacher at St. Mark Baptist Church for most of her adult life. (Barber family collection.)

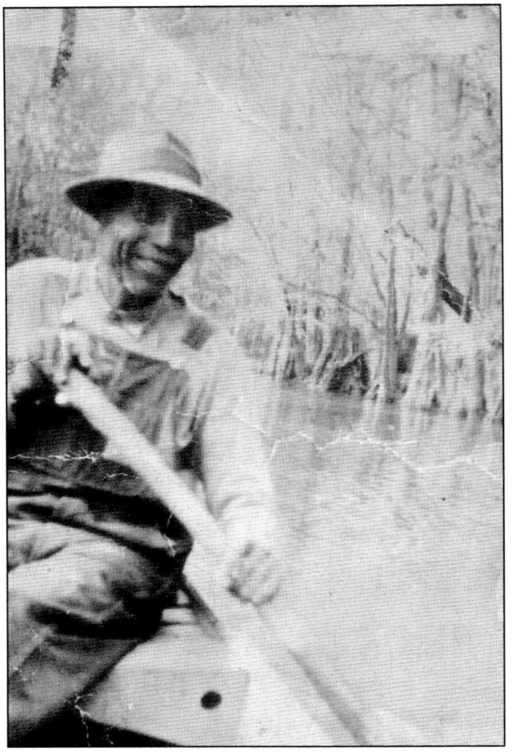

Irvin Portee was remembered as the local animal doctor, caring for the farm animals in the Lower Richland community. His skill in treating sick animals included dispensing medicines as well as performing emergency surgery to save the lives of valuable farm animals. His astute knowledge of veterinary medicine, hunting, and fishing made him an unforgettable legend in the Gadsden community. (Barber family collection.)

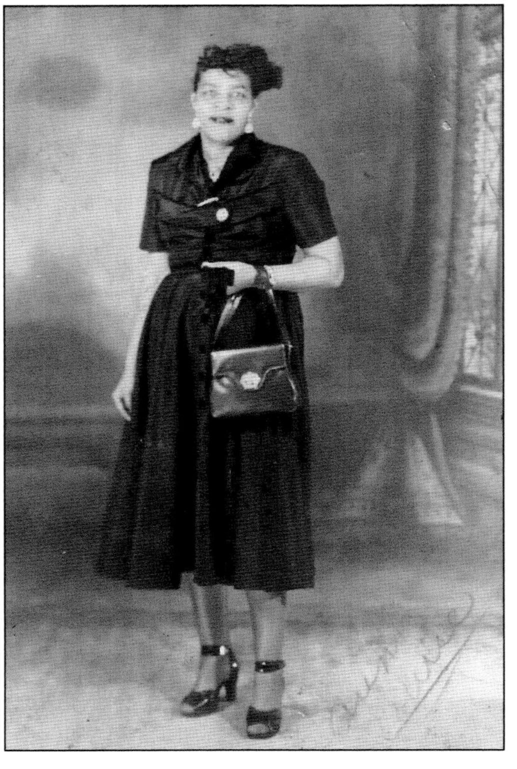

Eloise Portee Gaillard, like other young African Americans, joined the northern migration to find better opportunities than she had in the South, found a home in Philadelphia, and continued to support her family in Gadsden. The average daily wage in the South in 1924 was about $1 a day. Workers could receive more than twice that amount in northern factories during that time. (Rachel Simpson.)

Annie Mae Allen was the daughter of Elouise Allen and the Reverend John Allen Sr. She was a tall, pretty lady with a beautiful voice. Family members recall her singing talent in church services and other programs in the community. She was married to Robert Reeves, and from this union, two children were born: Rachel and Robert. (Rachel Simpson.)

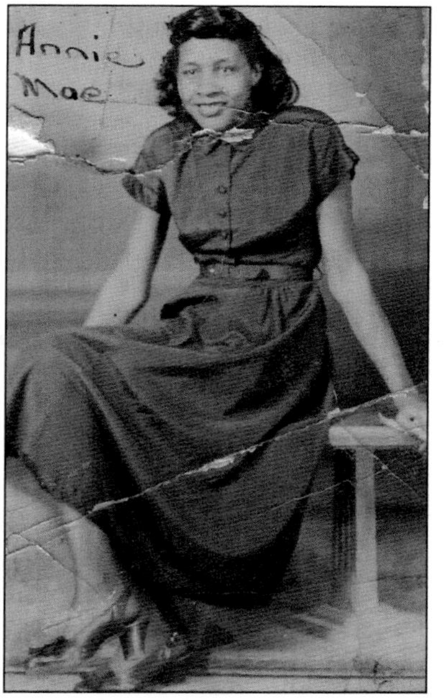

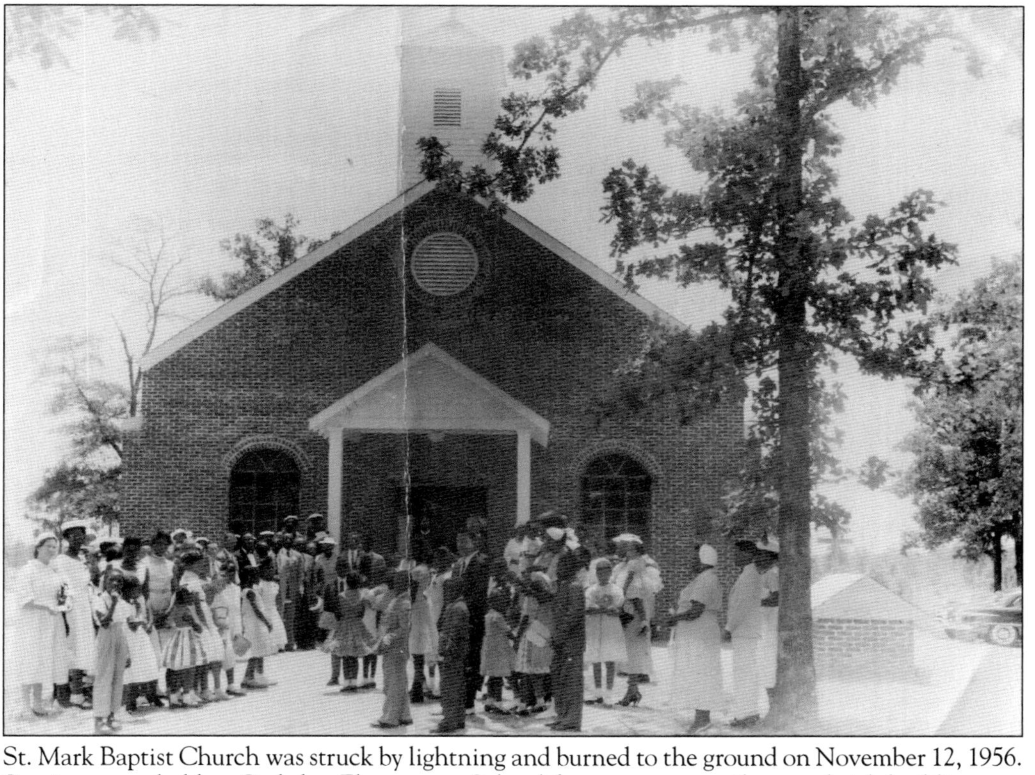

St. Mark Baptist Church was struck by lightning and burned to the ground on November 12, 1956. Services were held at Gadsden Elementary School for two years until a new brick building was completed. Rev. John B. Barber had served as pastor until the new church was completed. After declining health, Reverend Barber turned over the leadership of the church to Rev. Simon Moore in 1958. The church celebrated its 100th anniversary in 1983. (Barber family collection.)

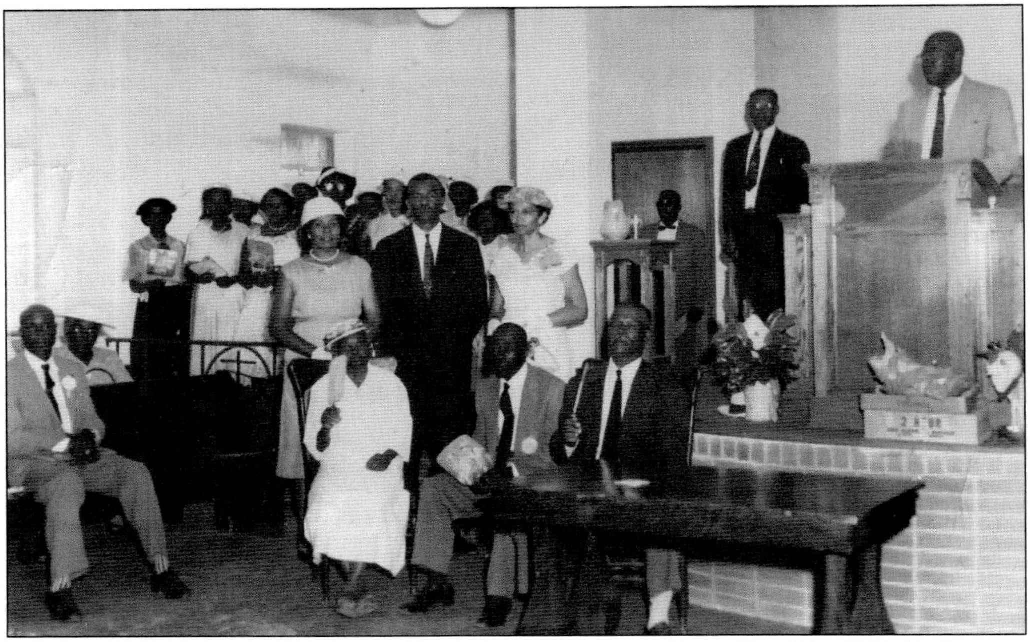

After the terms of Rev. Andrew C. Richbourg and Rev. Seymore Jones, Rev. John B. Barber became pastor of St. Mark in 1927. Deacons working under his leadership included Jacob Garrick, John Garrick, Sam Perkins, Doctor Sims Sr., Hamp Sumter, Joseph Sumter, and Jube Taylor. James Portee, Beverly Garrick Sr., Jimmie Williams, Frank Adams, Doctor Sims Jr., and William Mosley were added to the deacon board a few years later. (Barber family collection.)

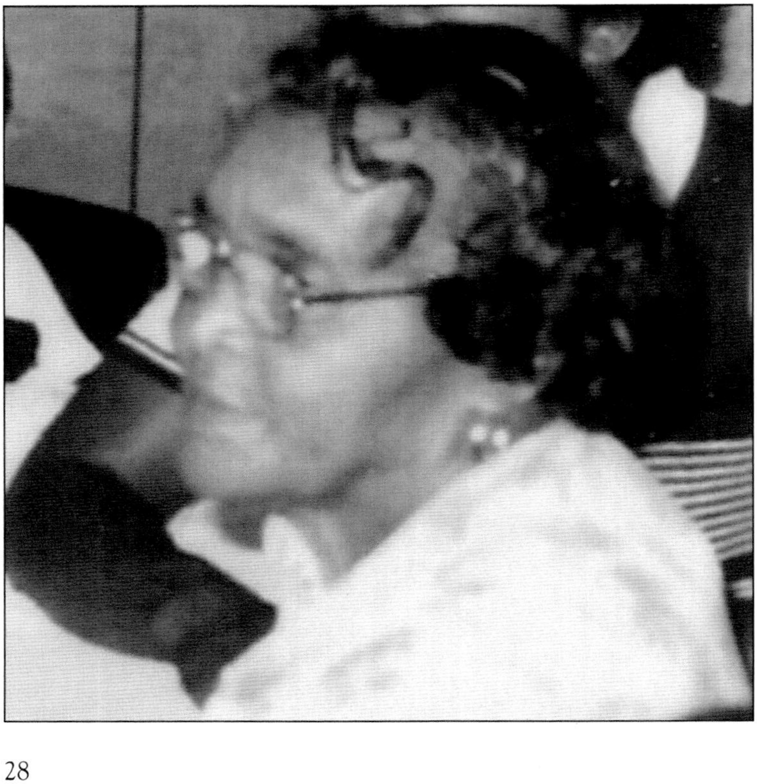

Lessie Portee Rice was the wife of Edward Rice Jr., a descendant of Ellen Cole, who was born in 1839. Ellen married H. W. Rice, her second husband, in 1860. Their son Zack Rice Sr. was the father of Edward. Lessie and Edward's children were Annie Mae, Ellen, Edna, Della, Edward Jr., Ulysses, Ruby, and Jimmy. (Barber family collection.)

Louise Portee Blakely lived in Gadsden until her marriage to Herbert Blakely. She and her husband owned and operated a successful neighborhood store on Bluff Road near Atlas Road. Their children were Herbert Jr., Earl, Leroy, and Carolyn. (Rachel Simpson.)

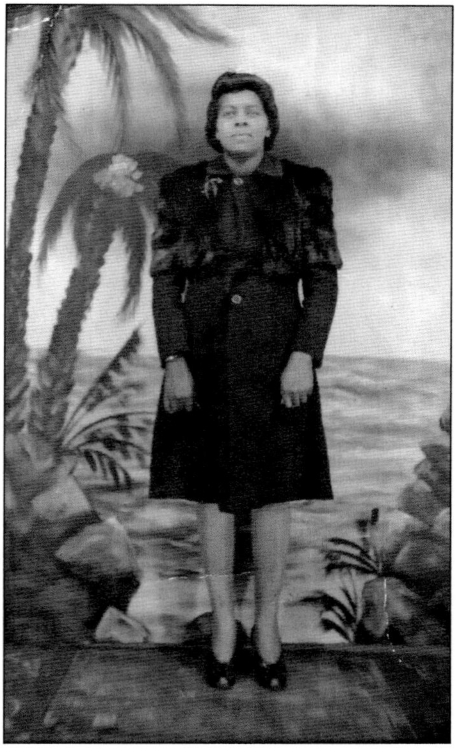

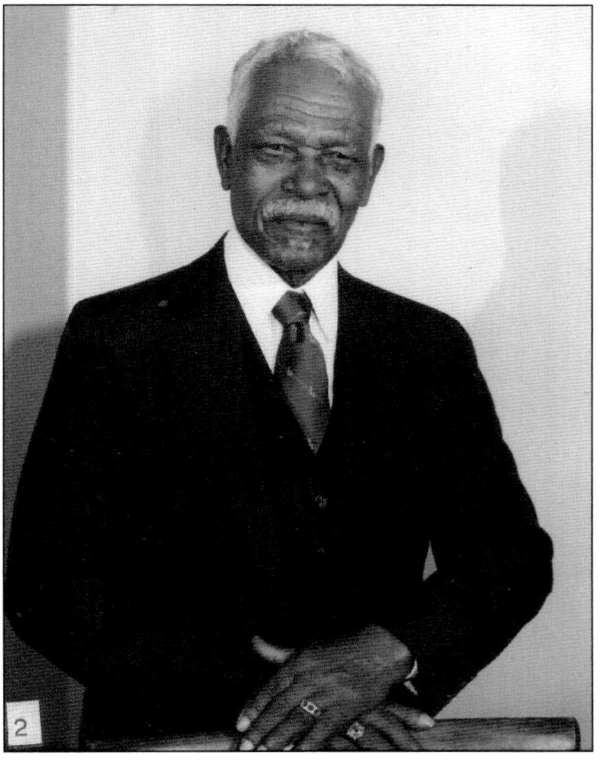

Frank Adams Sr., who lived to be 104, could trace his family back to David Hopkins Adams, one of the Lower Richland planters, and Eve Gates. Frank Sr.'s parents were John and Millie Brown Adams. He married Dorcas Sims; their children were Millie, Margaret, Mary Jane, Doctor, Darcus, John, Sarah, Annie, and Robert. (Doctor Adams Jr.)

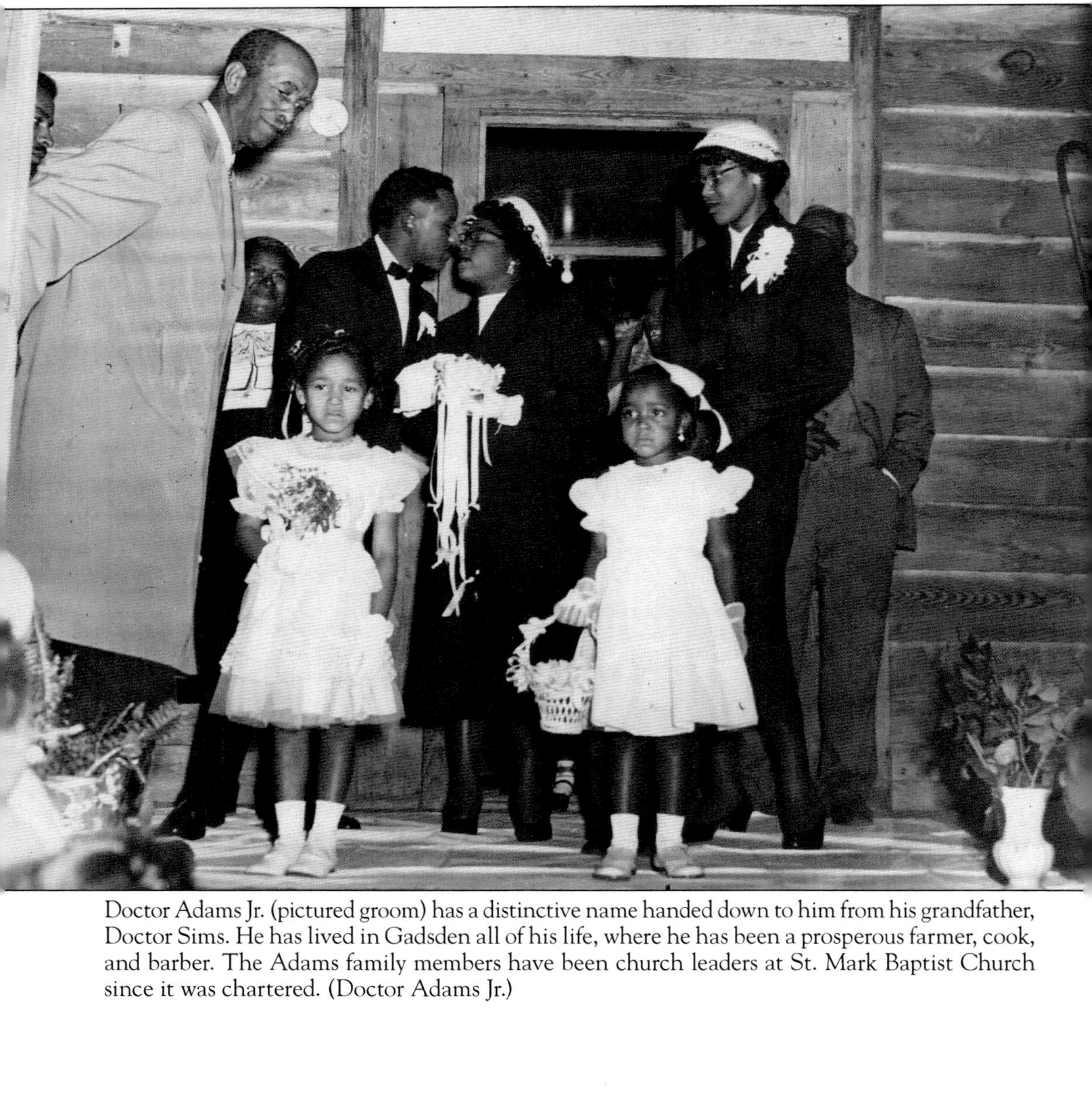

Doctor Adams Jr. (pictured groom) has a distinctive name handed down to him from his grandfather, Doctor Sims. He has lived in Gadsden all of his life, where he has been a prosperous farmer, cook, and barber. The Adams family members have been church leaders at St. Mark Baptist Church since it was chartered. (Doctor Adams Jr.)

Mary Williams Adams married Doctor Adams Jr. at St. Mark Baptist Church. The Reverend John B. Barber officiated the marriage. Their sons are Melvin, Greg, Doctor Jr., and Anthony. (Doctor Adams Jr.)

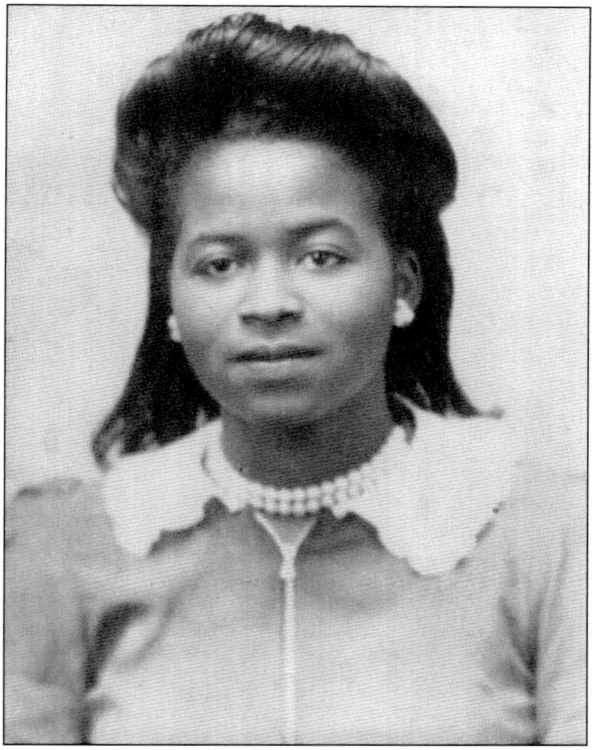

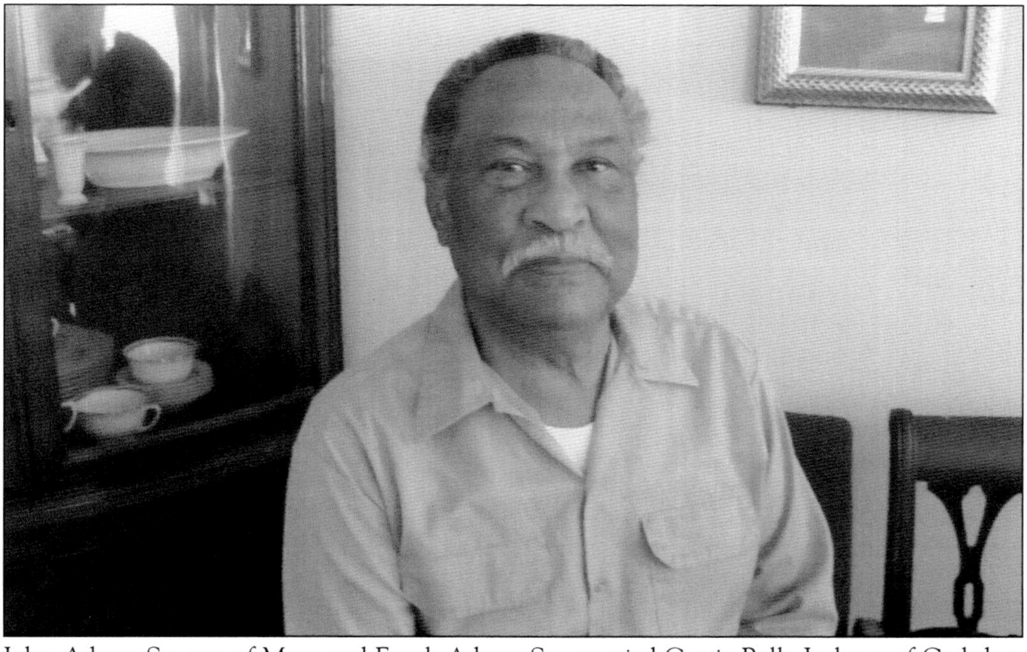

John Adams Sr., son of Mary and Frank Adams Sr., married Carrie Belle Jackson of Gadsden. Their children are Dorcas, John Jr., Ronald, and Frank. John and his brother Doctor Adams continued the farming tradition started by their father, Frank. The farm included livestock as well as hay, cotton, and vegetables. (Photograph by Deborah Scott Brooks.)

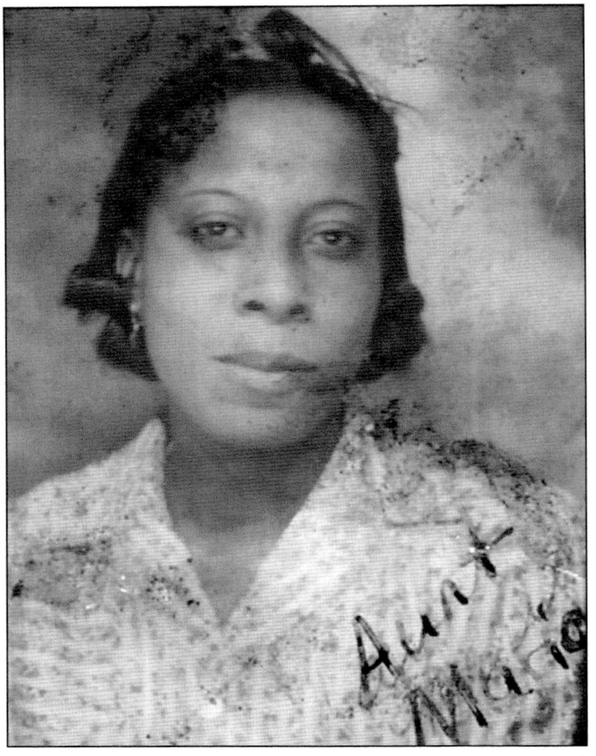

Lula Mosley and Jim Shiver were married in Gadsden, South Carolina, and their children were Maria, Nancy, Margaret, William, Jim, and Eddie. Pictured here is Maria, who married Richard Chandler, whose family originally came from Charleston. Maria and Richard's children are Richard Jr,. Charles, James, Nelson, and Tonney. (Barber family collection.)

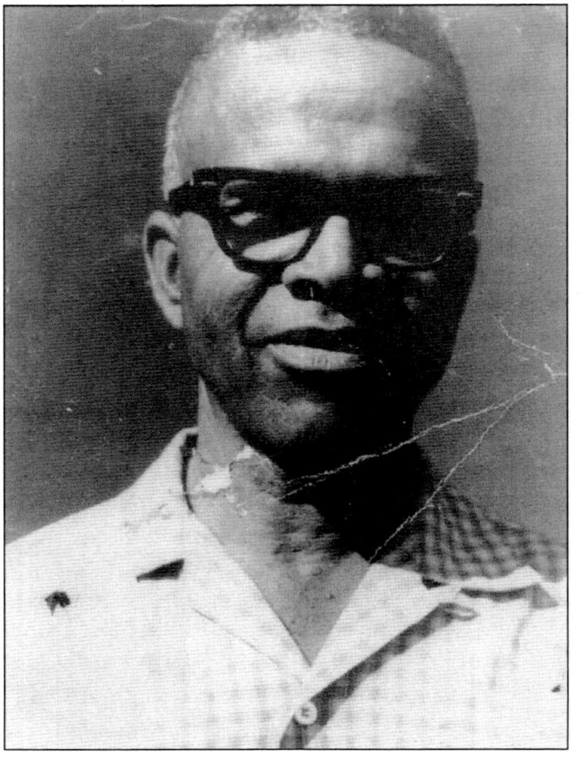

Robert Lee Taylor Sr. was born in Gadsden in 1914. He was the son of Zachary and Lula Taylor. Affectionately known as "Pink" Taylor, he was a master electrician and builder. He was employed by Congaree Iron and Steel Company until his retirement. In 1938, he married Lillian Reese of Eastover, and to this union, six children were born: Zack, Lillian, Betty, Margie, Edith, and Vivian. Active in his church and community, he played a leadership role in the Gadsden Community Development Club. (Zack and Levola Taylor.)

Doctor Sims Sr., born in 1865, was the son of Jesse Lloyd Sims. Doctor and Betty Campbell Sims were the parents of Margaret, Dorcas, and Doctor Jr. Doctor Sims Jr. married Ollie Marshall, and their children were Henry, Margaret, Ollie, and Doctor David. The Sims family members were leaders at St. Mark Baptist Church. (Margaret Sims Goodwin.)

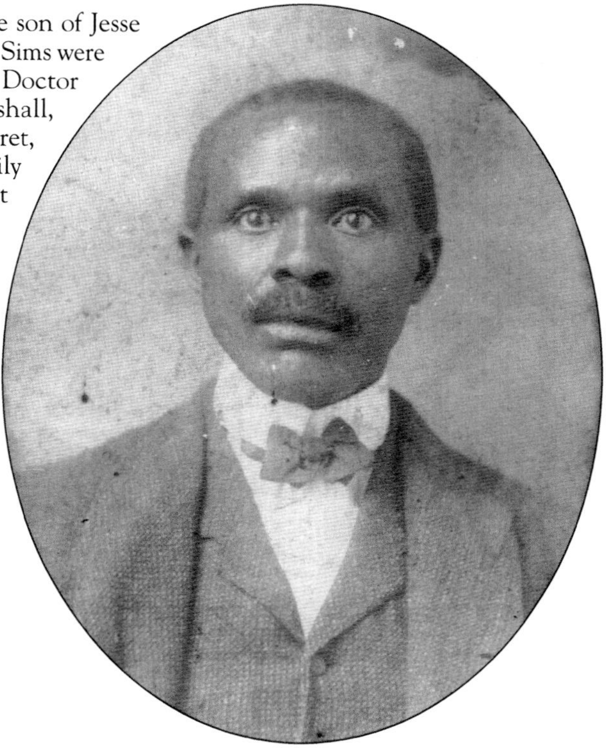

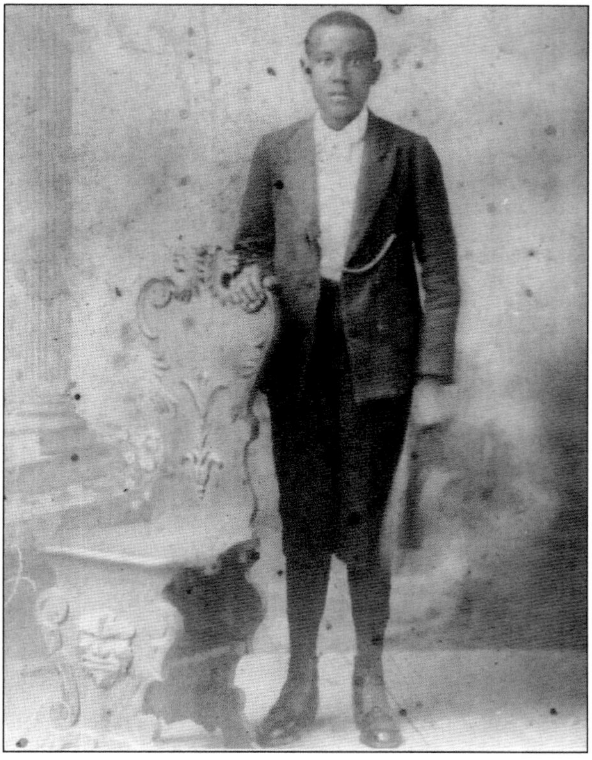

Doctor Sims Jr. carried the name of his father and continued the tradition of farming in the Gadsden community. He purchased land in Gadsden on Bluff Road and established a farm there on 200 acres. He and his wife, Ollie Marshall Sims, were the parents of Henry, Margaret, Ollie, and Doctor David. Henry and Margaret became educators in Richland County. (Margaret Sims Goodwin.)

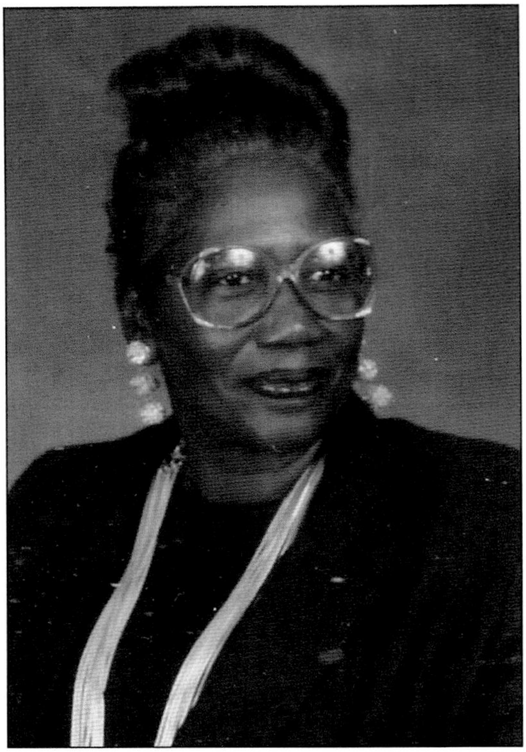

Hattie Jacques Sims became the first female magistrate in Gadsden and the first African American to hold that office. A graduate of Benedict College, she served in this capacity from 1983 until her retirement. Hattie married Doctor Sims Jr. (Herbert Sims.)

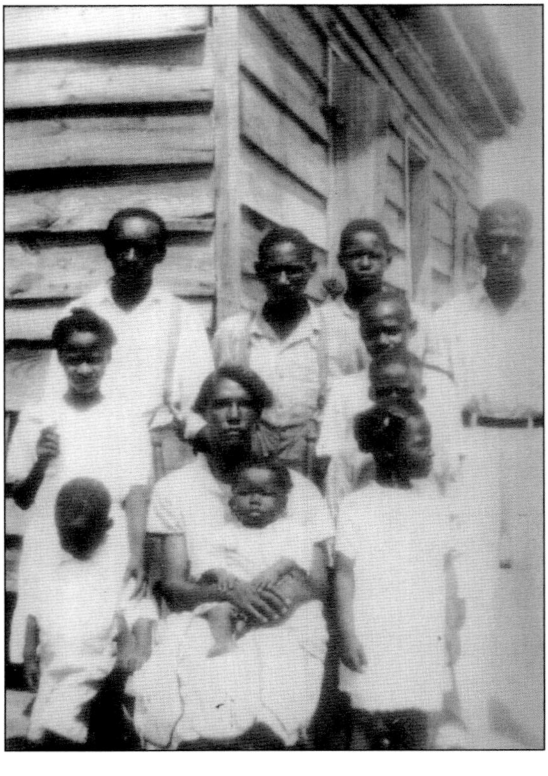

The Richard "Money" Jackson family lived in Gadsden during the 1920s and 1930s, and they made a living farming cotton and other crops. Children were expected to do most of the planting, cultivating, and harvesting along with their parents and other relatives. One of the sons, Richard Jackson Jr., continued the family farming tradition on land located on Bluff Road. (Marie Barber Adams.)

Jimmie Portee, the sharply dressed man pictured here, was somehow connected to the Willie Portee family. He was listed as a deacon at St. Mark in 1927; however, little is known about his immediate family. A large number of Portees lived in Gadsden as well as Kingville from 1870 until the 1930s. (Barber family collection.)

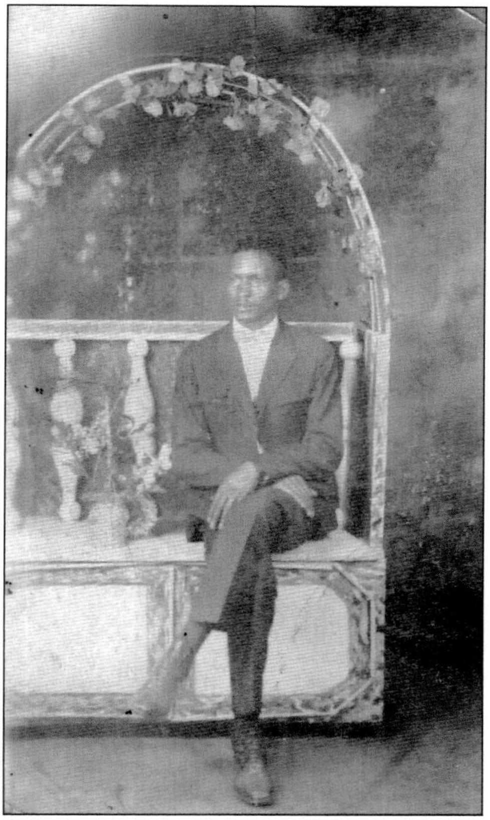

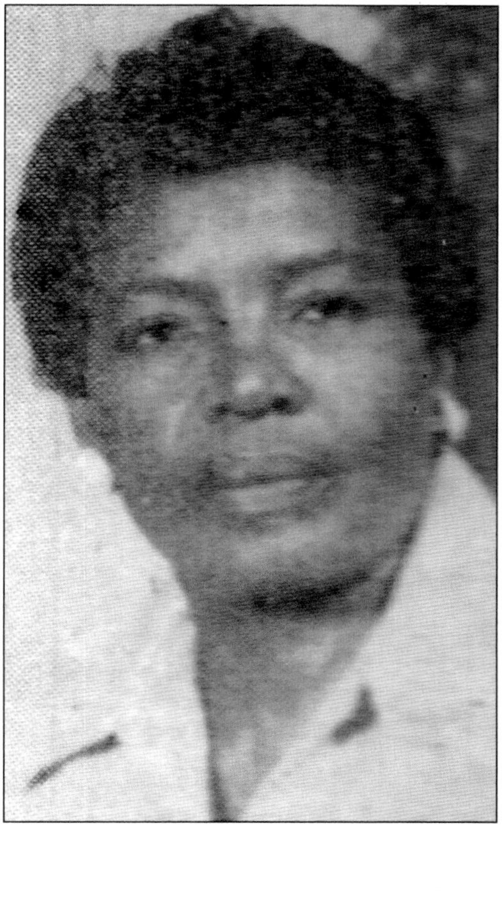

Frankie Brooks Brunson was the daughter of Lee and Malissa Brown Brooks and the wife of Charlie Brunson Jr. She attended Gadsden Elementary and Booker Washington High School and earned her bachelor of arts and master of arts degrees at South Carolina State College. Frankie taught in Richland County schools. She established the South Carolina State College home economics scholarship for Richland County students. She was appointed to national education boards and was vice chairman of the Richland County Democratic Party. (Neal-Scott family collection.)

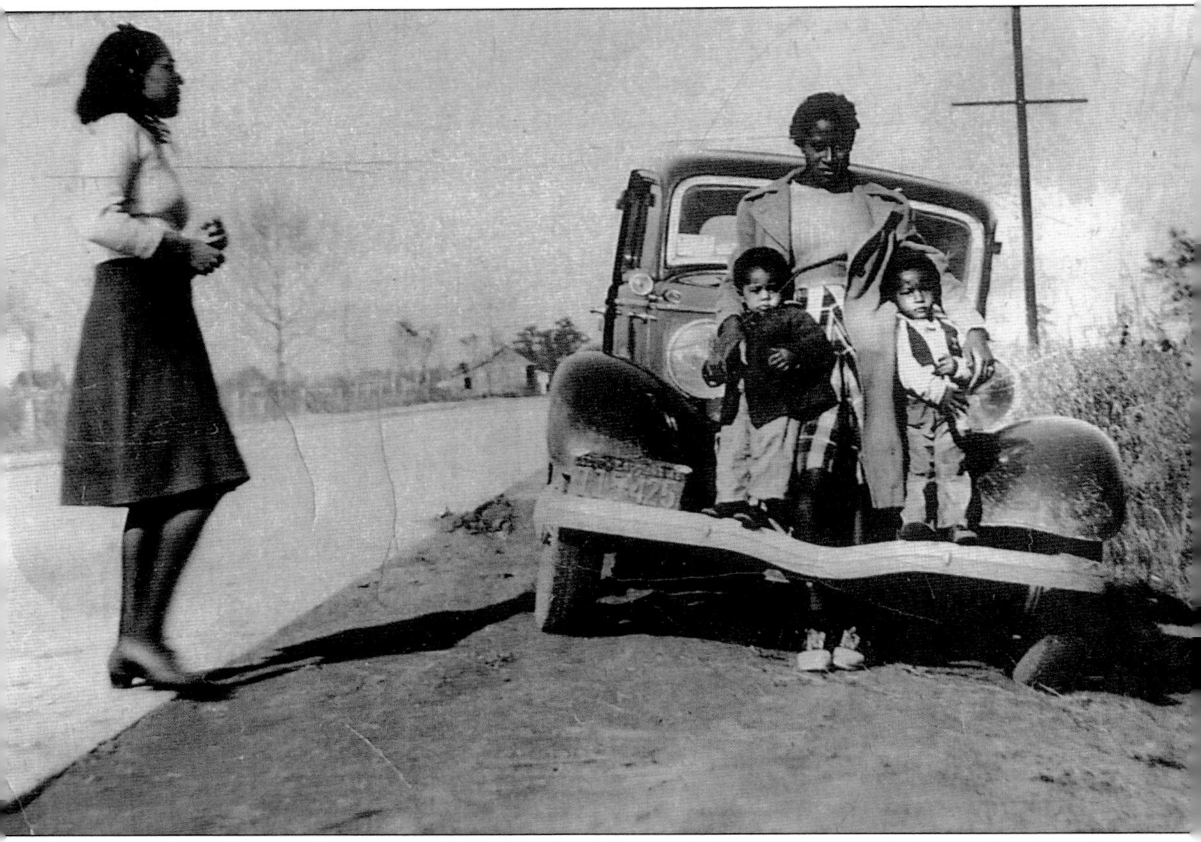

People in this picture are not identified. The automobile license plate reads South Carolina 1942. It should be noted that one lady is standing inside the bumper space. (Rachel Simpson.)

Three

Congaree/Weston

Large plantation owners, including Gov. James Hopkins Adams, grew wealthy in this part of Lower Richland. African Americans of Lower Richland before the Civil War attended predominately white churches established by plantation owners for their families as well as their slaves. The Congaree Baptist Church was first established in 1765 with Rev. Joseph Reese as the first pastor. The church was moved to its location on Tom's Creek around 1800. Membership was made up of slaves, who were allowed to worship in the gallery upstairs, and their owners, who lived in this area around the Congaree settlement and the Minervaville Academy.

Organized in 1806, a branch of the Congaree Baptist Church, named Beulah Baptist Church, worshipped in the Minerva Academy with 31 African American slaves and 9 white members. In their application for admission into the Charleston Association of Churches, it was noted that the congregation adopted the name Beaula (Beulah). The application listed the following slaves as charter members of Beulah Baptist Church: Raiford's Gambo, Jacob, Dinah, and Peggy; J. Adams's John, Jack, Sarah, and Rachel; R. Hail's Peter, Satirah, and Binah; John Pierce's Jack; estate of James Taylor's Miley, Bet, and Jenny; B. Waring's Sancho and Dinah; R. Howell's Humphrey; S. Roach's Jose; T. J. Howell's Monday; W. R. Tucker's Gambo; W. Fitzpatrick's Phillis; T. Taylor's Suckey and Eve; Robert Stark's Clarissa and Shamony; W. Taylor's Ishmael; Wade's Tangy; V. Center's Nancy; Green's Aggy; John Hart's Miley; and estate of W. Howell's Jack.

Grovewood was constructed around 1765 in what was called the Congaree settlement. African American families who lived and worked on this plantation included Tansey Davis, Julius Goodwin, Dolly and Simon Hayne, John Jenkins, Jane and Joshua King, Henry and Dianah Mosley, Grace Sumter, Samuel Sumter, Phillip Taylor, Suckey Tucker, Jannie Tucker, Celia Weston, Isam Williams, and Rose Williams.

Families who lived and worked on the Magnolia (Wavering Place) plantation included Alfred Bush, Ben Goodwin, Peter Goodwin, Affie Grant, Robert Hopkins, Warick Howell, Hannah Jamison, Andrew Moye, Elsey Tucker, Matilda Tucker, Katie Ward, and William Washington.

Many of these families prospered on the same lands once owned by slave owners. Their children were given the opportunity to get an education, acquire property, and serve in various political roles in the community.

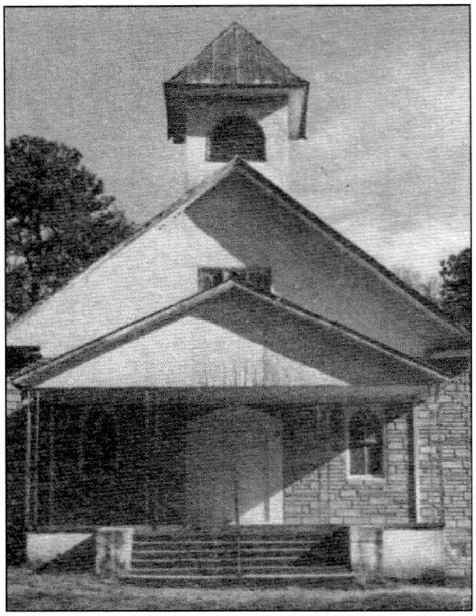

The New Light Beulah Baptist Church began in a brush arbor, and baptisms were held in nearby Cedar Creek. In 1871, former slaves who had worshipped with their slave masters at Beulah Baptist Church established themselves as a separate congregation. The Reverend William W. Adams and the New Light Beulah Baptist Church leaders worshipped on the land owned by Deacon Pharoah Smith until a building was constructed. (Blanch McRant McFadden.)

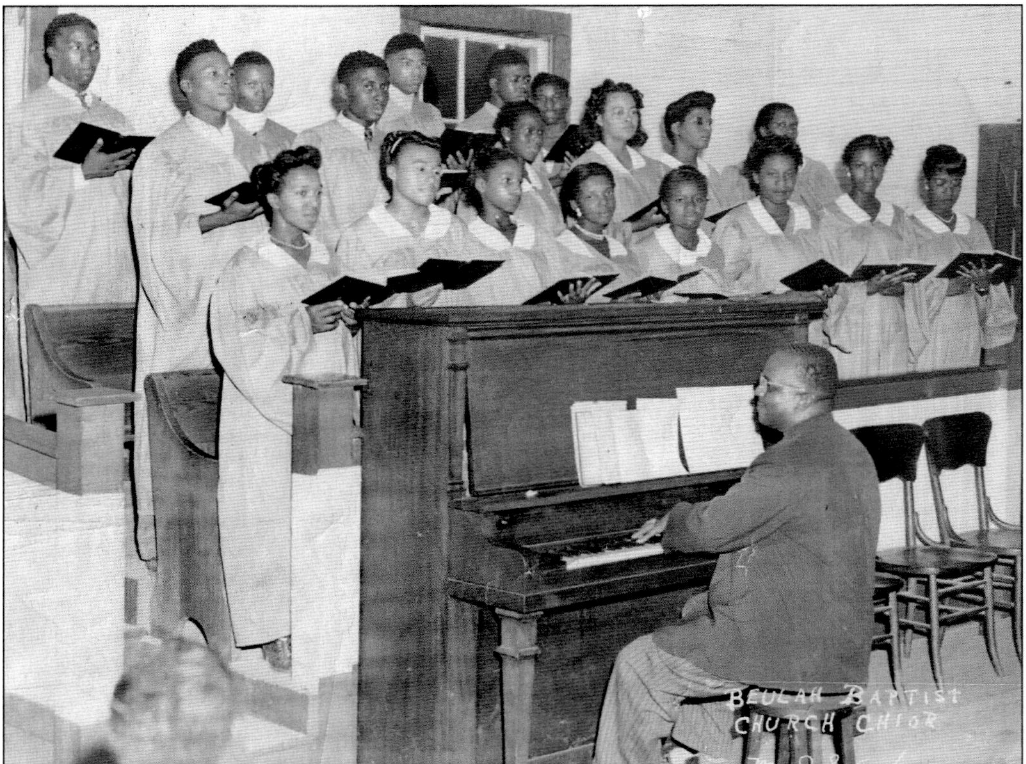

In 1886, New Light Beulah purchased 2 acres of land at a cost of $25. Trustees signing the deed on December 23, 1886, were Abram Weston, Jacob Golman, Pompey Smith, Thomas Stocker, Warrick Howell, Hamilton Jamison, and Julius Goodwin. The church building was used for both a place of worship and a school. New Light Beulah's membership continued to grow with new church leadership and new ministries. (Barber family collection.)

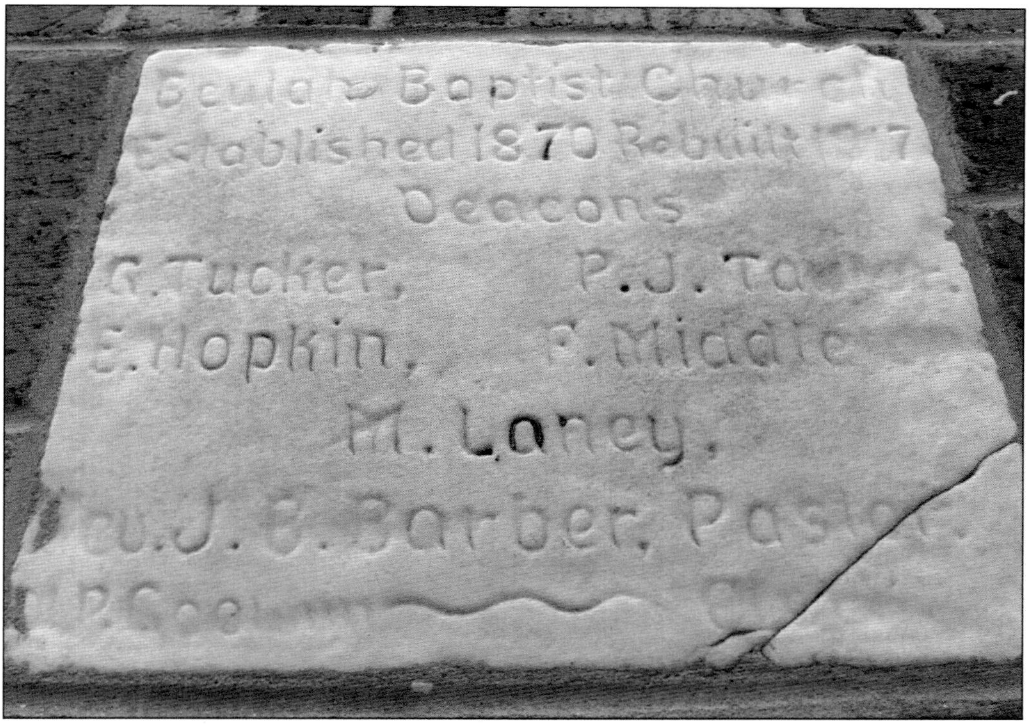

In 1902, a two-story school building was constructed next to Beulah Baptist Church. Spencer Adams was the first teacher in the school. The building remained on the property until the late 1930s. In 1916, a fire destroyed the church building, but a year later, a new granite structure was completed. The congregation celebrated its 140th anniversary in 2007. (Photograph by Deborah Scott Brooks.)

Peter Middleton was born in 1875, the grandson of Ned Edward Middleton, one of the founders of New Light Beulah. Pictured here with his friend Jake Johnson on his right, Peter and his wife, Mary, were the parents of Moses, Charles, Alexander, Peter, Arthur, Sylvia, William, Willie Ethel, Andrew, James, Simon, Pinkie, John, Leon, and Joseph. (Blanch McRant McFadden.)

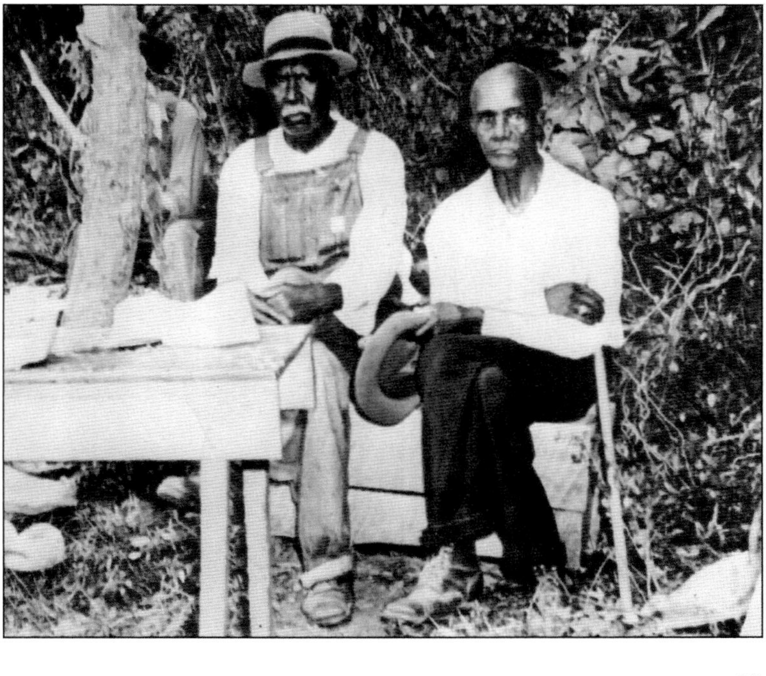

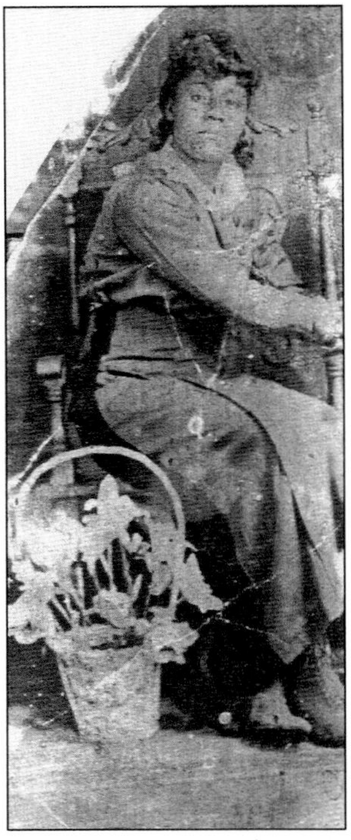

Maggie Johnson Hayes, born in Richland County in 1893, was the daughter of Jacob "Jake" and Fannie Goodwin Johnson. Affectionately known as "Miss Bing," she was a valued church worker and missionary throughout the community. Having been involved in civic and community activities, she worked diligently toward the success of many local politicians. (Blanch McRant McFadden.)

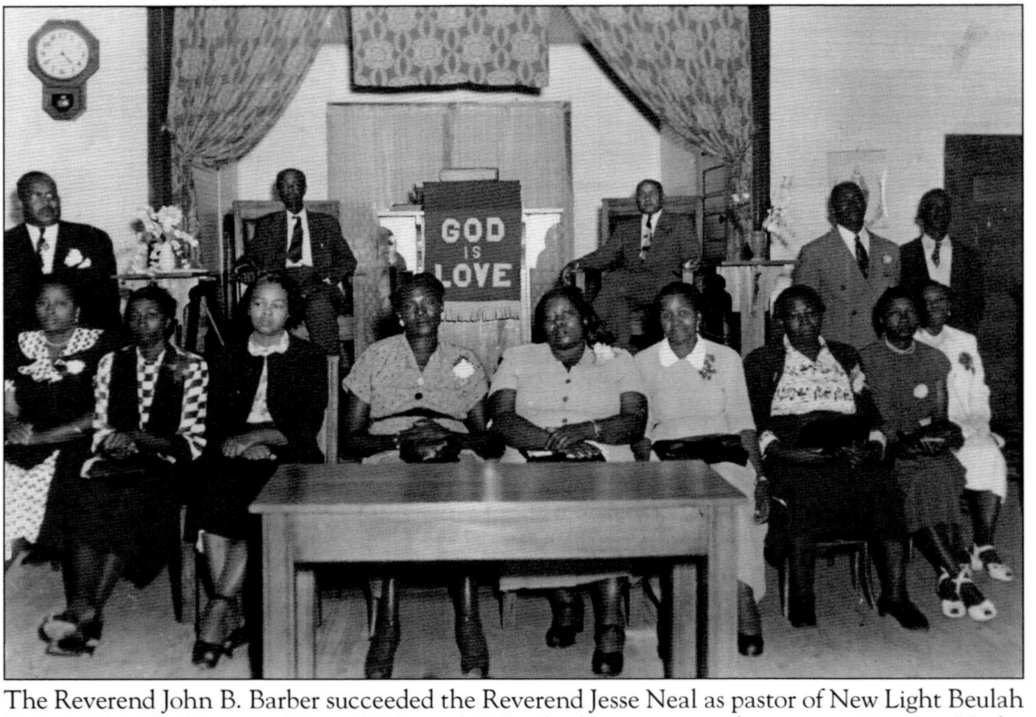

The Reverend John B. Barber succeeded the Reverend Jesse Neal as pastor of New Light Beulah Baptist Church. He served from 1909 until 1957, the longest term of service at 48 years. Under his leadership, the church continued to grow, with new church auxiliaries and organizations created. (Barber family collection.)

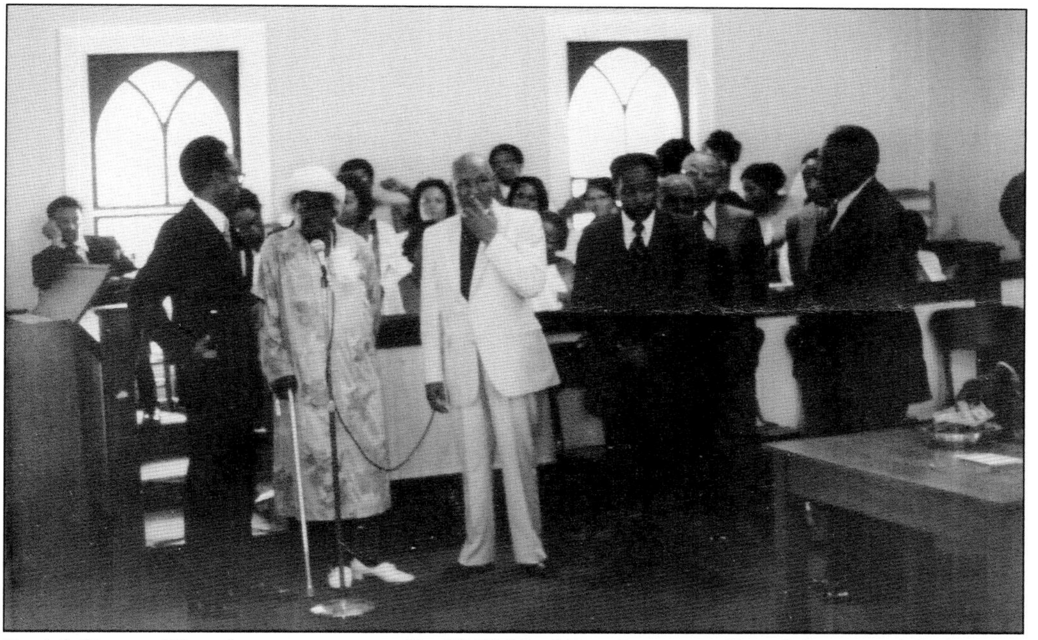

Beulah Baptist Church pastors emeriti Dr. W. H. Neal, Rev. Lawrence David, Rev. Mack Robinson, and Rev. Willie James Goodwin made a special presentation to Maggie Johnson Hayes inside the historic church building before it was torn down when the new church was completed. (Blanch McRant McFadden.)

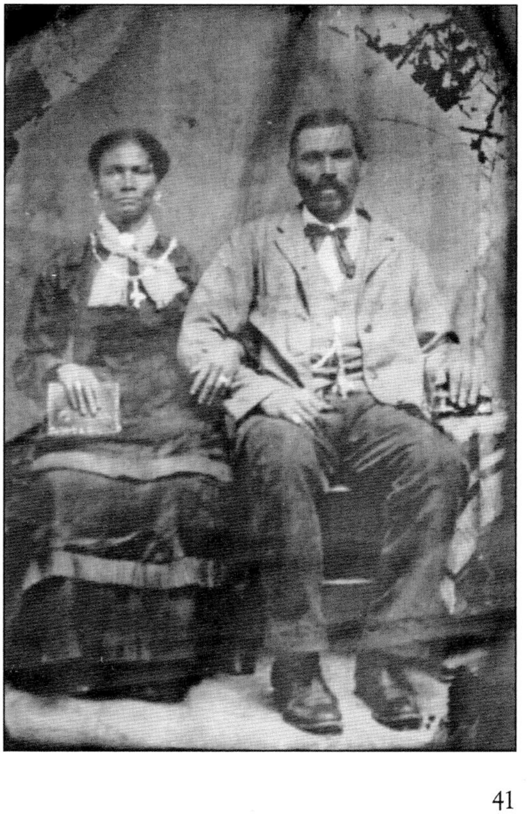

Peter Adams, born in 1834, was believed to be the son of a slave named Lucy from the McLaughlin Farm. His father was the plantation owner, Joel Adams. Peter is pictured here with his third wife, Laura Weston Adams. Their children were Tally, Celia, and Adell. (Wayne and Hazel Adams.)

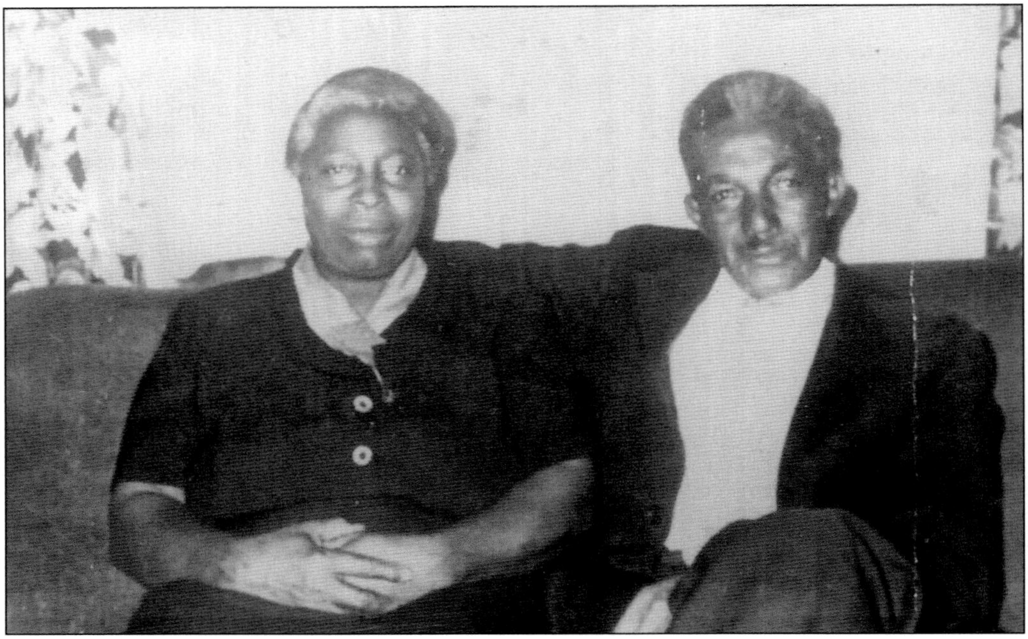

Tally Adams Sr. was one of three children born to Peter and Laura Weston. Peter Adams was a slave on the Joel Adams plantation, Grovewood. Tally married Lucille Herbert, and from this union, 13 children were born. The children were Lillie, Cleveland, Lugenia, Tally Jr., James, Lucille, Cornell, Peter, John (1931–1931), Maxie, Essie, Cephas, and John (1940). (Dorothy Adams.)

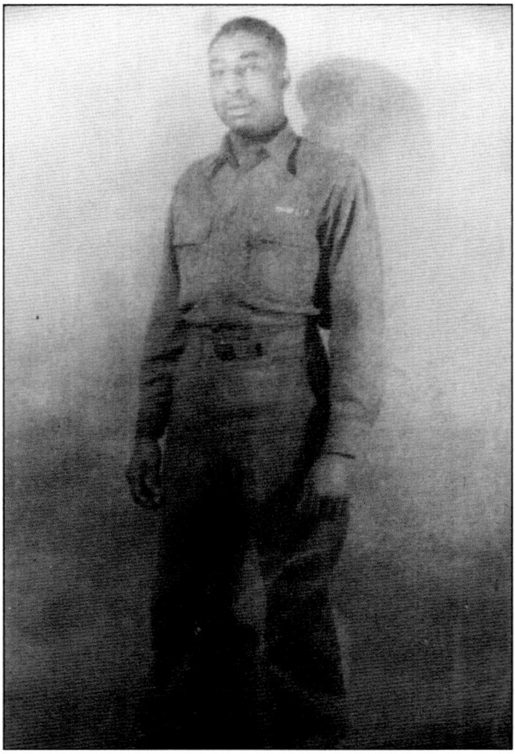

Tally Adams Jr. was the son of Tally Adams and Lucille Herbert Adams of Eastover. Among his accomplishments were Parent-Teacher-Student Association (PTSA) president, farmer, New Light Beulah Baptist Church deacon, Sunday school superintendent, and teacher. Two of his children were two of the first African American students to integrate Lower Richland High School in Hopkins. All 10 of his children received college degrees. In 2002, he was named Father of the Year by the South Carolina Attorney General's Office. (Wayne and Hazel Adams.)

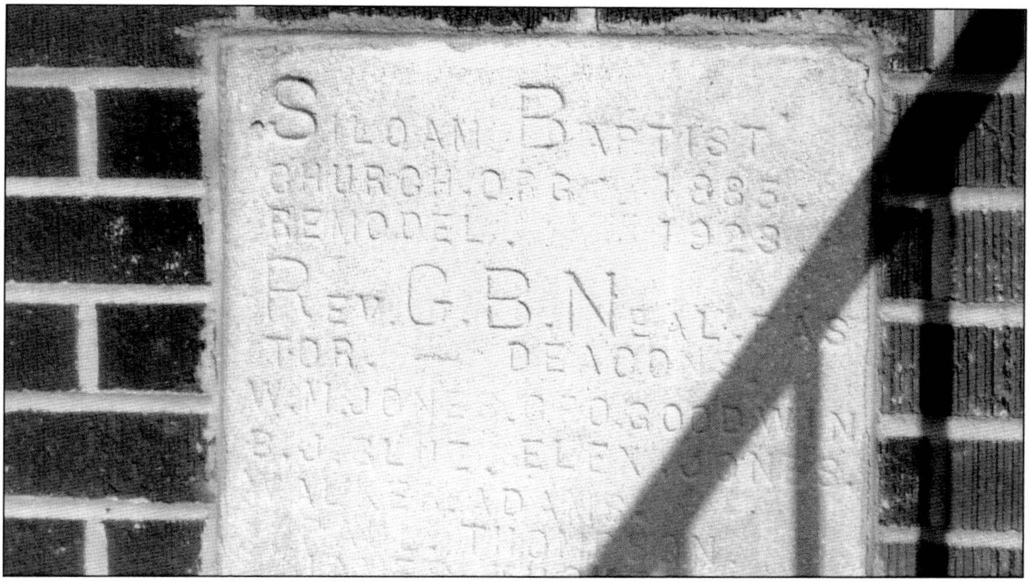

Siloam Baptist Church was formed when Pastor Daniel Boyd and members from New Light Beulah Baptist Church withdrew to form their new church in 1885. Deacons John Dinkins and Lewis Tucker were in leadership roles. This cornerstone indicates that Siloam was bricked in 1923, while Rev. G. B. Neal was pastor. After several years in the location just a short distance from Beulah, a school was built at Siloam, and Beulah students were transferred to Siloam. (Photograph by Marie Barber Adams.)

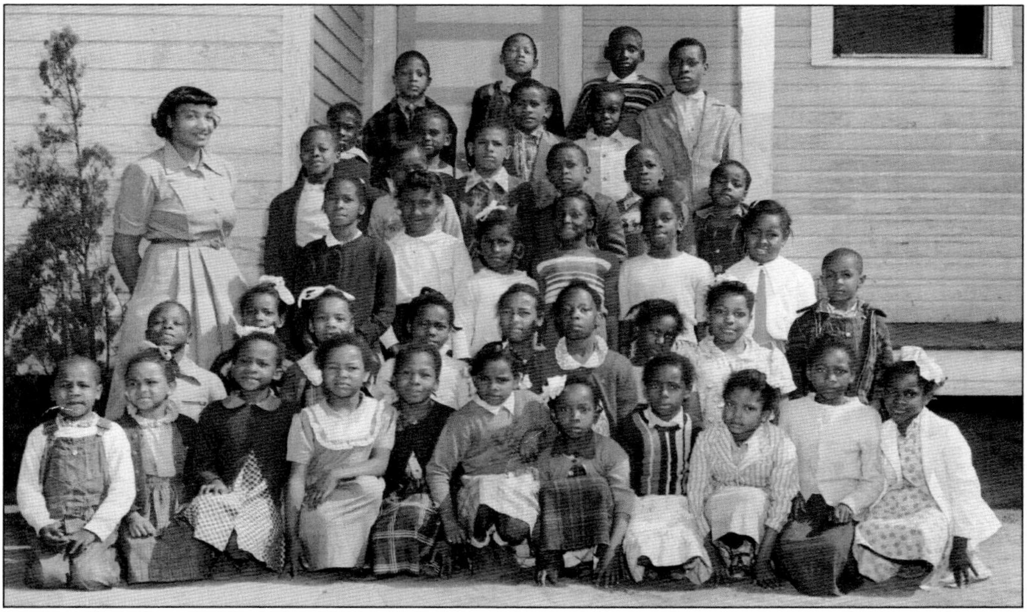

Siloam School is pictured here after a restoration in 1936 with funds from the Works Progress Administration for rural African American students. It served the residents in this area until 1956, when small community schools were consolidated. The teacher shown on the left is Lillie Neal Scott. The school started out like most in the county—within churches and serving the members of the congregation in the same building with one teacher. (Neal-Scott family collection.)

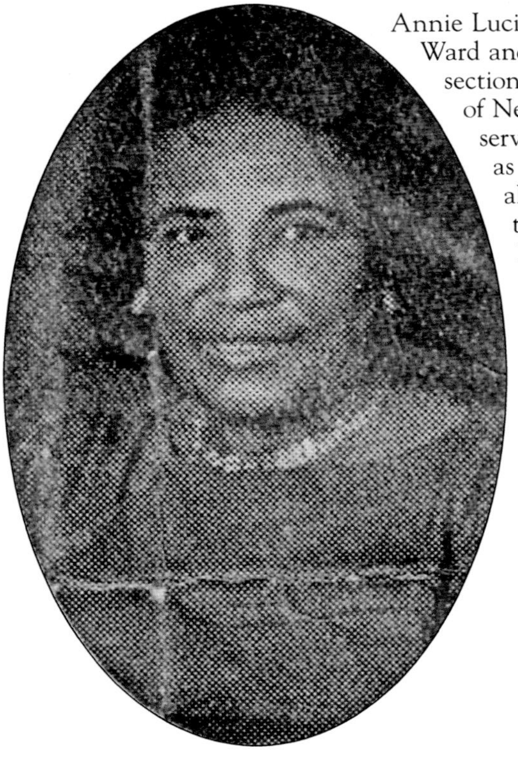

Annie Lucinda Ward White was the daughter of David Ward and Ella Brawley Ward. Living in the Congaree section, her family members were among the founders of New Light Beulah. Her husband, Ernest White, served the community on the election commission as the Lower Richland Citizens Committee. He also organized and coached baseball and softball teams for the youth in this area. (Blanch McRant McFadden.)

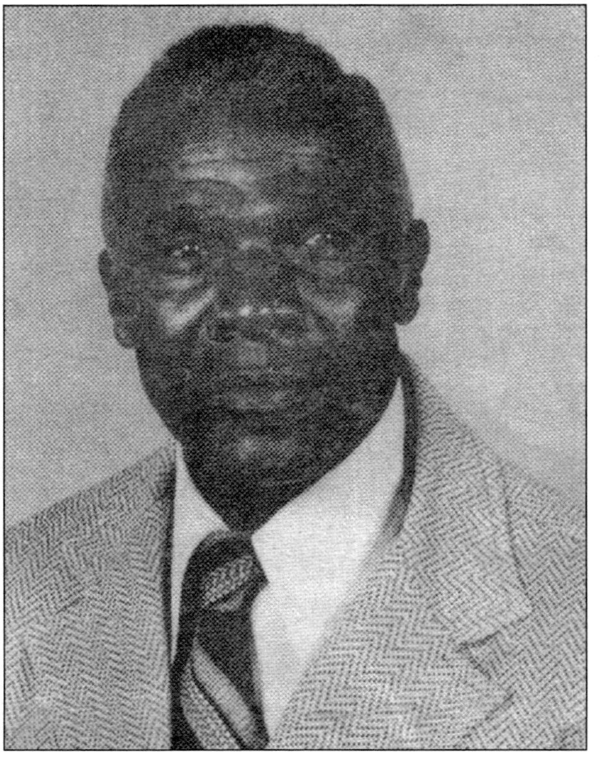

Boston Myers was among the early deacons ordained at New Light Beulah. He was married to Evelyn Smith Myers, and they were the parents of 16 children, including Leroy, Thomas, Lawrence, Pelham, Powell, Boston Jr., Joseph, John, Nathaniel, Samuel, Rebecca, and Queenie. Several of his sons formed a gospel quartet group, some of whom still perform. (Blanch McRant McFadden.)

Four

Hopkins

The history of the town of Hopkins can be traced to the family of John Hopkins, who was born in Hanover County, Virginia. This is the site of the Hopkins Turnout, a station built after the Minervaville site was abandoned in 1834. Many stories are told about the train turning around at the Hopkins station to go back to Charleston before the railroad was connected to Columbia. Hopkins, however, had its humble beginnings before the Revolutionary War. Through land grants, inheritance, the acquisition of slaves, and the marriages between the early settlers, the growth of Hopkins continued.

The Lower Richland planters included Hopkins, Adams, Weston, Clarkson, Gorman, Bush, Chappell, Myers, and others who acquired slaves to clear land, plant crops, build houses, and perform other work necessary for survival and economic growth in the Hopkins area. The various sections of Hopkins included Meeting House, Bannister Bridge, Divers, Old Field, Meadow Brook, Joel Adams, Fannie Hopkins, the Tipen, Chappell, Pinette, Weston, Flowers, Reeves, Minervaville, Dry Branch, Taylor Ford, McLemore, James Crossing, Hospen Branch, Bluff, Duffie, Bruno, Sand Hill, Baker's Level, and Chappell Creek. After the Emancipation Proclamation ended slavery, many families remained in these areas where they were once held as slaves.

Eventually jobs for African Americans became available in various industries throughout the area. Pinette and Tipen were noted for the production of turpentine. Long staple cotton was grown in Reeves and Flowers. The Neufus Mills Lumber Company had processing mills in Pin Cushion and Divers, and the dry kiln was alongside the Southern Railroad. The mill's tract extended from the mill to the Congaree River. In the location named Macamore's Corner, the mill employed over 150 workers. Over 50 dwellings were built and owned by the mill group. After the end of World War I, many African Americans had become prosperous business owners in this location. This included Willie Young and Dolly King's blacksmith shops, Joe McRant's Valet Shop, Martha Ann McRant's variety store, Fred Alston's barbershop, Phyllis Alston's cafe and lounge, Alex Smith's butcher shop, and a number of neighborhood variety stores.

The late Dr. W. H. Neal would often say, "If you plan to go to heaven, you have to stop by Hopkins on your way!"

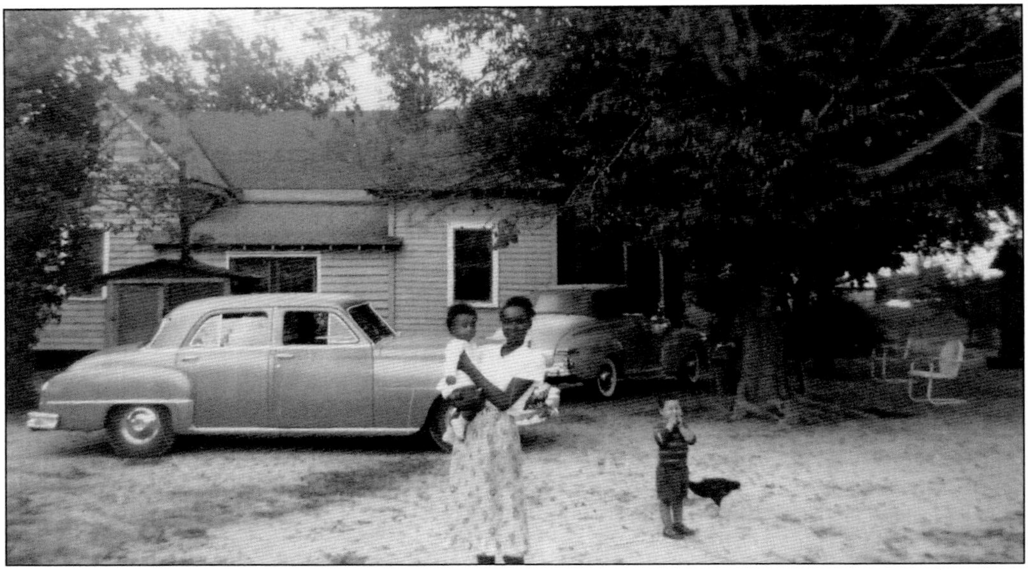

The Harriet Barber House started out as a log cabin built by former slaves Samuel and Harriet Barber in 1872 when they purchased 42.5 acres of land from the state's land commission, created during the Reconstruction years. Although many freedmen eventually lost their land, the land on which the Barber House is located has remained in the same family since 1872. A two-room home replaced the original log cabin, and additional rooms were built onto the structure as the family grew over the years. The present house was listed in the National Register of Historic Places on March 27, 1986. It appears to be the only freedman's dwelling still remaining from the land commission program. (John Barber Jr.)

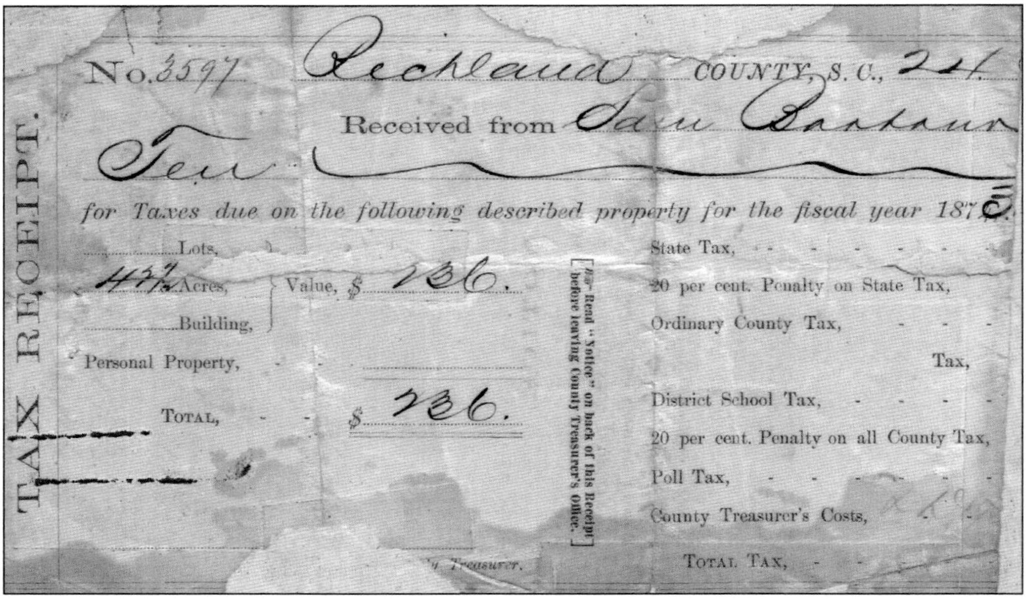

TAX RECEIPT.

No. 3597 Richland COUNTY, S. C., 24

Received from Sam Barbour

Ten

*for Taxes due on the following described property for the fiscal year 187*5

Lots,	State Tax,
42½ Acres, Value, $ 136.	20 per cent. Penalty on State Tax,
Building,	Ordinary County Tax,
Personal Property,	Tax,
TOTAL, $ 136.	District School Tax,
	20 per cent. Penalty on all County Tax,
	Poll Tax,
	County Treasurer's Costs,
Treasurer.	TOTAL TAX,

☞ Read "Notice" on back of this Receipt before leaving County Treasurer's Office.

Sam Barber made the first payment on this property, and his wife Harriet made the final payment in May 1879. A tax receipt is pictured. Generations of the Barber family lived in the house and farmed the land until the late 1950s. The restoration of the house was completed in 2009. (Barber family collection.)

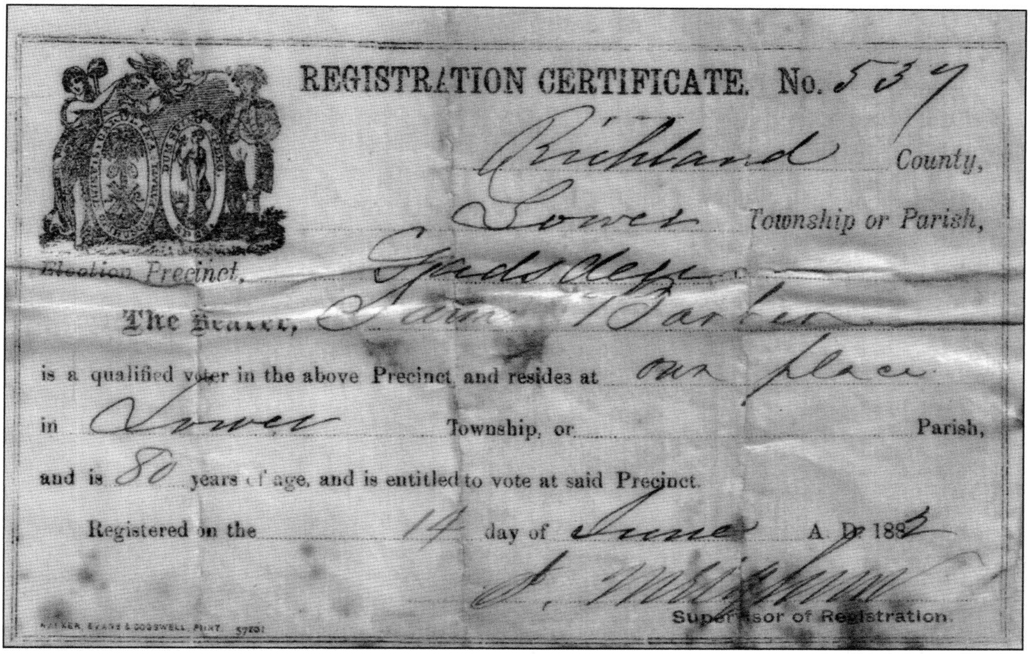
REGISTRATION CERTIFICATE. No. 537

Richland County,

Lower Township or Parish,

Election Precinct, [illegible]

The Bearer, Sam Barber

is a qualified voter in the above Precinct and resides at our place

in Lower Township, or Parish,

and is 80 years of age, and is entitled to vote at said Precinct.

Registered on the 14 day of June A. D. 1882

[illegible]

Supervisor of Registration.

Walker, Evans & Cogswell, Print. [illegible]

Samuel Barber was born in Blackstone, Virginia. He came to the Lower Richland area with one of the plantation families from Virginia who settled here in the early 1800s. This document shows his age of 80 years when he registered to vote on June 14, 1882. He was a well digger by trade, but he was also a minister and a farmer. He and his family moved to the Hopkins community and led a campaign to establish St. John Baptist Church by 1875 after meeting in a bush arbor by an old oak tree off Clarkson Road. (Barber family collection.)

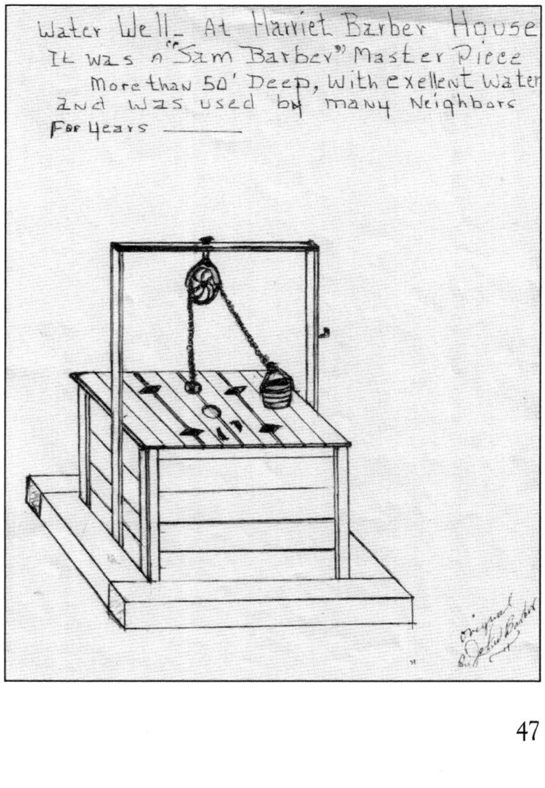

According to family lore, Sam gained his freedom before settling in Kingville. He had permission during slavery to travel from place to place when new wells were needed. John B. Barber Jr., at age 88, sketched this drawing of his grandfather's first well in Hopkins. (John B. Barber Jr.)

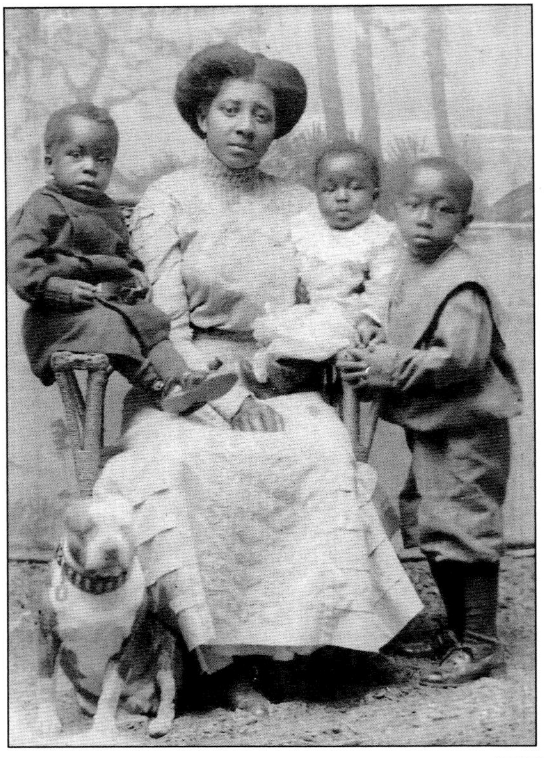

Nancy Barber Jeter was born in Richland County in 1865 in the Kingville community. Nancy was listed in the pupil roster in 1870 at the Red Hill School. She moved with her parents, Sam and Harriet Barber, to the Hopkins community in 1872. She later married John Henry Jeter, and they lived in their house on the Barber tract of land. John Henry Jeter worked for the railroad, and some time after 1880, he and Nancy sold their home to the McCracken family and moved to Jacksonville, Florida. (Barber family collection.)

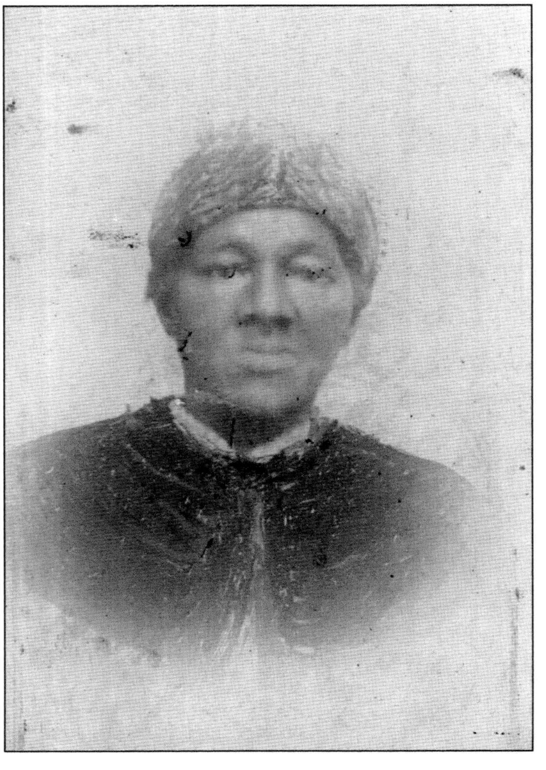

Sarah Barber Johnson was born in February 1854. She was living in the Kingville area with her parents, Rev. Sam Barber and his first wife, Rachel. She married deacon Sandy Johnson in 1875, shortly after the Barber family moved to Hopkins. Sarah became active in St. John Baptist Church, and there she became the first Sunday school teacher. (Blanch McRant McFadden.)

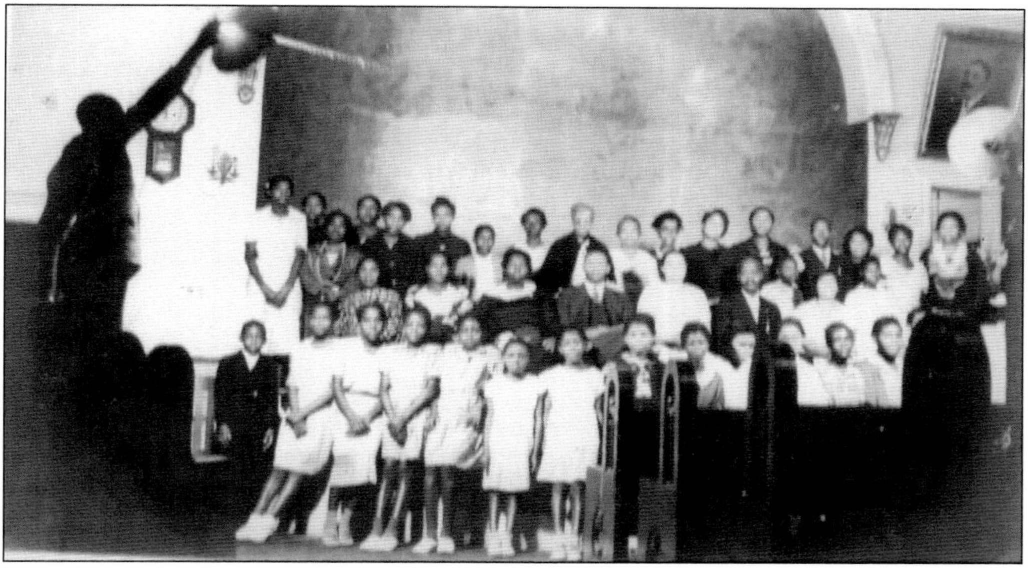

Maria Barber Goodwin was one of the daughters born to Samuel and Rachel Barber in 1855, while the family was living in the Kingville community. By the 1860s, Samuel was married to Harriet, and Maria was a teenager when the family moved to Hopkins in 1872. When Maria married Korsuit Goodwin, a Benedict Institute student, the couple moved to Columbia, where she worked for a florist on Main Street. She is pictured in the center of the third row, a statuesque 6-foot-tall lady, at the Zion Baptist Church. (Barber family collection.)

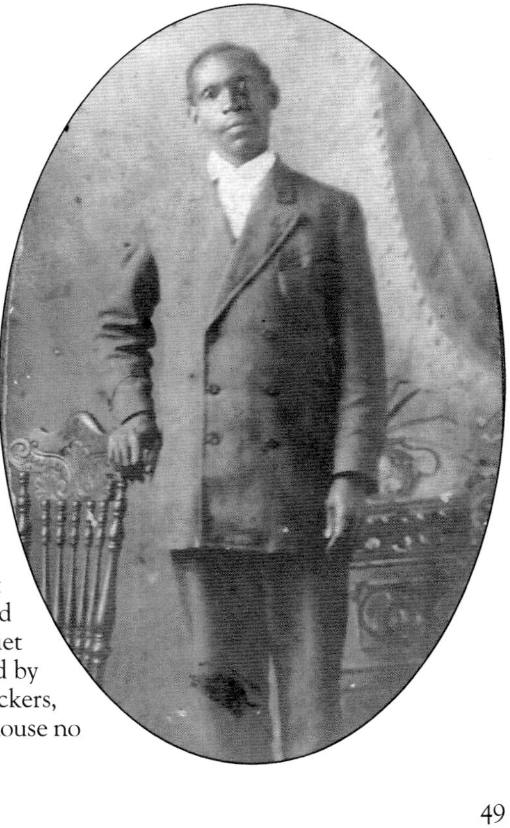

Washington Tucker was born in Lower Richland in 1864. He was a Benedict Institute student from 1883 to 1884. He taught at the Beulah School in the Congaree community. In 1896, he married Frances Barber, the daughter of Sam and Harriet Barber. Washington and his wife, Frances, lived on a portion of the Barber tract behind the Harriet Barber House. Although the house was occupied by other family members after the death of the Tuckers, the property still remains in the family, but the house no longer exists. (Barber family collection.)

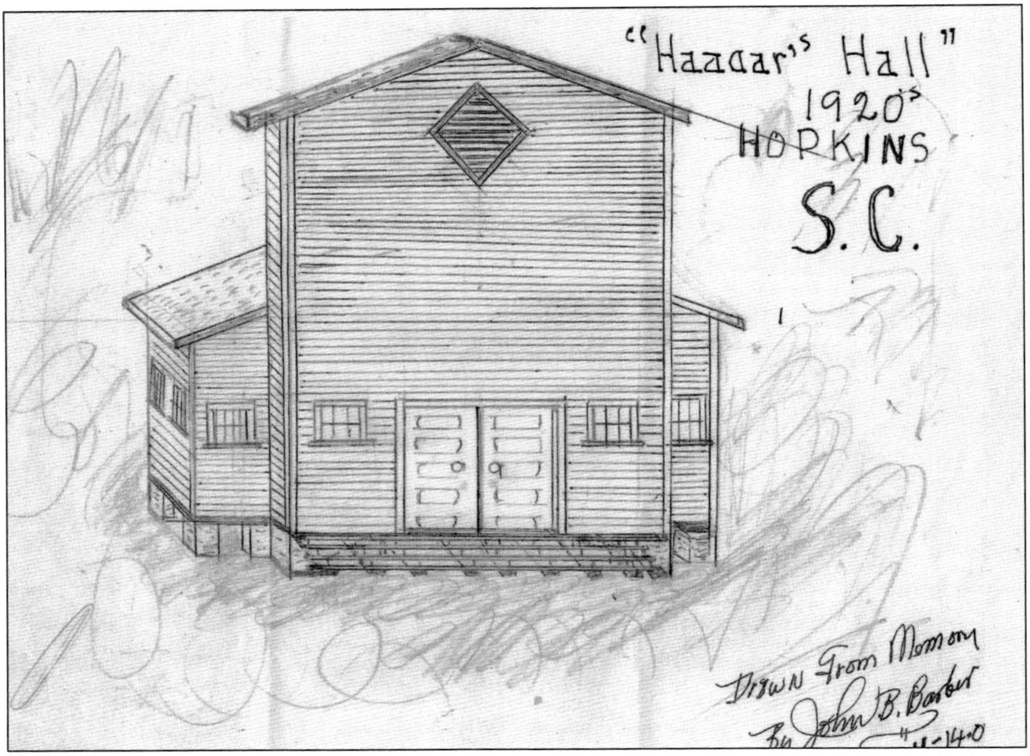

The Hicks Chappell House is one of the oldest dwellings in Richland County. It was also the home of Hagar Chappell, who resided there as the housekeeper for the family of Maj. Hicks Chappell, a Revolutionary War officer and wealthy landowner. Hagar lived in a house built next to the main house. After slavery ended, she became a successful business lady along with her husband, Brazell Alston. Hagar donated the lumber to build the depicted meeting hall. (John B. Barber Jr.)

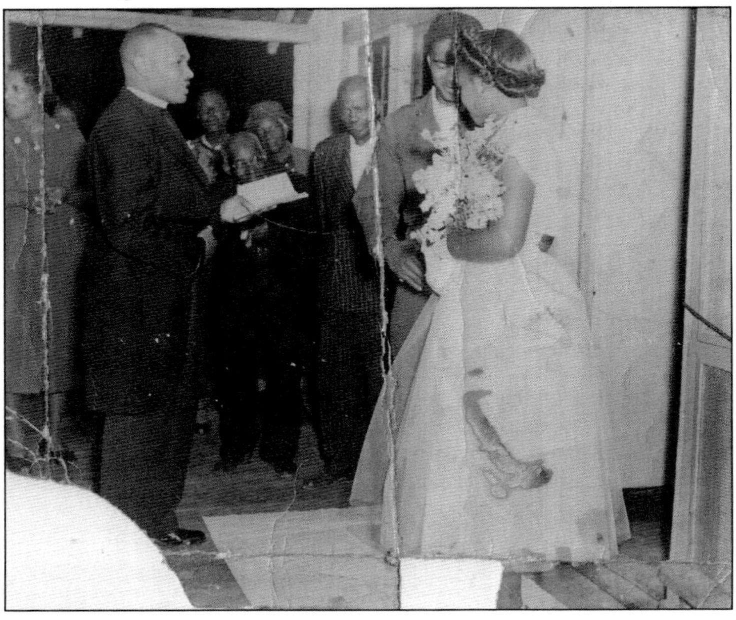

Israel Alston (center) was the son of Hagar and Brazell Alston. Alston was regarded as a big farmer with hired workers. Alston, a well-known singer and choir leader, performed in a singing group across the county with his brothers Cyrus, Brazell, Sam, and Richard. Many older residents recall him as a well-dressed man riding about in a rubber-tired buggy pulled by his horse, named Dan. (Ernestine Alston.)

Clarissa Mack (McPherson) Barber was the daughter of George McPherson. She was born in 1852 and married Sam Barber Jr. in 1868. Clarissa was a well-known midwife in the Hopkins area. She was also known as a "healer" who created most of her medicines from herbs and plants grown locally. She was known to cure a sore throat by tying a string around the hair at the top of the head of a patient and pulling the hair in a snap. (Barber family collection.)

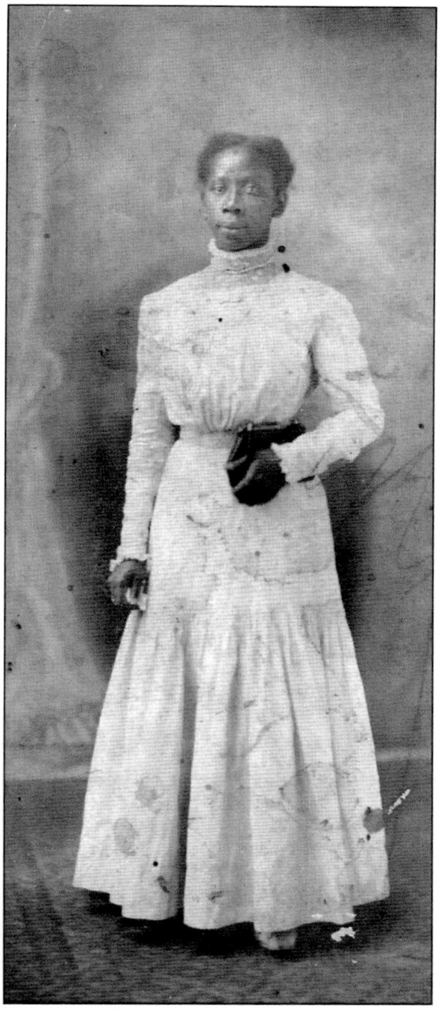

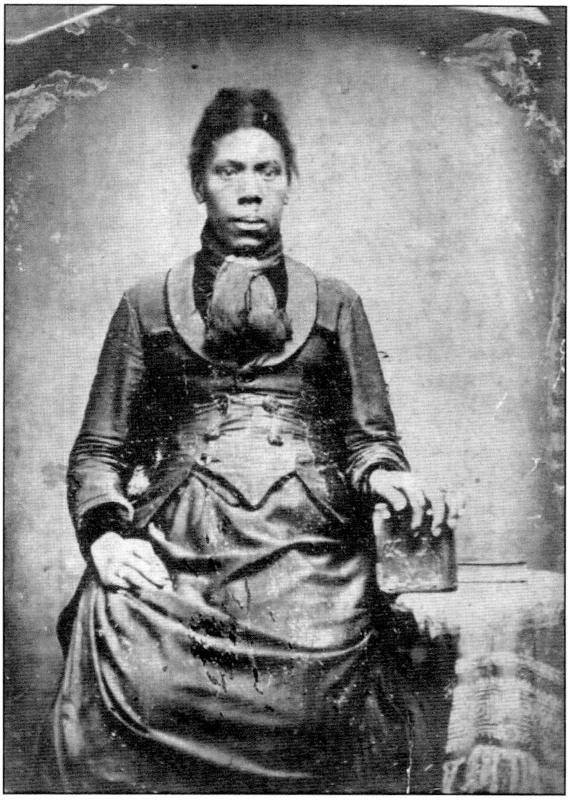

Alice Barber is pictured here in a striking pose with one hand on the Bible. Alice was the wife of Henry Barber, son of Rev. Sam Barber and his first wife. Alice and Henry were married in 1884, and they lived on the tract of land in Hopkins belonging to the Barber family. (Barber family collection.)

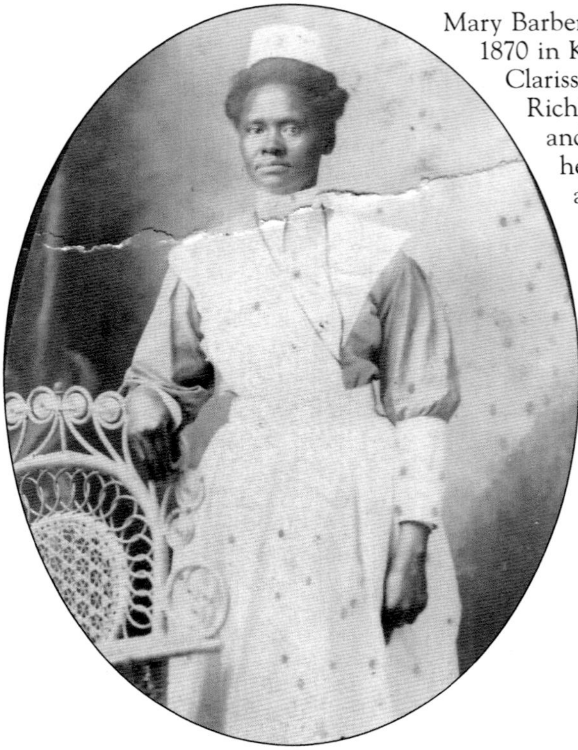

Mary Barber, also known as Tay Mary, was born in 1870 in Kingville to Sam Barber Jr. and his wife, Clarissa, who was known throughout the Lower Richland area as a healer who used local herbs and plants to treat the sick. Mary, pictured here in a nurse's uniform, also worked as a midwife like her mother. According to Barber family records, Mary Barber had served as a nurse in the Spanish-American War. (Barber family collection.)

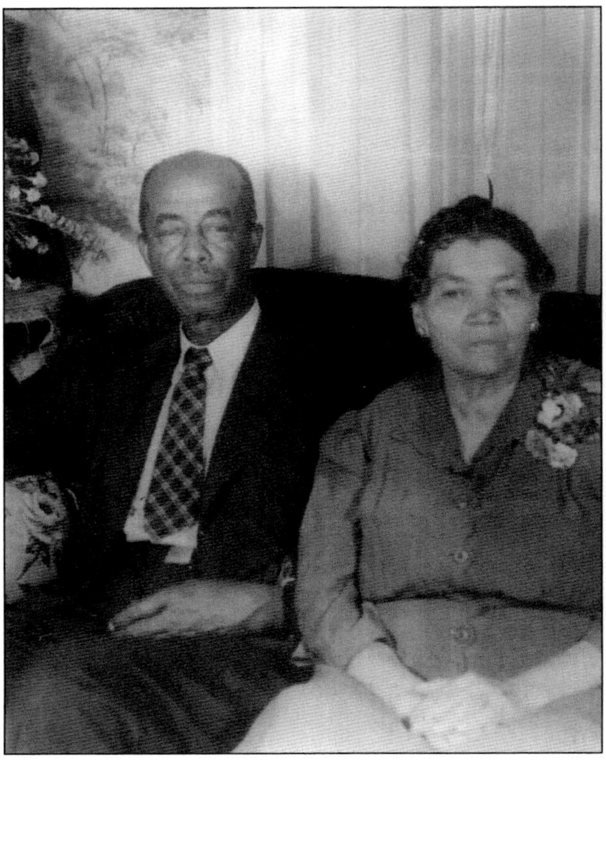

John Benjamin Barber was born in 1872, the son of Sam and Harriet Barber. He attended the Hopkins School from 1879 to 1886. He completed his high school training at Benedict Institute in 1900. Barber continued his education there, pursuing the normal course for teaching and other courses leading to the divinity degree. State Department of Education records show that he taught in the Killian School from 1898 to 1903, St. James from 1904 to 1907, Egypt Hill from 1908 to 1910, Friendship from 1911 to 1914, Flatlake from 1915 to 1923, and Hopkins School from 1923 until his retirement in 1940. (Barber family collection.)

Rev. John Barber was ordained in 1902 and served as pastor of the following churches: Capernaum Baptist Church in Eastover, St. James in Hopkins, Beulah Baptist in Hopkins, St. Mark in Gadsden, and Pleasant Grove in Gadsden. He was highly esteemed, not only locally but also generally in the county and state through his leadership with the Wateree Baptist Association Upper Division. (Barber family collection.)

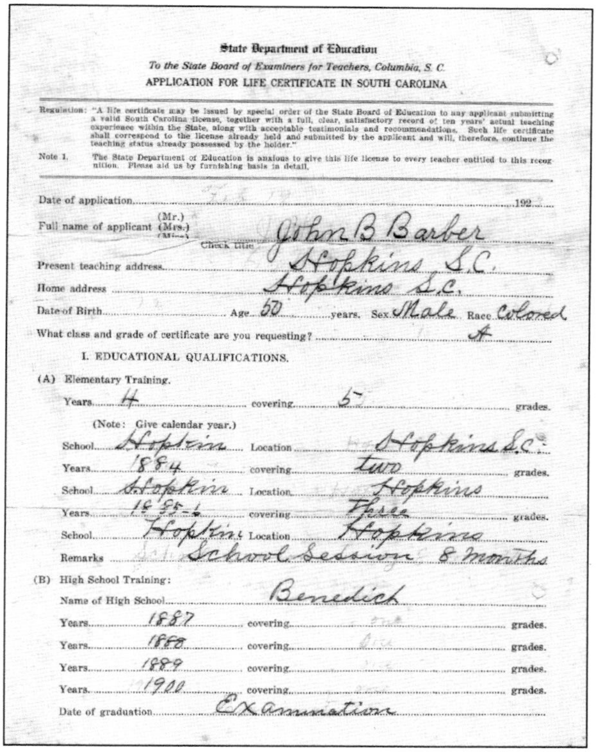

State Department of Education

To the State Board of Examiners for Teachers, Columbia, S. C.

APPLICATION FOR LIFE CERTIFICATE IN SOUTH CAROLINA

Regulation: "A life certificate may be issued by special order of the State Board of Education to any applicant submitting a valid South Carolina license, together with a full, clear, satisfactory record of ten years' actual teaching experience within the State, along with acceptable testimonials and recommendations. Such life certificate shall correspond to the license already held and submitted by the applicant and will, therefore, continue the teaching status already possessed by the holder."

Note 1. The State Department of Education is anxious to give this life license to every teacher entitled to this recognition. Please aid us by furnishing basis in detail.

Date of application.................192....

Full name of applicant (Mr.) (Mrs.) (Miss) Check title John B Barber

Present teaching address Hopkins S.C.

Home address Hopkins S.C.

Date of Birth.......... Age 50 years. Sex Male Race Colored

What class and grade of certificate are you requesting? A

I. EDUCATIONAL QUALIFICATIONS.

(A) Elementary Training.

Years 4 covering 5 grades.

(Note: Give calendar year.)

School Hopkin Location Hopkins S.C.

Years 1884 covering two grades.

School Hopkin Location Hopkins

Years 1885-6 covering Three grades.

School Hopkins Location Hopkins

Remarks School Session 8 months

(B) High School Training:

Name of High School Benedict

Years 1887 covering .... grades.

Years 1888 covering .... grades.

Years 1889 covering .... grades.

Years 1900 covering .... grades.

Date of graduation Examination

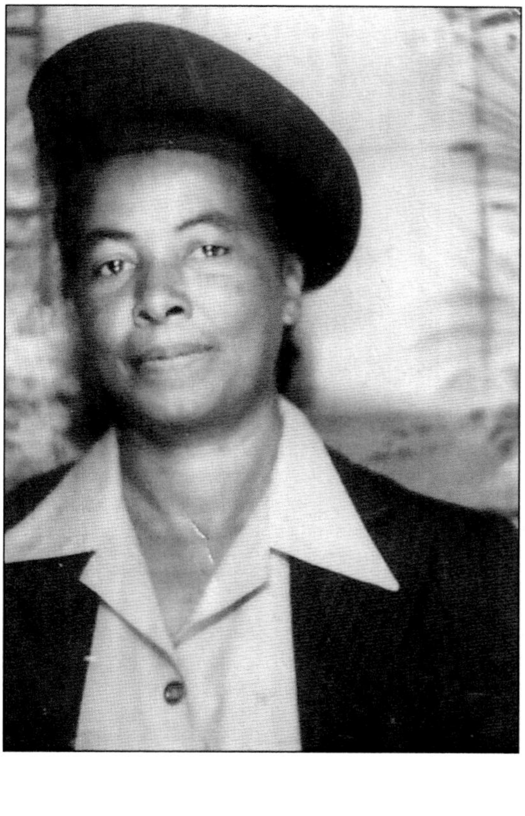

Celestine Louise Barber Daniels (1899–1978) was the first child born to Rev. John B. Barber and his wife, Mamie Holley Barber. She was educated at Benedict Normal School, where she was listed as a graduate in the class of 1918. By 1924, she had completed the requirements to teach. She began teaching at Siloam School and later taught at Flat Lake, Hopkins, and Claytor Schools. Celestine Barber married Edward Daniels, the local train or tram driver. (Barber family collection.)

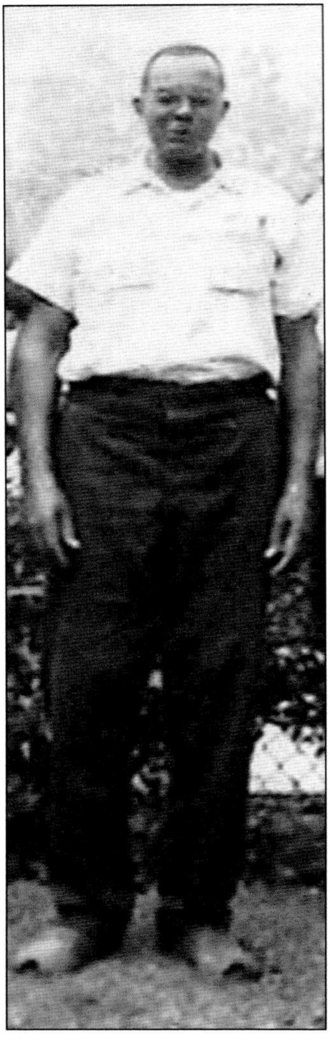

Sandy Fletcher Barber was born in Hopkins in 1905. His parents were the Reverend John B. Barber and Mamie Holly Barber. He received his formal education in Hopkins and attended South Carolina State College in Orangeburg. By 1924, Sandy had left Hopkins to find work first in North Carolina and later in Pittsburgh, Pennsylvania. He finally settled in Detroit, Michigan, where he found a passion for working with automobiles at the Ford Motor Company. (Barber family collection.)

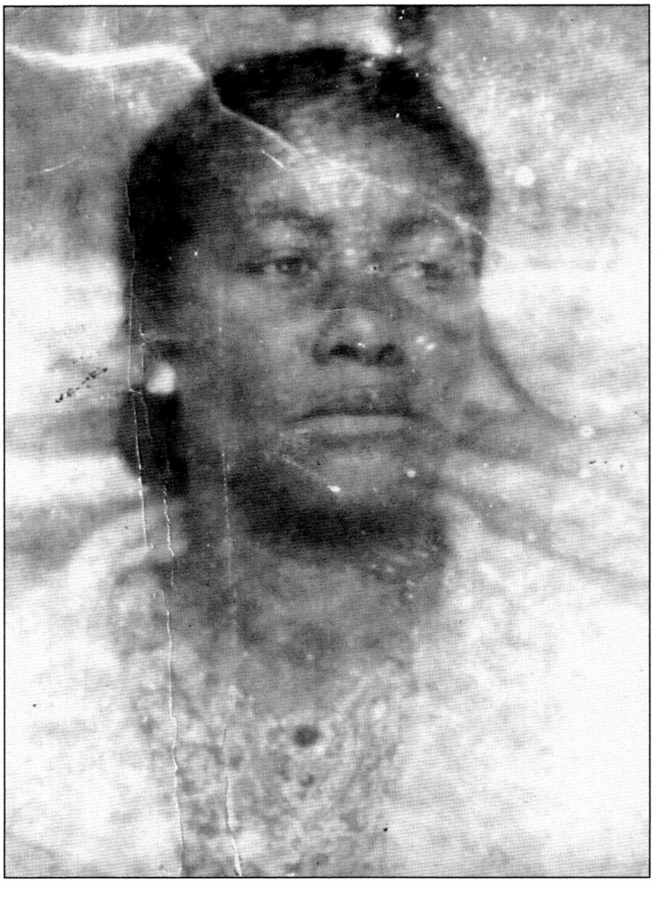

Portia Barber married Israel Alston on the front porch of the Harriet Barber House. It was a wedding attended by many family members who came from far and near. Alston was considered by many as a "well-to-do" farmer and businessman. Portia and her husband were faithful members of St. John Baptist Church, where she played the organ and he sang in the choir. Portia was born in 1903. (Barber family collection.)

Edith Barber Newton Rawlinson was a professional beautician with a shop built onto her home in Hopkins. She became founder and president of the Church Aid Club at St. John Baptist Church. She also held leadership positions in other church organizations as well as the Wateree Sunday School Convention and the Eastern Stars. Rawlinson also served as a foster parent and advocate, treasurer of the Lower Richland NAACP, and member of the Lower Richland Community Club, Inc. (Barber family collection.)

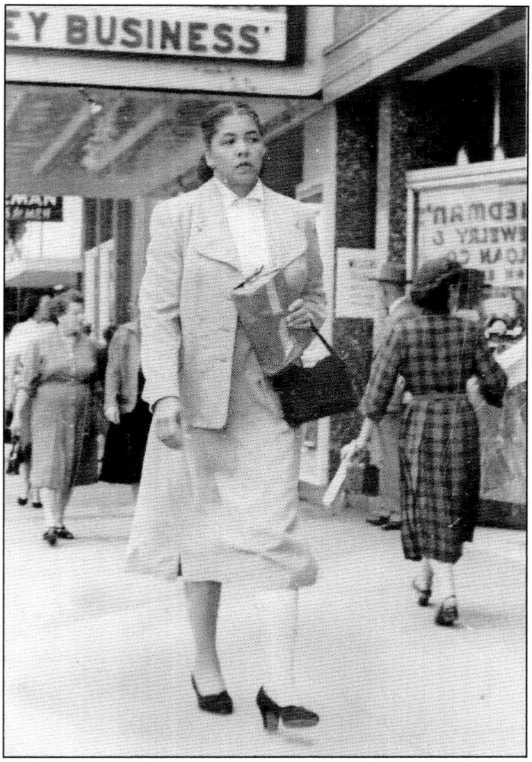

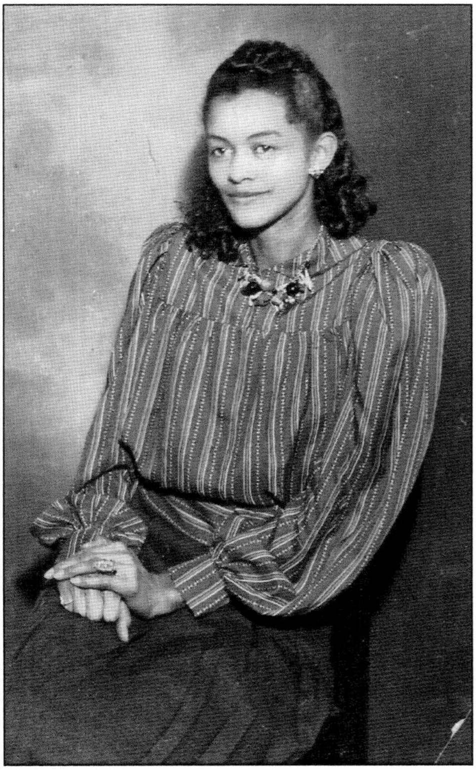

Mable Barber was born in 1907, daughter of the Reverend John B. Barber and Mamie Holley Barber. She graduated from Booker T. Washington High School, Allen University, and New York University, where she earned her master of arts degree in education. The wife of Russell Hagood, she began teaching at Friendship and Siloam Schools in the Lower Richland community. She worked as a first-grade teacher until her retirement from Hopkins Elementary School in 1976. (Barber family collection.)

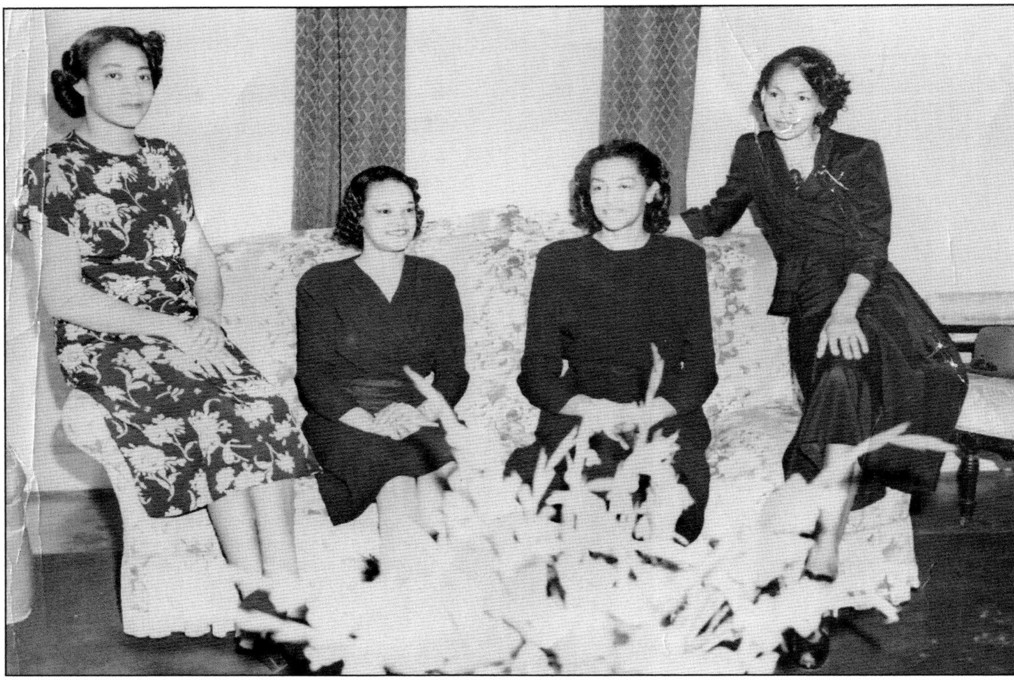

Mable Barber Hagood was affiliated with several civic organizations, including the education associations at the national, state and county levels, the Zeta Phi Beta Sorority, Inc, and the Hopkins Senior Citizens Club. She also worked as a wedding director and consultant throughout the local area. She held several leadership positions at her family church, St. John Baptist Church in Hopkins. (Barber family collection.)

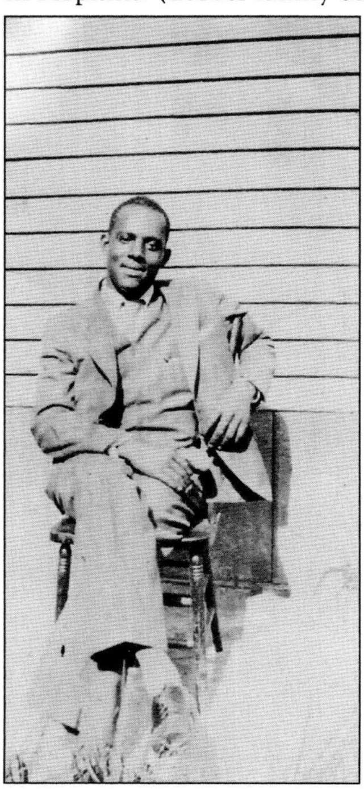

Russell Hagood was united in matrimony to Mable Barber in 1948. Together they reared one son, Sandy Odell Hagood. Russell grew up in Columbia, where he was born in 1910. After completing Booker T. Washington High School and Allen University, he moved to New York and began operating several businesses and worked as a carpenter. With his wife, Mable, he settled in the Hopkins community, where he operated a successful interstate trucking business for 35 years and the first convenience store on Cabin Creek Road. (Barber family collection.)

Marie Barber Jones was born in Hopkins in 1909. She was a talented seamstress. She was married to Pelham Jones of Hopkins, and the couple lived most of their lives in Columbia on Pine Street. They were the parents of Pelham Jr. and Sylvester. (Barber family collection.)

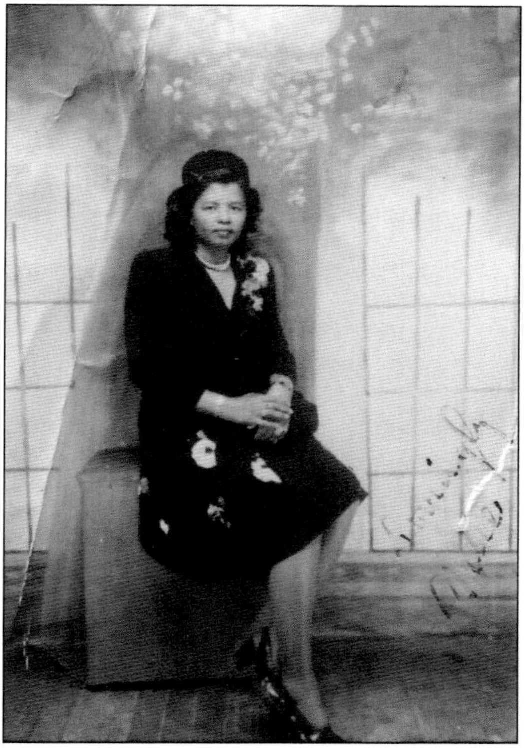

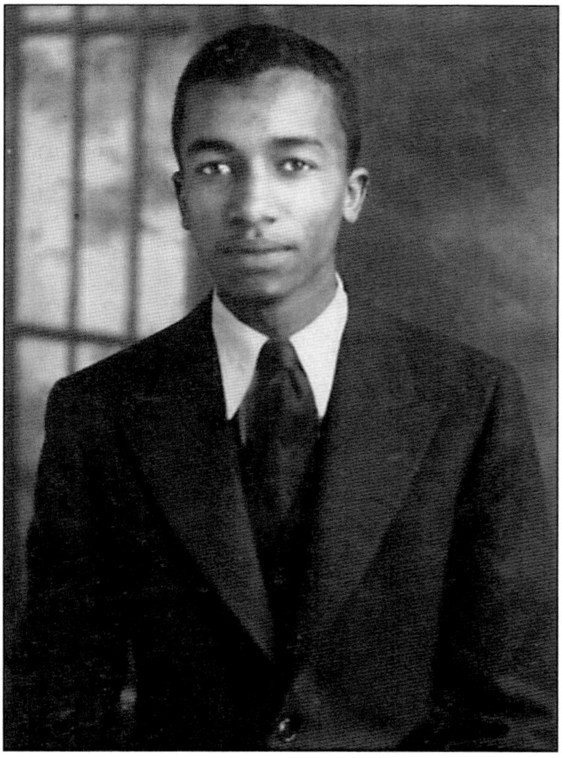

Melvin Wilson Barber Sr. was born in Hopkins in 1916. He graduated from Booker T. Washington High School in Columbia, where he excelled in academics. He became a master carpenter and a building construction superintendent for various companies in the Detroit area. He and his cousin, Sylvester Jones, created the B&J Construction Company, and together they built Detroit's Sherwood Hospital and Hitsville USA, home of Motown. (Barber family collection.)

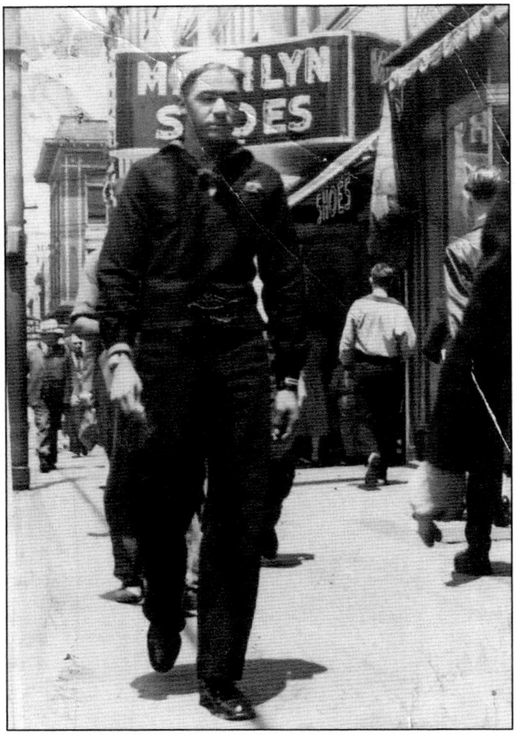

John Benjamin Barber Jr. joined the U.S. Navy out of Booker T. Washington High School in Columbia and traveled the world before settling down in Detroit with his older brothers Sandy and Melvin. He soon became a part of the B&J Construction Company, applying his skills as a carpenter. He also found employment with the Ford Motor Company, which undoubtedly inspired him to be a "tinkerer and putterer" with electronic gadgets. At the age of 89, he is an expert with the computer and any other technology associated with it. A talented artist as well, John has a photographic memory of his early life in Hopkins. (Barber family collection.)

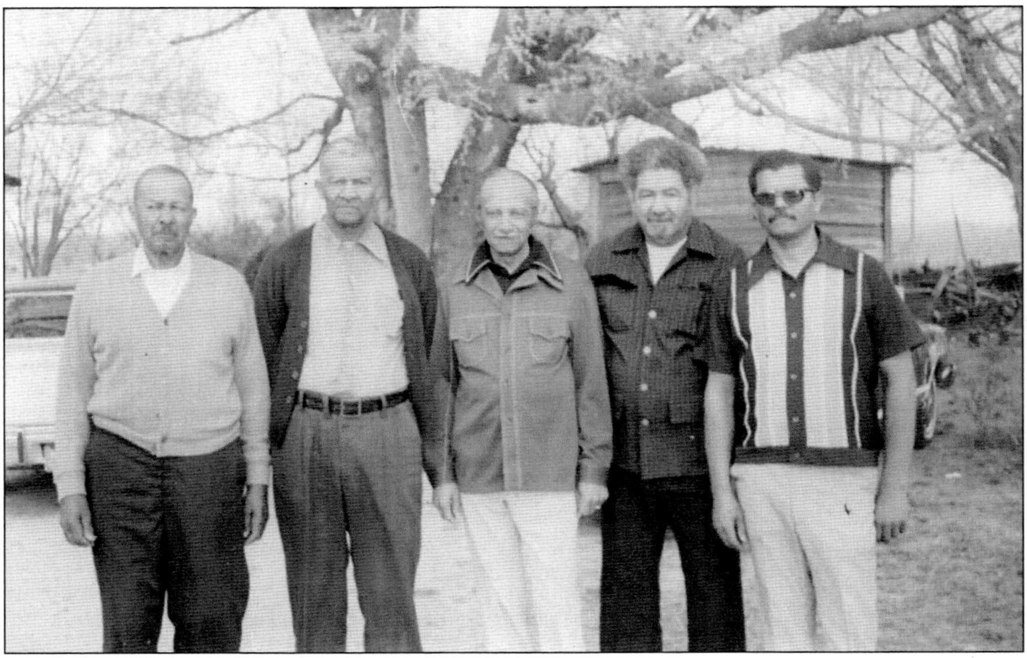

Barber brothers are pictured standing in front of the historic sugarberry tree at the Harriet Barber House. The brothers traveled the world, but they always found time to return home, where Ulysses remained all of his life, to keep the birthplace maintained. Pictured from left to right are Sandy, Ulysses, Melvin, Johnny, and Odell. (Barber family collection.)

Odell Sandy Barber joined the U.S. Navy after high school and served a tour of duty during World War II. He worked in the accounting field for a number of years and later worked for the U.S. Postal Service until his retirement. (Barber family collection.)

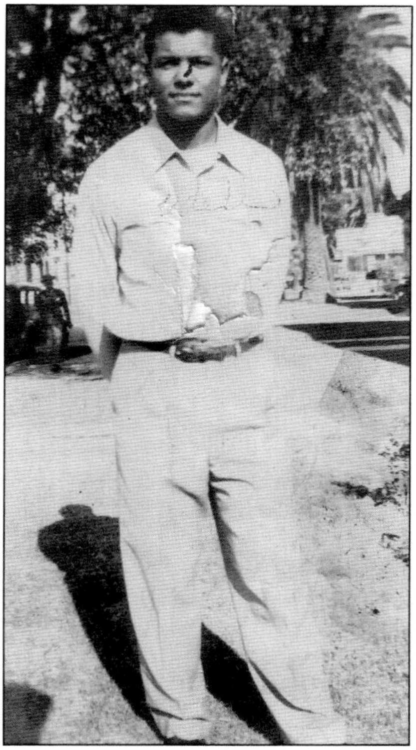

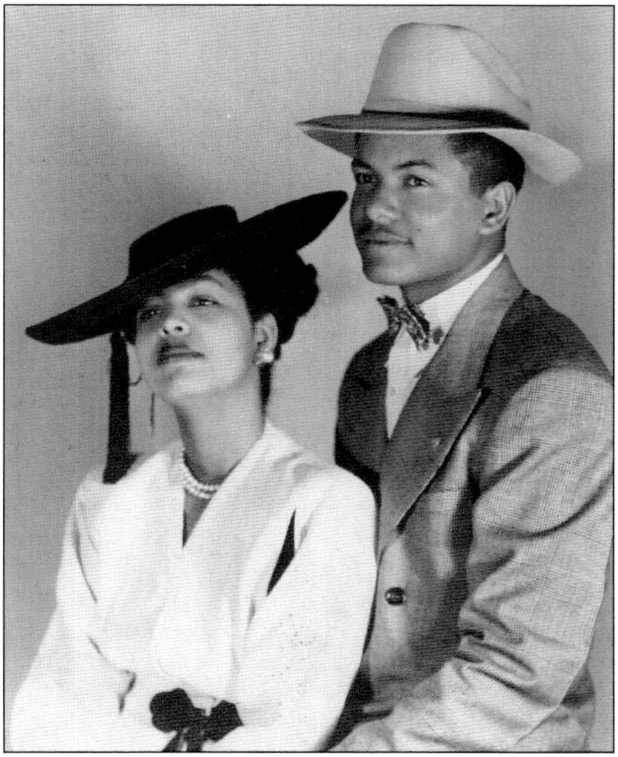

Odell and Ruth Barber met in California, where Odell was stationed at the U.S. Navy base in San Diego. After his tour of duty in the service, he settled in Los Angeles, where he met and later married an attractive lady named Ruth. Ginger was their only child. (Barber family collection.)

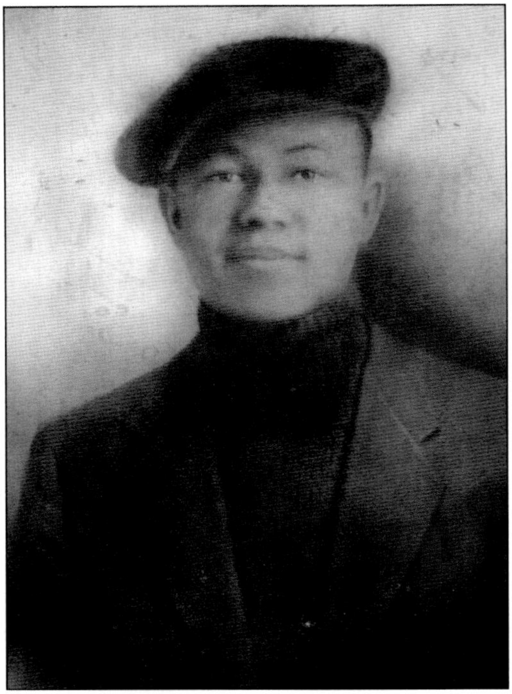

James "L. D." Henderson Barber was the ninth child born to Rev. John B. Barber and his wife, Mamie Holley Barber. He was born in Hopkins in 1919 and died in a tragic accident in 1937. Pictured as a young man in this photograph, he was an adventurous teenager who stood 6 feet 7 inches tall and weighed over 300 pounds. (Barber family collection.)

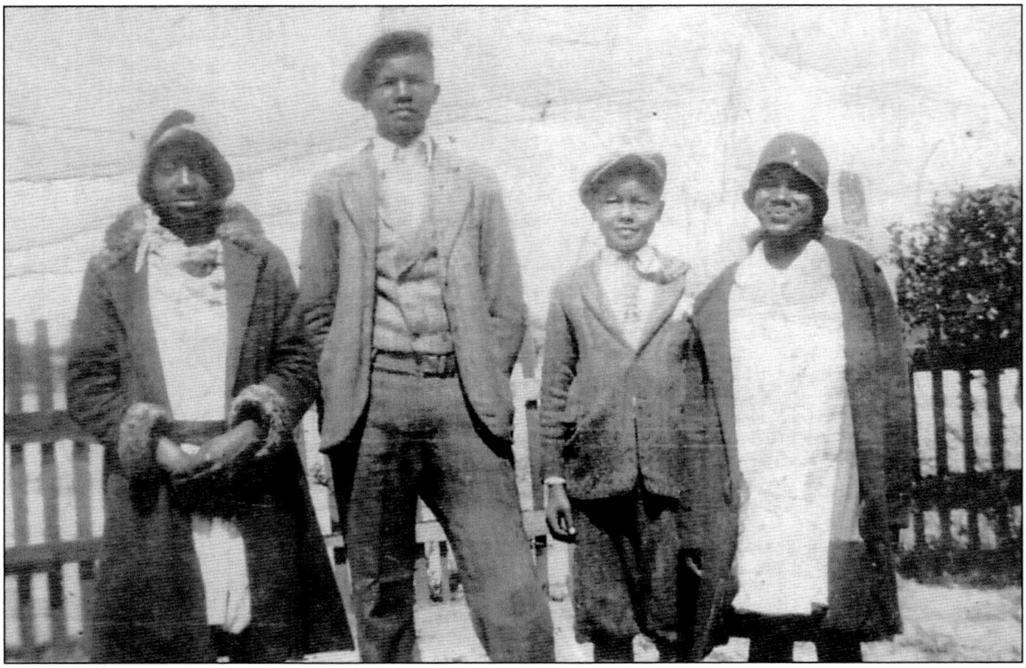

Ulysses R. Barber, the seventh child of Rev. and Mrs. John B. Barber, was given the title "professor." When he entered Allen University, he was a scholar athlete. He excelled in math and science, and his first teaching job was at Waverley School in Columbia. In 1941, his father was retiring from the Hopkins School, and Ulysses became the teaching principal at Hopkins that year. (Barber family collection.)

"Professor" Ulysses R. Barber received numerous awards during his years of teaching in Hopkins and Gadsden. In 1972, his greatest achievements included the Richland County Education Association Human Relations award, the Teacher of the Year Award for Gadsden Elementary and for Richland School District One, the 1973 Teacher of the Year Award for Richland School District One, the Greater Columbia Chamber of Commerce Outstanding Teacher of the Year, and a nominee for the South Carolina Teacher of the Year. (Barber family collection.)

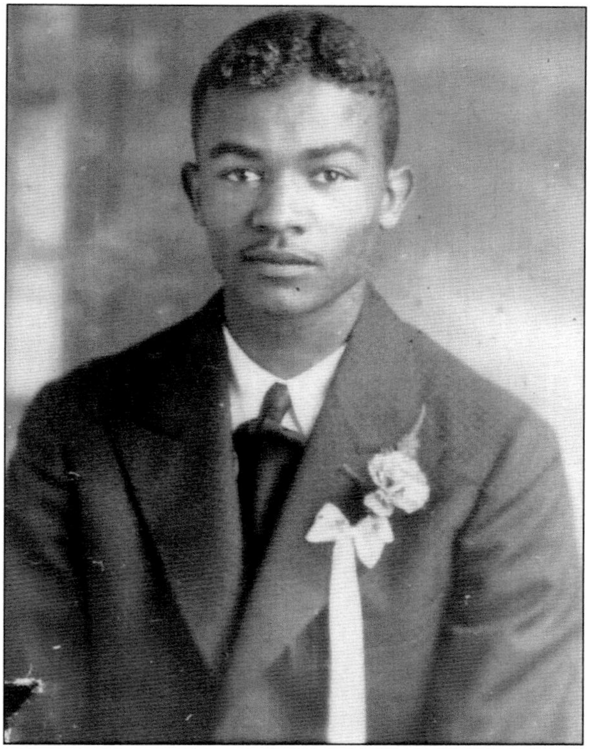

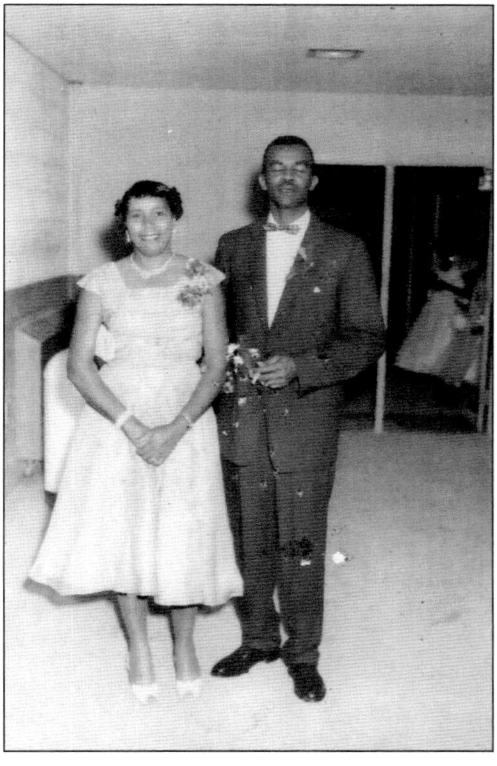

U. R. Barber and Ann Portee Barber were married in 1941. They lived in the Harriet Barber House with his parents until they were able to build a house of their own. Ulysses continued to teach and farm year-round, just as his father and grandfather had done. Daughters Carrie, Mary, Marie, and Jean were born to this union, and they all became school teachers except the youngest, who became a social worker. (Barber family collection.)

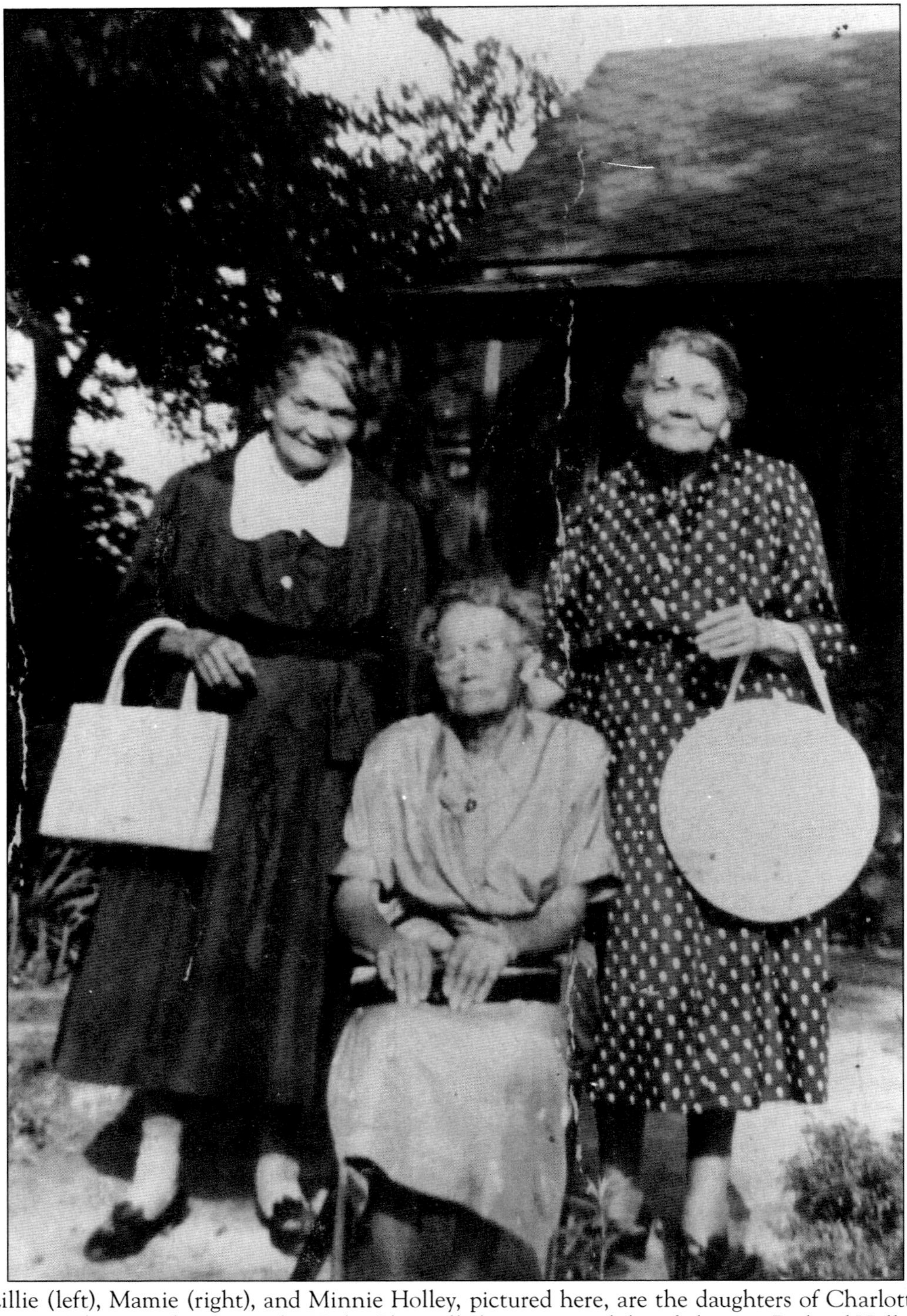

Lillie (left), Mamie (right), and Minnie Holley, pictured here, are the daughters of Charlotte Sumter. They were born near the Hicks-Chappell plantation, and their father was Richard Holley, a white businessman from Columbia. Minnie was the oldest daughter and was born in 1880, and the twins Mamie and Lillie were born in 1884. (Barber family collection.)

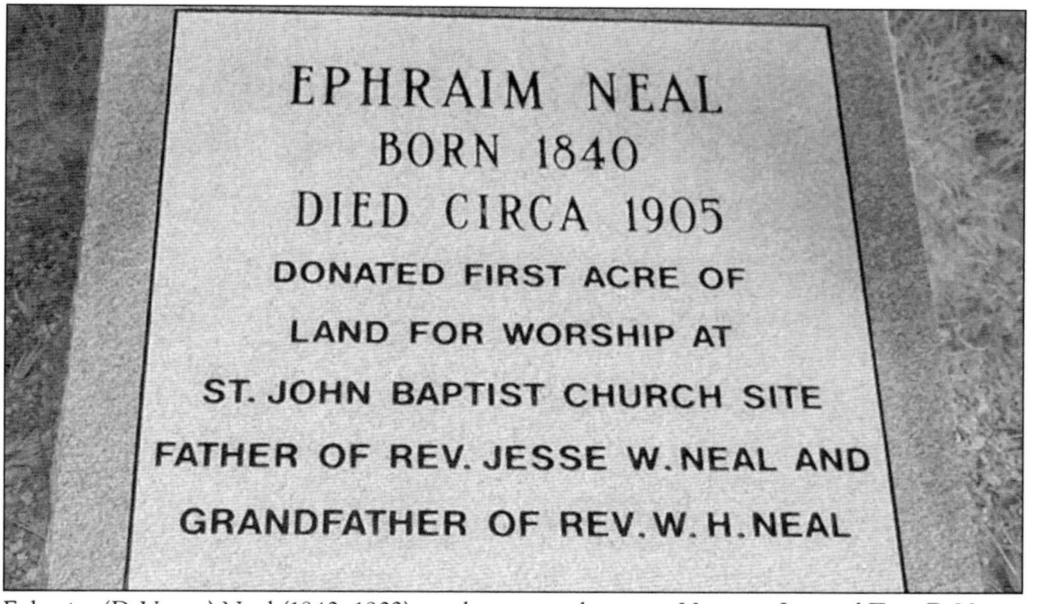

Ephraim (DeVeaux) Neal (1840–1903) was born into slavery in Virginia. Jim and Tina DeVeaux and eight children were sold to James Neale in Kingville. After emancipation, six siblings retained the DeVeaux name. Ephraim and brother Caleb assumed the Neal name. He worked his way to Hopkins clearing trees for the railroad. In 1872, Ephraim Neal purchased 75.5 acres through the South Carolina Land Commission. The first school for area children of ex-slaves was located in his fodder barn along Cedar Creek in 1875. Ephraim married Eliza Eikerenkoetter from Beaufort; their children were James, Joseph, Jesse (a reverend), Weston, Green (a reverend), and Frances. (Photograph by Ken James.)

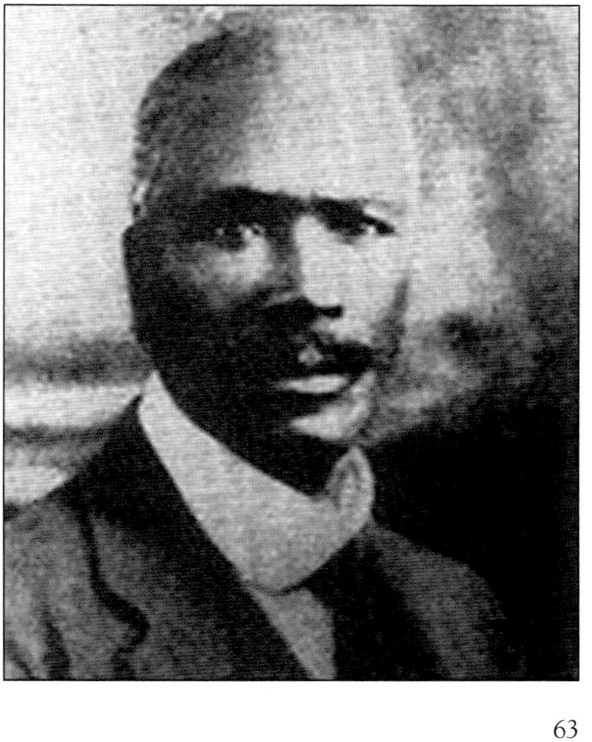

Rev. Jesse William Neal (1870–1943) was the son of Eliza and Ephraim Neal. He graduated from Benedict College in 1891, passed the teachers examination, and was a teacher and principal at Hopkins Colored School. His first wife was Benedict graduate Mary Howard; she died shortly after the birth of their son John. (Neal-Scott family collection.)

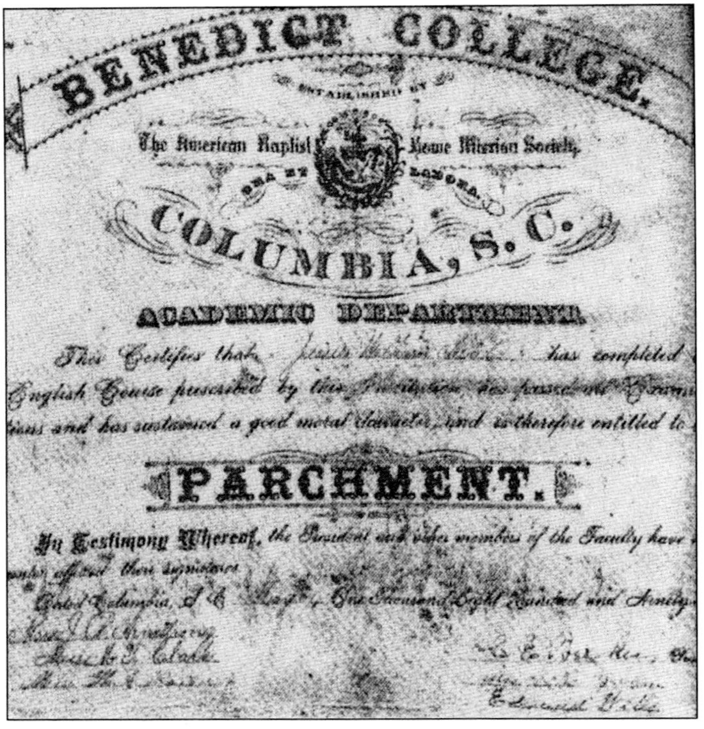

BENEDICT COLLEGE.

ESTABLISHED BY

The American Baptist Home Mission Society.

COLUMBIA, S.C.

ACADEMIC DEPARTMENT.

This Certifies that [illegible] has completed English Course prescribed by this Institution, has passed the Examinations and has sustained a good moral character, and is therefore entitled to

PARCHMENT.

In Testimony Whereof, the President and other members of the Faculty have hereunto affixed their signatures.

Dated Columbia, S.C. [illegible] One Thousand Eight Hundred and Ninety [illegible]

Rev. Jesse William Neal had a strong calling at an early age and began preaching in 1892. He was ordained in 1897 by the Wateree Association. By 1899, he was elected and held the position of assistant clerk for several years. He also served as pastor of Columbia's Antioch Baptist (10 years), New Light Beaulah (10 years), and Zion Benevolent (26 years). (Neal-Scott Collection/*Palmetto Leader* newspaper.)

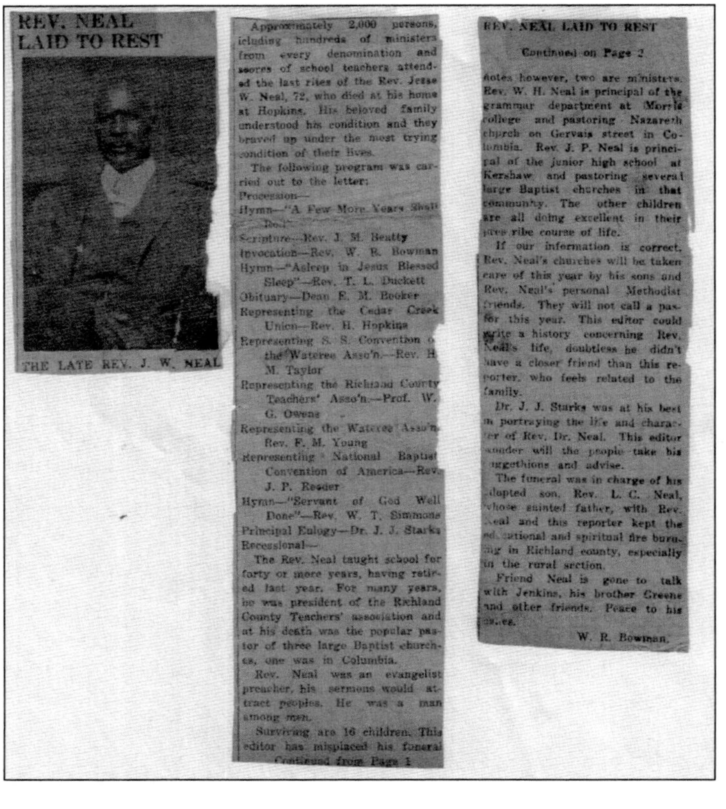

REV. NEAL LAID TO REST

THE LATE REV. J. W. NEAL

Approximately 2,000 persons, icluding hundreds of ministers from every denomination and scores of school teachers attended the last rites of the Rev. Jesse W. Neal, 72, who died at his home at Hopkins. His beloved family understood his condition and they braved up under the most trying condition of their lives.

The following program was carried out to the letter:

Procession—

Hymn—"A Few More Years Shall Roll"

Scripture—Rev. J. M. Beatty

Invocation—Rev. W. R. Bowman

Hymn—"Asleep in Jesus Blessed Sleep"—Rev. T. L. Duckett

Obituary—Dean E. M. Booker

Representing the Cedar Creek Union—Rev. H. Hopkins

Representing S. S. Convention of the Wateree Asso'n.—Rev. H. M. Taylor

Representing the Richland County Teachers' Asso'n.—Prof. W. G. Owens

Representing the Wateree Asso'n. Rev. F. M. Young

Representing National Baptist Convention of America—Rev. J. P. Reeder

Hymn—"Servant of God Well Done"—Rev. W. T. Simmons

Principal Eulogy—Dr. J. J. Starks

Recessional—

The Rev. Neal taught school for forty or more years, having retired last year. For many years, he was president of the Richland County Teachers' association and at his death was the popular pastor of three large Baptist churches, one was in Columbia.

Rev. Neal was an evangelist preacher, his sermons would attract peoples. He was a man among men.

Surviving are 16 children. This editor has misplaced his funeral

Continued from Page 1

REV. NEAL LAID TO REST

Continued on Page 2

notes however, two are ministers. Rev. W. H. Neal is principal of the grammar department at Morris college and pastoring Nazareth church on Gervais street in Columbia. Rev. J. P. Neal is principal of the junior high school at Kershaw and pastoring several large Baptist churches in that community. The other children are all doing excellent in their prescribe course of life.

If our information is correct, Rev. Neal's churches will be taken care of this year by his sons and Rev. Neal's personal Methodist friends. They will not call a pastor this year. This editor could write a history concerning Rev. Neal's life, doubtless he didn't have a closer friend than this reporter, who feels related to the family.

Dr. J. J. Starks was at his best in portraying the life and character of Rev. Dr. Neal. This editor wonder will the people take his suggethions and advise.

The funeral was in charge of his adopted son, Rev. L. C. Neal, whose sainted father, with Rev. Neal and this reporter kept the educational and spiritual fire burning in Richland county, especially in the rural section.

Friend Neal is gone to talk with Jenkins, his brother Greene and other friends. Peace to his ashes.

W. R. Bowman.

Rev. Jesse William Neal married his second wife, Minnie Holley, in 1895, and they had 15 children: Eliza, Javan, Jesse, James (a reverend), Earl, Fred, Helen, Westberry (a reverend), Albert, Ruben, Minnie, Avery, Lillie, Rosa, and Wendell. He was active in politics, serving as the 1892 Hopkins Republican organization chairman. He was also a 1900 Census enumerator. (James B. Neal Jr.)

Rev. Dr. Westberry Homer Neal was the eighth of Rev. Jesse W. and Minnie Holley Neal's 15 children. He earned bachelor of arts, bachelor of divinity, and honorary doctor of divinity degrees from Morris College. He was a teacher and principal for 37 years; pastor of Mount Zion Baptist and Weeping Mary; and pastor emeritus of First Nazareth, Mount Moriah, New Light Beulah, and St. John Baptist Churches. Westberry was St. John's pastor for 57 years. (Neal-Scott family collection.)

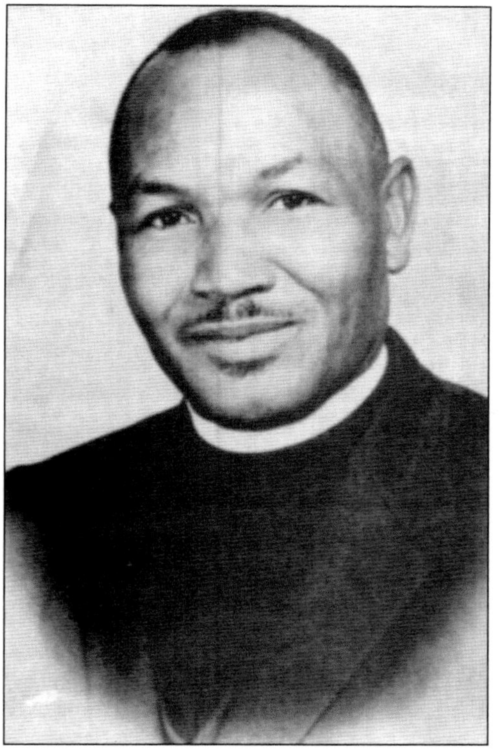

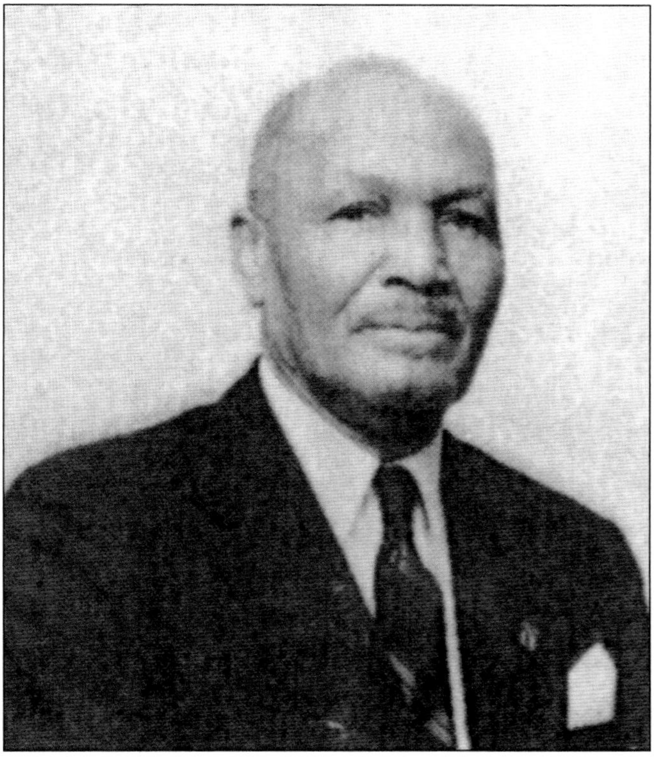

Rev. Dr. Westberry Homer Neal was Morris College's trustee board chairman for 46 years, holding the nation's longest higher education chairmanship record. He received the Order of the Palmetto, the highest citizen honor given by South Carolina. Westberry married fellow student Mary Letman of Chicago, a Fairfield County educator. Their children are Marilyn Rochelle and Westberry Jr. After Mary's death, Westberry married Audrey Potts, an elementary school educator. (Neal-Scott family collection.)

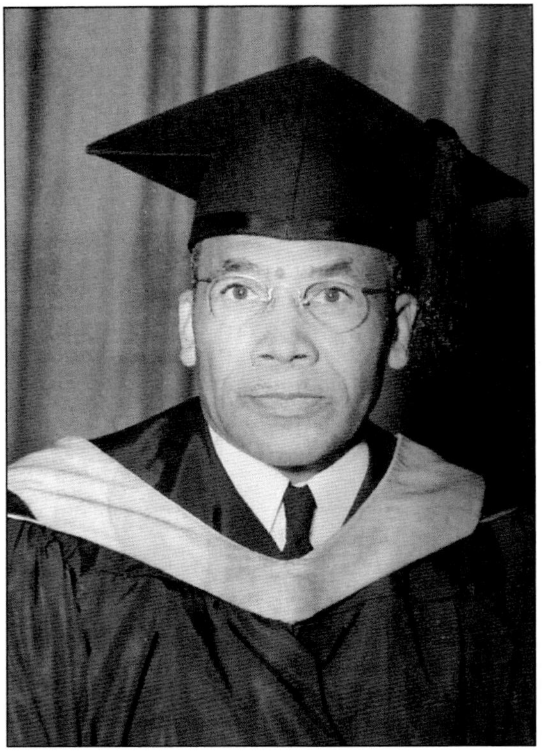

Rev. Dr. James Peter Neal Sr. was born in 1902 and was the son of Rev. Jesse W. and Minnie Holley Neal. He graduated from Morris College in 1930; completed studies at Fisk University and South Carolina State College; and was awarded the doctor of divinity degree in 1957. He was pastor of Capernaum, Lower Richland; First Baptist and Second Calvary, Kershaw; and Sutton Branch, Lugoff, and Antioch in Columbia. (Neal-Scott family collection.)

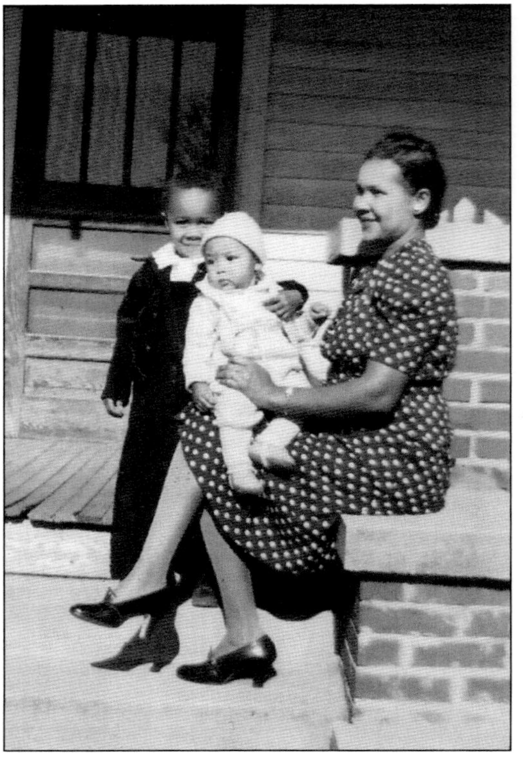

Rev. Dr. James Peter Neal Sr. was pastor, educator, civic leader, and college trustee. He was bestowed an honorary doctorate of humanity in 1980 and a distinguished alumnus award in 1983 by Morris College. He married Geneva Outen of Camden; they had three sons: Rev. James P. Jr., educator and pioneer television talk-show host; Rev. Talmadge J'Von (deceased); and Rev. Dr. Albert, Antioch Baptist's pastor and educator. (Neal-Scott family collection.)

Lillie Neal Scott was the 13th of 15 children born to Rev. Jesse and Minnie Holley Neal. She lived on the family's farm on Clarkson Road near Cabin Creek. She attended Hopkins Graded School, completed high school, earned a bachelor of arts degree at Morris College, and completed further studies at South Carolina State College. Her first teaching position was at Siloam School in Lower Richland. (Neal-Scott family collection.)

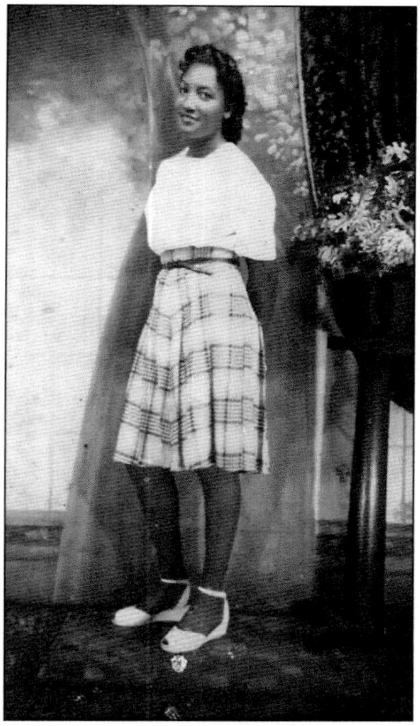

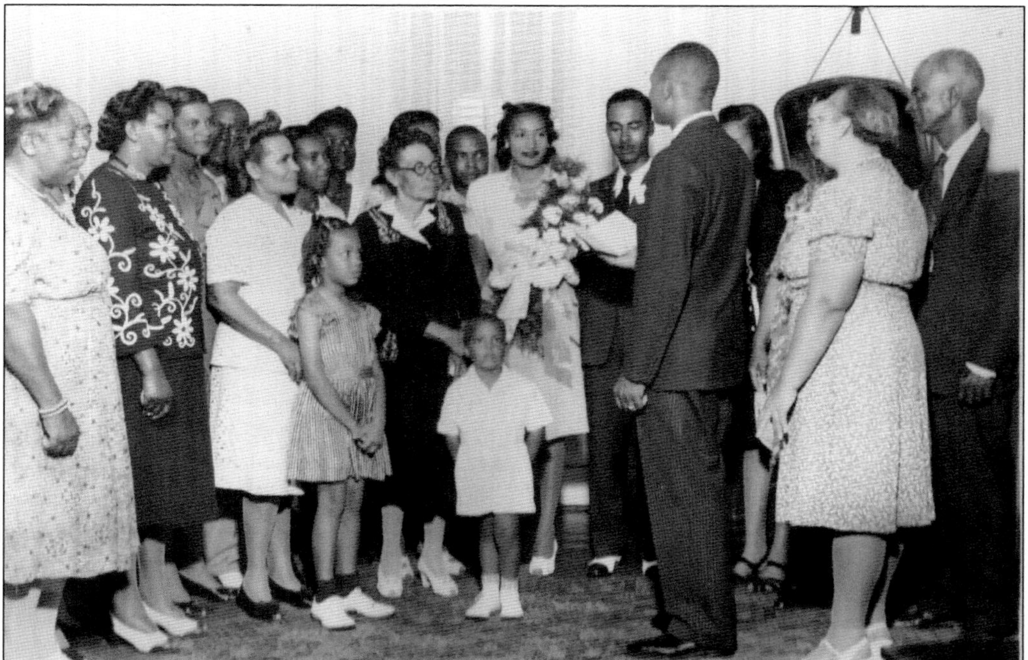

While Lillie Neal Scott was waiting for her father to complete a meeting in downtown Columbia, a passing young man introduced himself, asking if she was Reverend Neal's daughter; she married that young man, Blakely Scott Jr. from Eastover, shortly thereafter. She retired from Fairfield County Schools after 30 years. Lillie and Blakely Jr. had three children; they are Rev. Dr. Blakely III, Deborah, and Detra. (Neal-Scott family collection.)

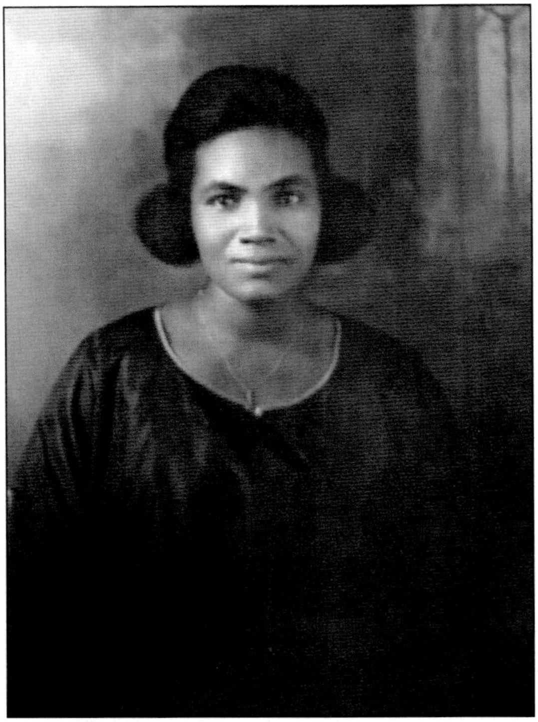

Eliza Neal Manigault was the first child born to Rev. Jesse and Minnie Holley Neal. After earning her bachelor of arts degree at Benedict College, she became an elementary school teacher in Fairfield County. This 1920s photograph of Eliza was included in "A True Likeness," featuring the photography of Richard Roberts. (Neal-Scott family collection.)

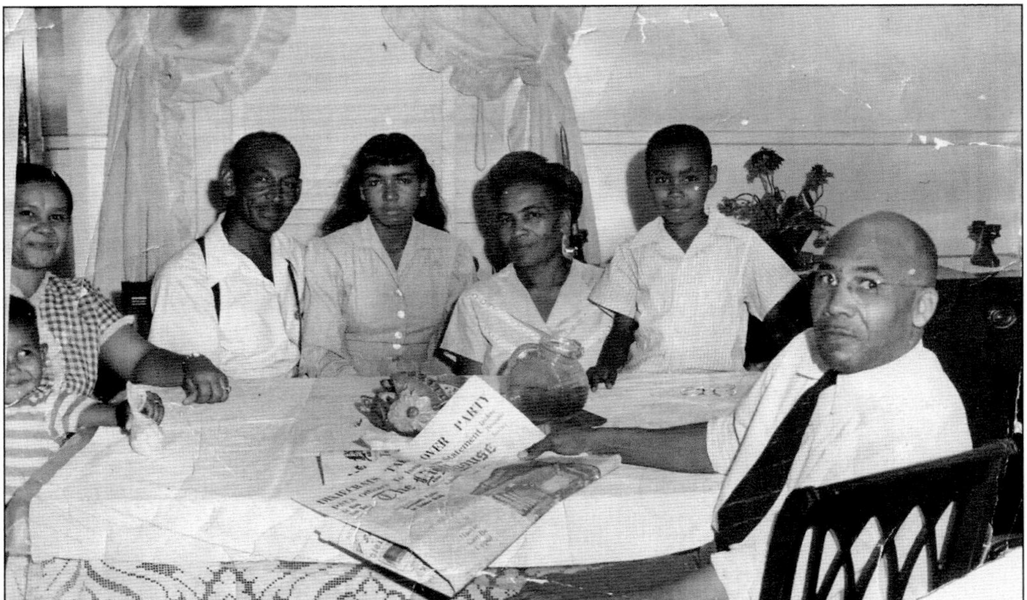

Eliza Neal is shown on the right with her spouse, Claude Manigault of Winnsboro, South Carolina. Claude and his brothers owned several businesses, including a funeral home. Seated on the left of Eliza and Claude is their daughter, Oscarola Manigault Pitt, who was an educator at South Carolina State College. Eliza's brother, Rev. James P. Neal, and his family are pictured during a visit to Winnsboro and are seated on the left. (Neal-Scott family collection.)

This picture features three of Rev. Jesse W. and Minnie H. Neal's daughters. From left to right, they are Rosa Lee Neal Boyd, Minnie Neal Johnson, and Lillie Neal Scott (featured before). Rosa married Jimmie L. Boyd and had three sons, Russell, Roland, and Kenneth; Minnie married Heyward Johnson and moved to Baltimore. They had eight children, Evelyn, Jesse, Christopher, Menard, Melvin, Heyward, Eugene, and Ernest. (R. Russell Boyd.)

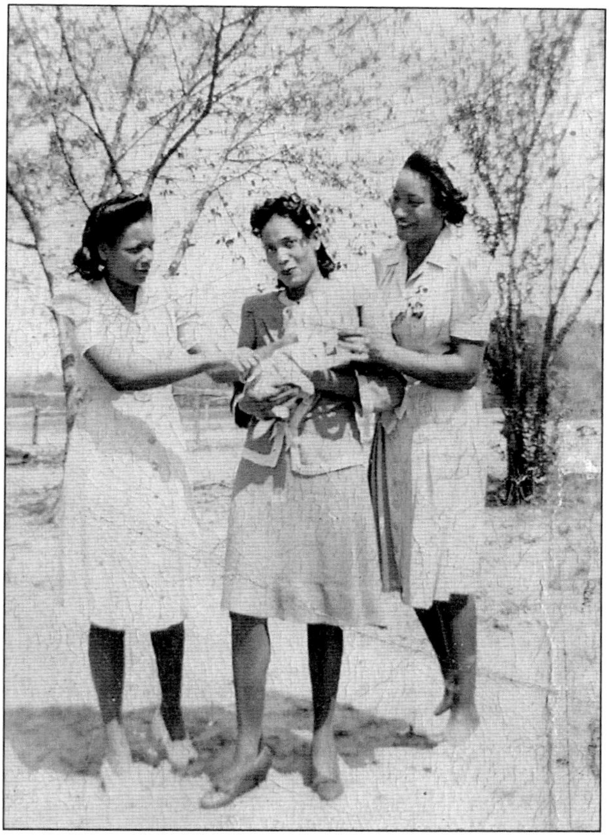

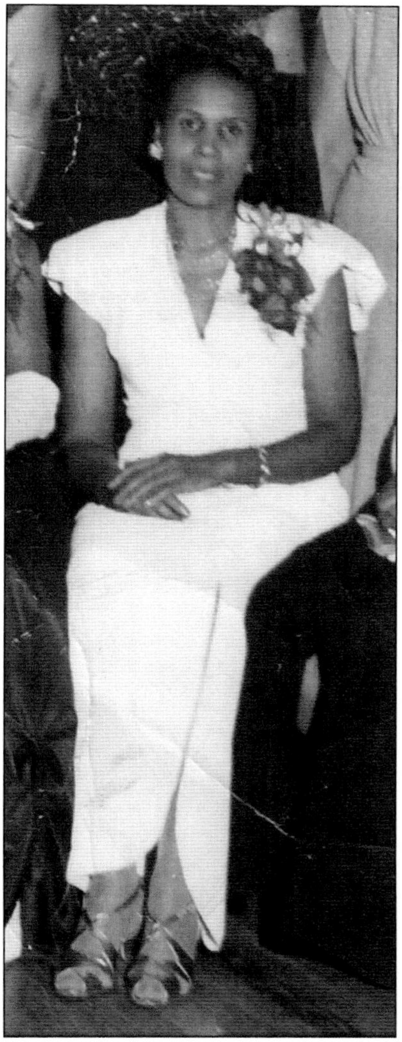

Helen L. Neal was born in 1908 and was the sixth child of Rev. Jesse and Minnie Holley Neal. She graduated Morris College in 1929 and moved to New York City, where she owned a beauty parlor and rental properties. Helen was known as the tall, glamorous, and generous big sister who sent dolls to her younger sisters at Christmas. (Neal-Scott family collection.)

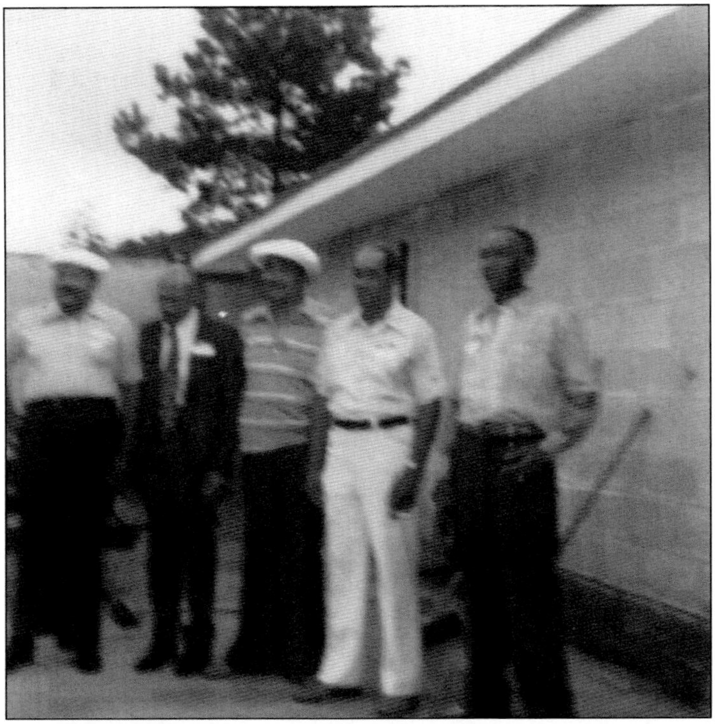

This 1978 photograph shows 5 of Jesse Neal's 10 sons: (from left to right) Wendell, Javan, Avery, Ruben, and Albert. Wendell retired from Baltimore Steel in Maryland; his daughter is Edith Jamison. Javan retired from Southern Railway in Asheville, North Carolina. Avery owned businesses in Texas. Rubin retired from Owen Steel; he married Julliette Davis, and their children are Ruby, Minnietta, and Herbert. One grandson is Zion Mill Creek Baptist's Bishop Wendell B. Sumter. Albert retired from Fort Jackson. (Kenneth B. James.)

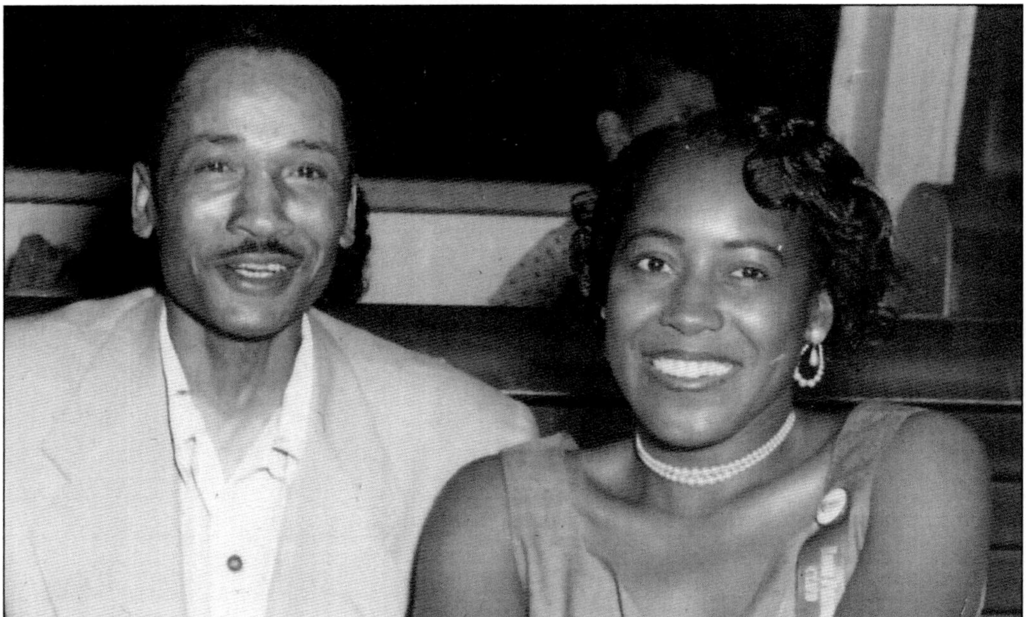

Frederick Douglas (Fay) Neal was born in 1907 and was the seventh child of Rev. Jesse and Minnie Holley Neal. As a youngster, he joined St. John, completed public school in Hopkins, and attended Morris College. Fred moved to New York seeking employment and married Maggie Ham of Timmonsville, South Carolina. He retired from the Manhattan Hotel Chain. The photograph shows him and his wife at the popular 3-Club in New York. (Neal-Scott family collection.)

Rev. Green B. Neal, son of Ephraim Neal, was educated at Benedict as a teacher and was credited with organizing the Rock Hill School in Lower Richland. Family history tells that the local school board initially denied funds for the school, declaring that there were not enough children in the area. Green B. drove a wagon door-to-door each morning collecting children and eventually proved the school board wrong. (Wilhelmina Neal Prioleau family collection.)

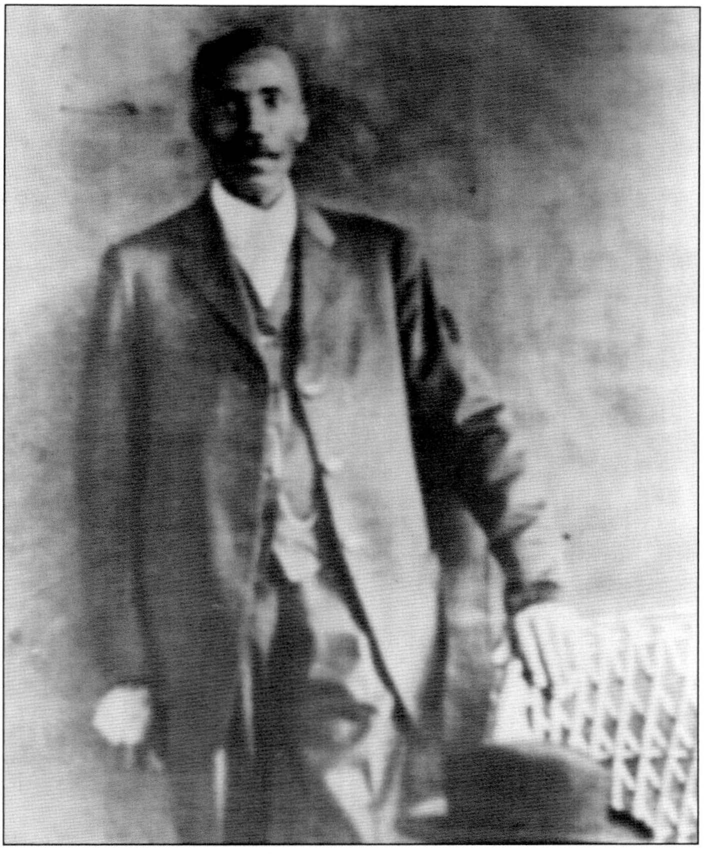

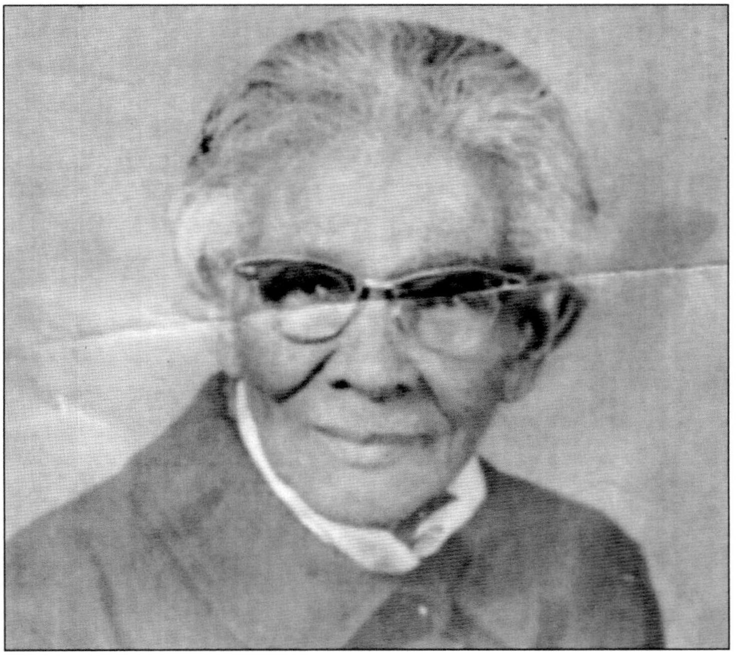

Clara E. Foster Neal was married to Rev. Green B. Neal from Hopkins. "Miss Clara," as she was affectionately called, was a member of St. John Baptist Church and taught Sunday school for over 50 years. She graduated from Benedict College and taught in Laurens and in Richland Counties. She was one of the founders of St. John's Excelsior Missionary Society. She founded the New Enterprise Society at Jerusalem Baptist Church. (Blanch McRant McFadden.)

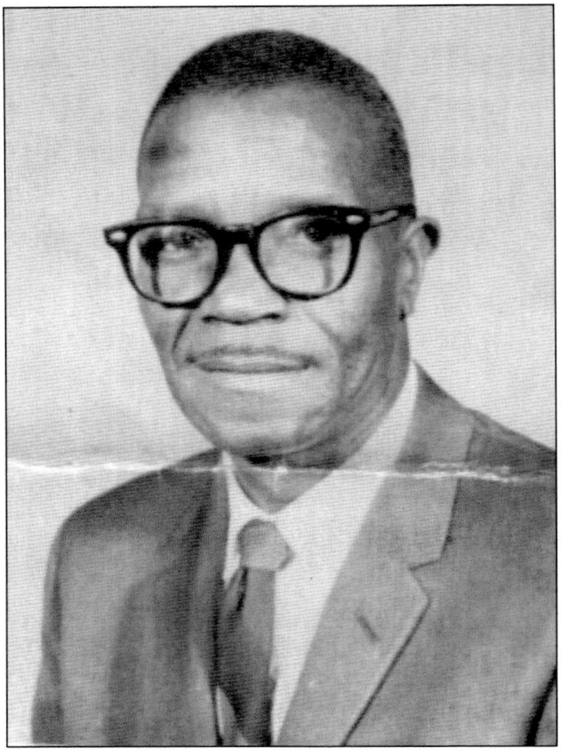

Eugene Emerson Neal was a son of Rev. Green B. and Clara Foster Neal and was born in 1913. Eugene earned his bachelor of science degree from Morris College, bachelor of arts degree from Benedict College, and master of arts degree from New York University. Eugene was assistant principal and coach at Jackson High School, Camden; principal of Michael C. Riley High School, Blufton; and retired as assistant superintendent of Barnwell County District 29 Schools. He married school teacher Sarah Miller of Gadsden; their daughter Vivian Neal Lowman also teaches school. (Neal-Scott family collection.)

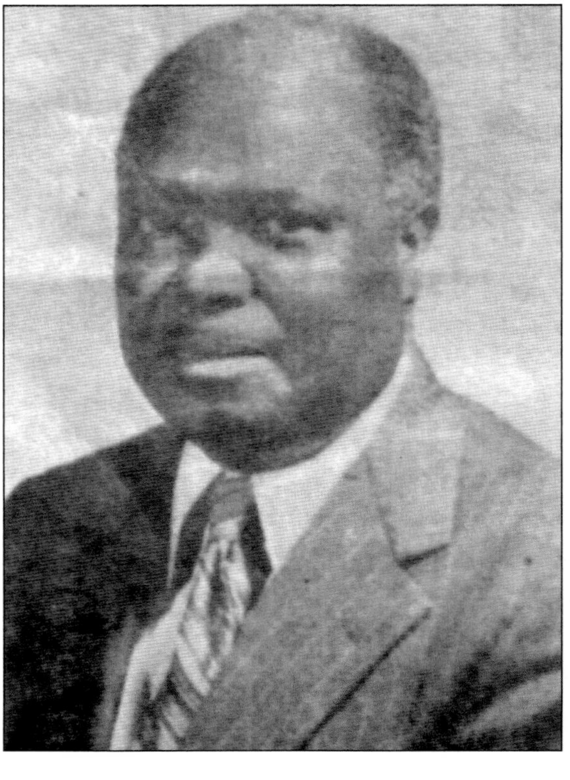

Rev. Choatte R. Neal Sr. was a son of Reverend Green B. and Clara Foster Neal and grandson of Ephraim Neal. He grew up on the Neal land tract and was a member of St. John Baptist Church. He earned his bachelor of arts degree from Morris College, a bachelor of divinity degree from Columbia University, and a master of engineering degree from South Carolina State College. He was pastor of Calvary Baptist Church in Chester, South Carolina, for 18 years. (Neal-Scott family collection.)

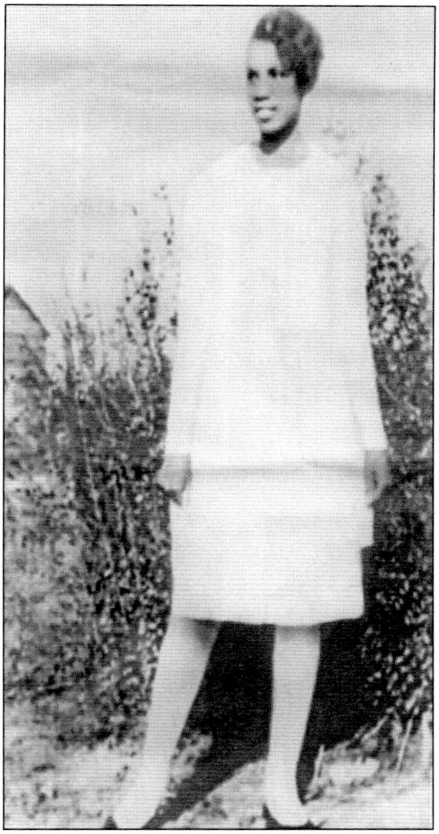

Wilhelmina Illora Neal Prioleau was the first of seven children born to Rev. Green B. and Clara Foster Neal. The year was 1905. She attended Rock Hill School in Lower Richland and Benedict College. She graduated from Morris College in Sumter with dual degrees in teaching and dressmaking. Wilhelmina began teaching at age 17. For 44 years, she taught children in Gadsden, Blufton, and Williston. She retired from Michael C. Riley, where she helped her entire class to obtain college scholarships. Her actual last year of teaching was in Williston, where she mentored white teachers during the early years of integration. She was the widow of Willie Prioleau; they had four children: Sarah, a retired dentist; Oscar Jr., a retired steel worker; Clara, an educator; and Hattie, an attorney. In 2009, she celebrated her 104th birthday with family and St. John Baptist Church members. Wilhelmina Prioleau died on July 3, 2010. (Both, Neal-Scott family collection.)

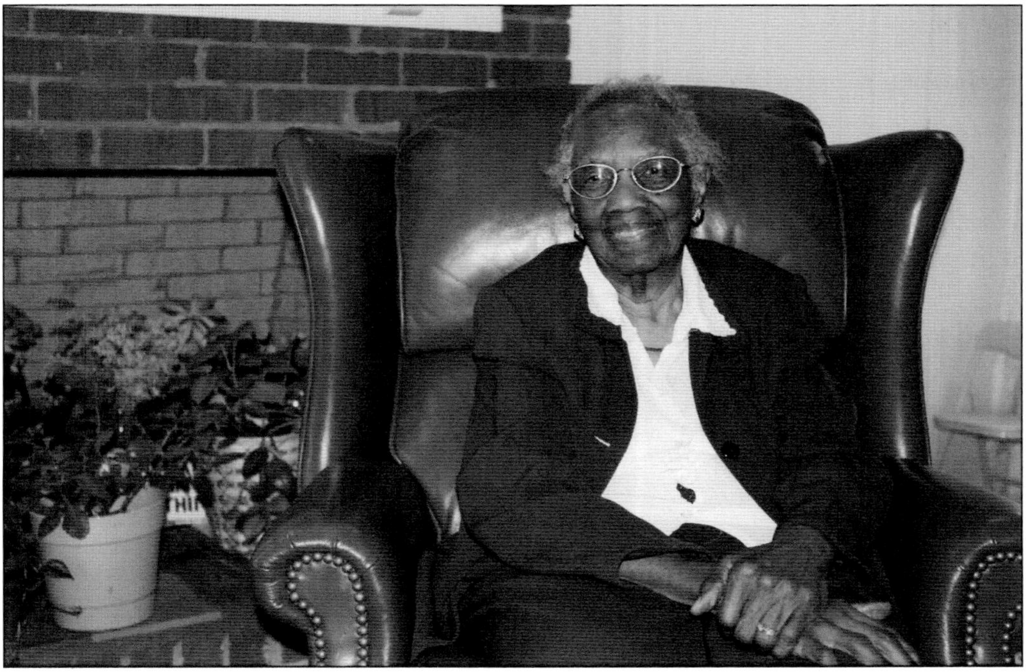

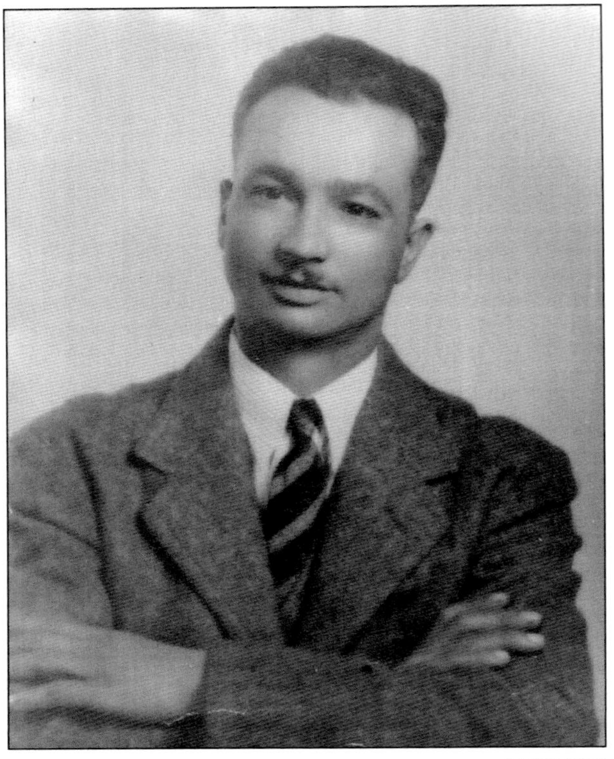

Willie Oree Prioleau Jr. was the husband of Wilhelmina Neal Prioleau and the son of Willie Sr. and Nellie Clarkson Prioleau Daniels Thompson. He was a farmer, owned a neighborhood store, and taught discharged African American veterans agriculture and farming techniques. (Wilhelmina Neal Prioleau family collection.)

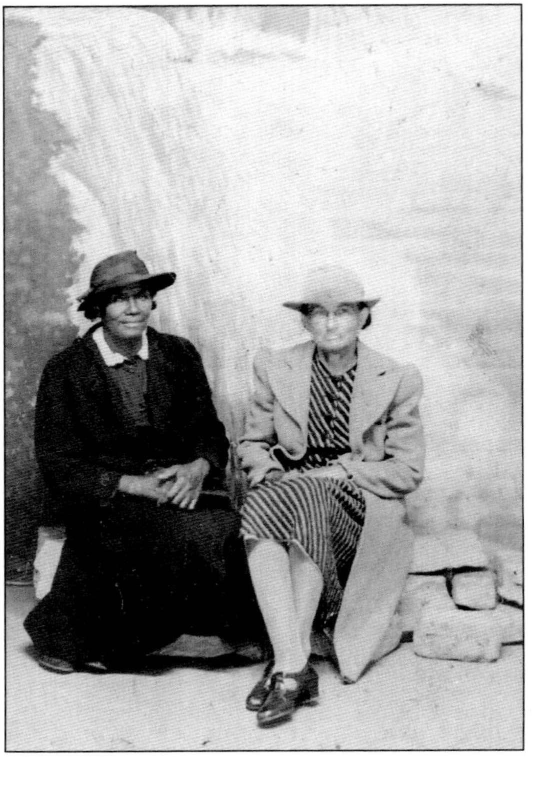

Clara Foster Neal (left) and Nellie Clarkson Prioleau Daniels (right) are shown in this 1940 photograph while they were traveling in Buffalo, New York. The grandmothers took Sarah, their infant granddaughter, to Buffalo, where the father Willie Oree Prioleau was working at the time, in order that he could see his first born. (Wilhelmina Neal Prioleau family collection.)

Hattie Neal Weston was Ephraim Neal's granddaughter and a daughter of Deacon Weston P. and Annie Garrick Neal. She married Robert Weston, who was a deacon at St. John Baptist Church. Hattie was known for baking magical pound cakes. She and Robert migrated to Columbia early in their married life seeking employment. Their daughters were Lillie Mae Weston Coles and Susanna Weston Williams; both became teachers in the public schools. (Neal-Scott family collection.)

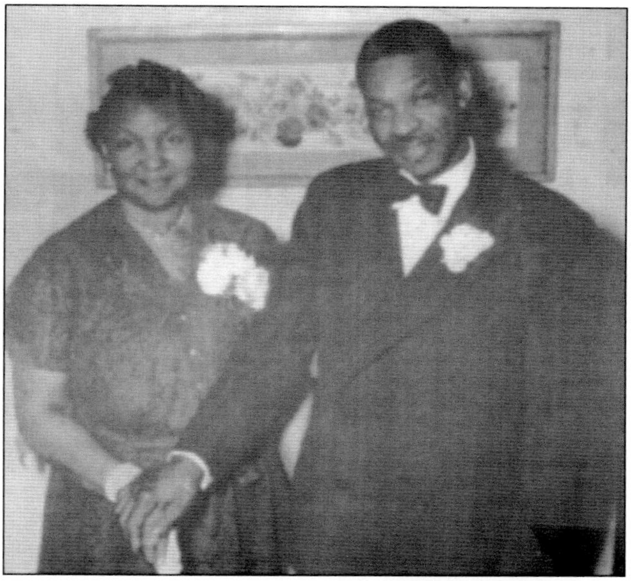

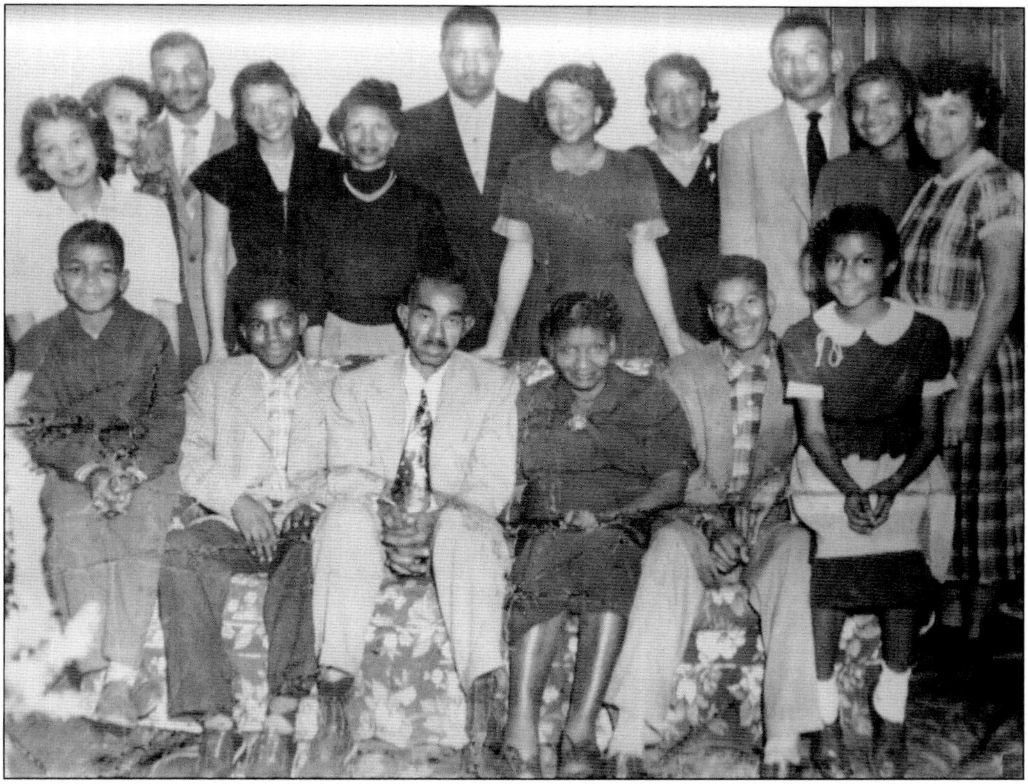

Josephine Neal Furgess was Ephraim Neal's granddaughter and a daughter of Deacon Weston P. and Annie Garrick Neal. She married Curtis Furgess Sr., and they were the parents of 15 children: Elizabeth, Curtis Jr, Weston, Mary, Martha, Mazie, Leon, Josephine, Annie, Albert, Frank, Hattie, Norma, Sarah, and John. Curtis was the longtime custodian of Waverly School in Columbia. (John Furgess Sr.)

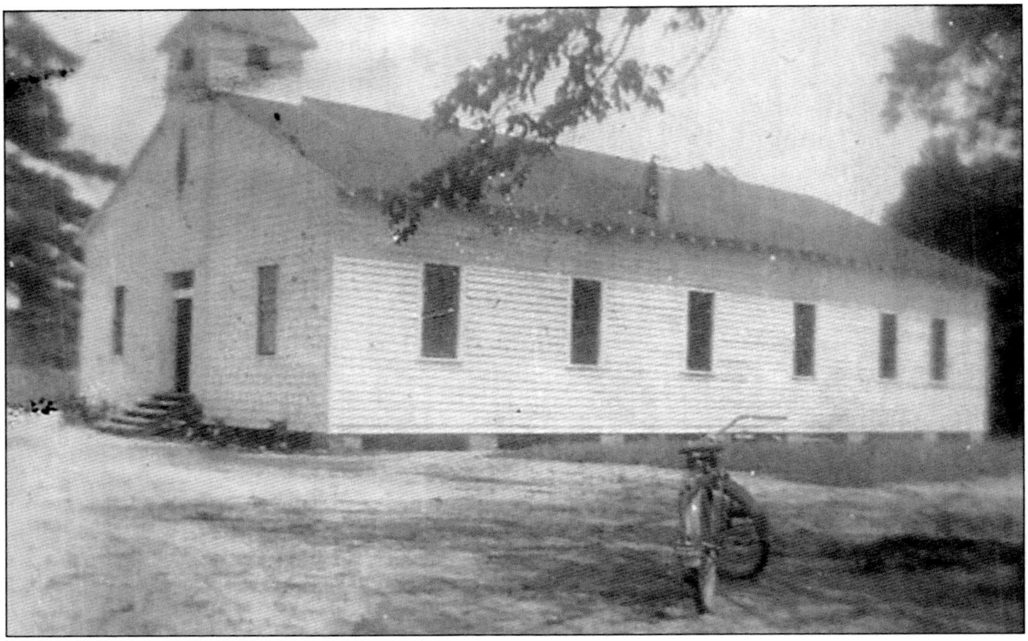

In 1872, Rev. Sam Barber led a campaign to establish a Hopkins community church. Rev. Phillip (Sip) Shiver became the first pastor; founding members met in a brush arbor. Ephraim Neal donated an acre of land, and the first church was built facing the railroad tracks. In 1911, a storm destroyed the structure. Rev. Jesse Neal, who was pastor for 51 years, provided personal labor to rebuild the church, as shown in the photograph. (Neal-Scott family collection.)

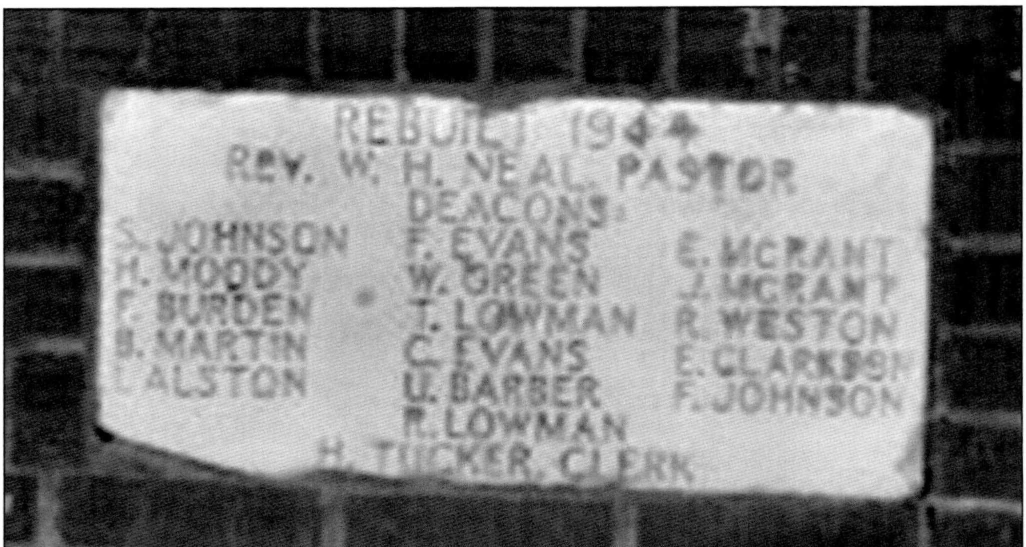

St. John Baptist Church is 135 years old; it was chartered in 1875. Rev. William Lowman was the first ordained pastor. The Alston, Barber, Brown, Green, Lowman, Neal, and Matthews families were among the founding families who left Zion Benevolent Baptist Church to create a church in a location near the Hopkins Turnout site. The church structure was bricked in 1944. (Photograph by Ken James.)

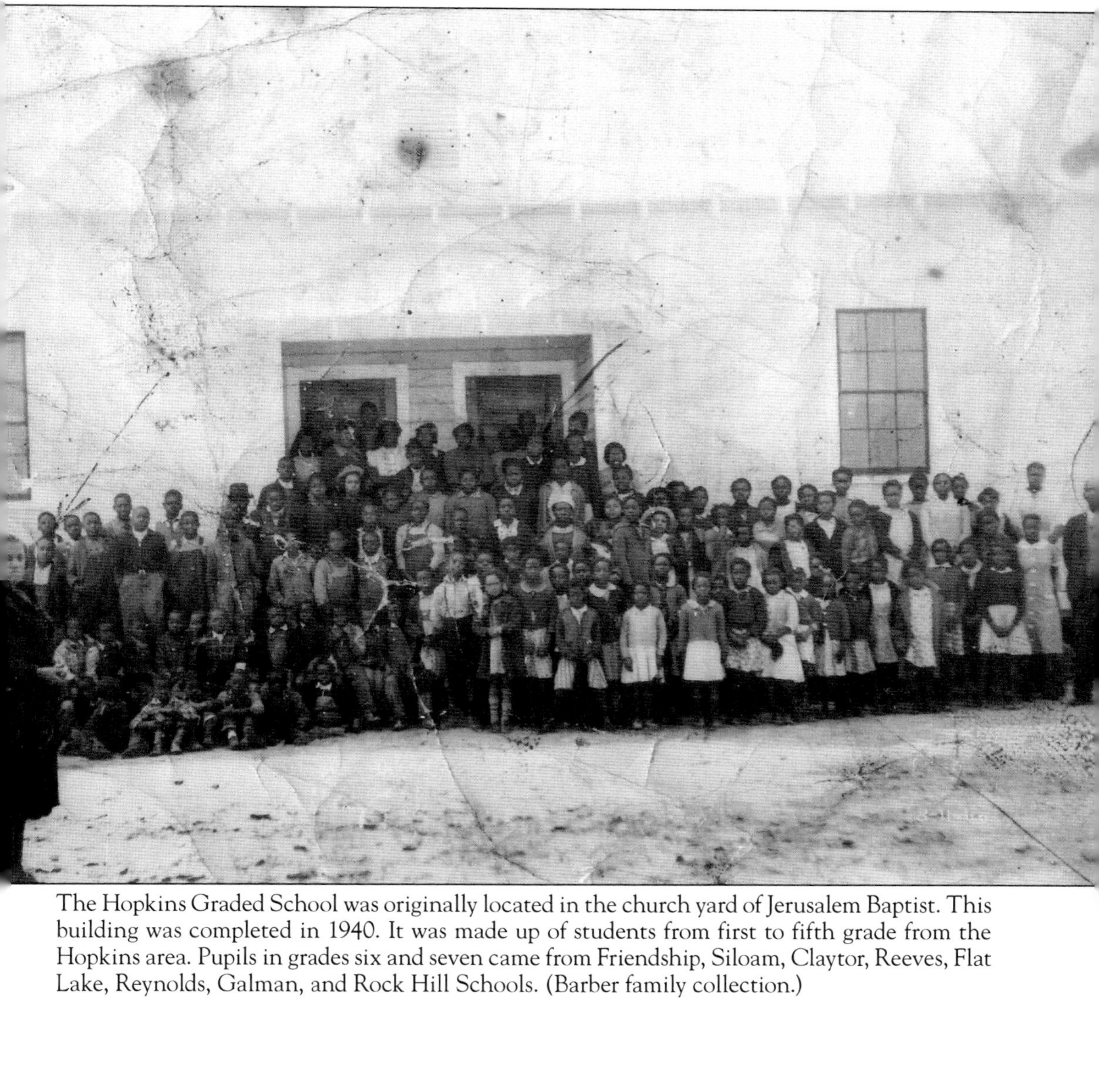

The Hopkins Graded School was originally located in the church yard of Jerusalem Baptist. This building was completed in 1940. It was made up of students from first to fifth grade from the Hopkins area. Pupils in grades six and seven came from Friendship, Siloam, Claytor, Reeves, Flat Lake, Reynolds, Galman, and Rock Hill Schools. (Barber family collection.)

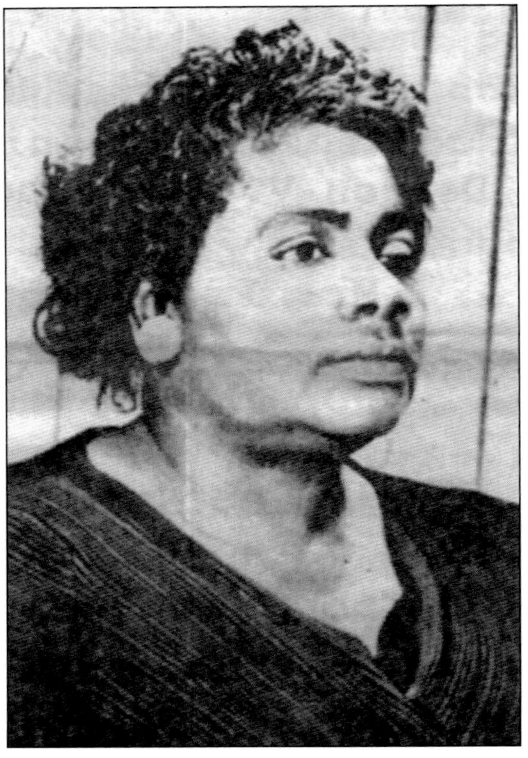

Elizabeth Newton Webber was the daughter of Peter and Mary Newton. She completed her early education at the Hopkins School and after high school earned her bachelor of science degree at Allen University. Webber taught in the public schools of Richland and Lexington Counties and later completed her master of arts degree at South Carolina State College. She became the first librarian at Hopkins High School until her death in 1970. She was married to Rainey Webber from Eastover. (Barber family collection.)

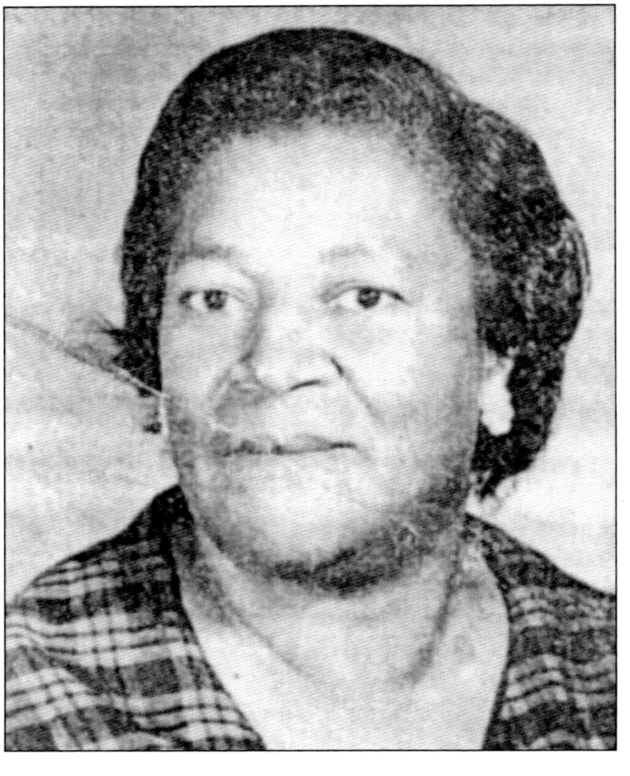

Nan Howell Middleton was born to Ishmael and Phyllis Castor Howell in 1910 in Hopkins. Upon completing her college education, Howell taught second grade at Hopkins Elementary School. She was a Brownie and Girl Scout leader for 20 years and received numerous meritorious awards for services to the American Red Cross. She was married to James P. Middleton. (Eugenia Middleton Griffin.)

Beverly Robinson Sr. was born in 1896 and was the son of Samuel and Mary Robinson. He was a veteran of World War I, and after his service in the army, he returned to Hopkins and became a farmer. His children included Margaret, Sarah, Leola, Beverly Jr., Walter, Samuel, John, and Willie. (Barber family collection.)

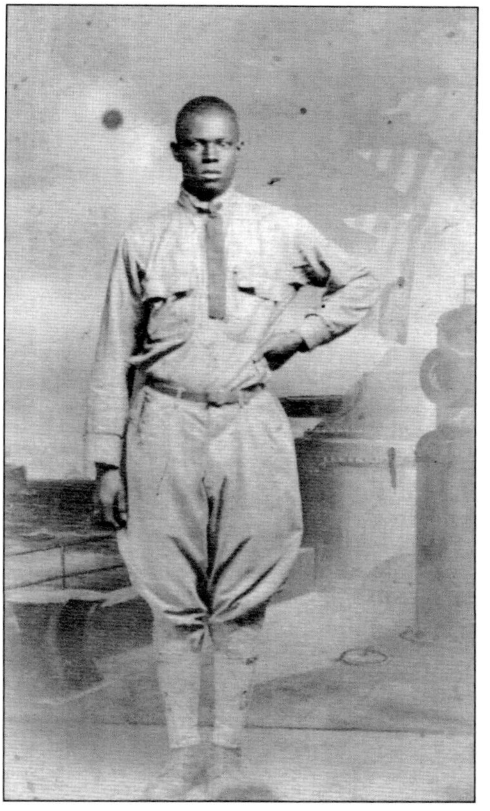

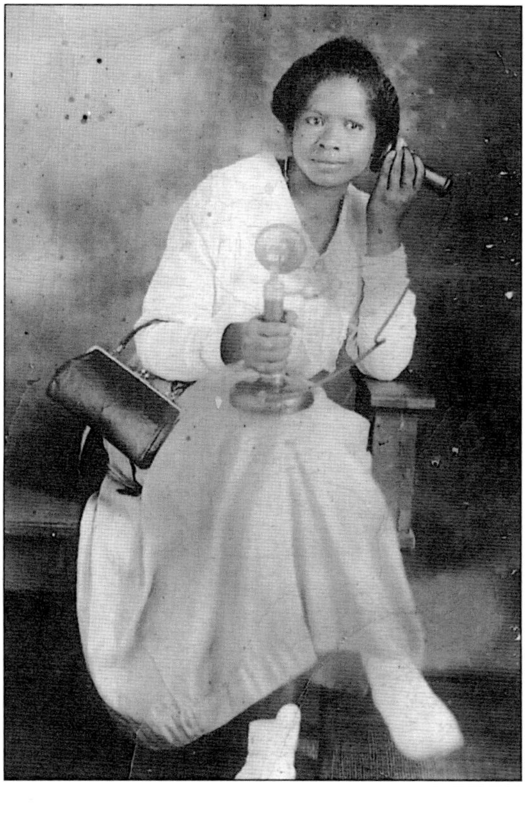

Gertrude Carter Martin was one of three children born to Thomas Carter and Charlotte Sumter Carter. Her mother, Charlotte, was also the mother of Mamie Holley, who married the Reverend John B. Barber of Hopkins. Gertrude married McDaniel Edmond of Hopkins. Their children were Alberta, Allen, Julius, McDaniel Jr., Lillie Bell, Pink Phyllis, and Bertha. (Barber family collection.)

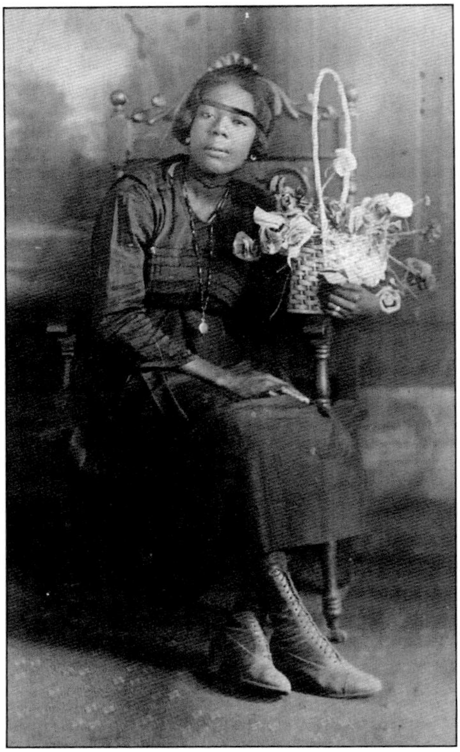

Jennie Alston was the daughter of Cyrus Alston, son of Brazell and Hagar Alston. Cyrus was remembered as a friendly clerk at the Gormans Store in the village of Hopkins. He could be seen picking flowers for his daughters on his way home from work. (Barber family collection.)

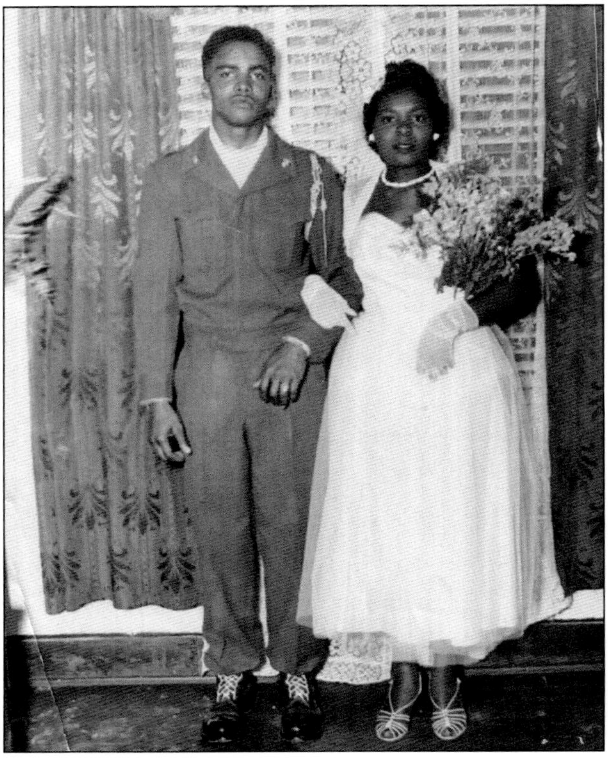

Rev. Johnie B. Alston returned after his tour of duty in the army to Hopkins and the land he inherited from his father, Israel Alston. Alston married Ernestine Evans, and they maintained the farm started by his father. He became employed as a tailor at Fort Jackson, and his wife, Ernestine, was a talented seamstress. Alston served as the first black constable for the Lower Richland area since Reconstruction. In 1971, he received his contractor's license and is known to have built one of the first totally solar-heated homes in South Carolina. (Barber family collection.)

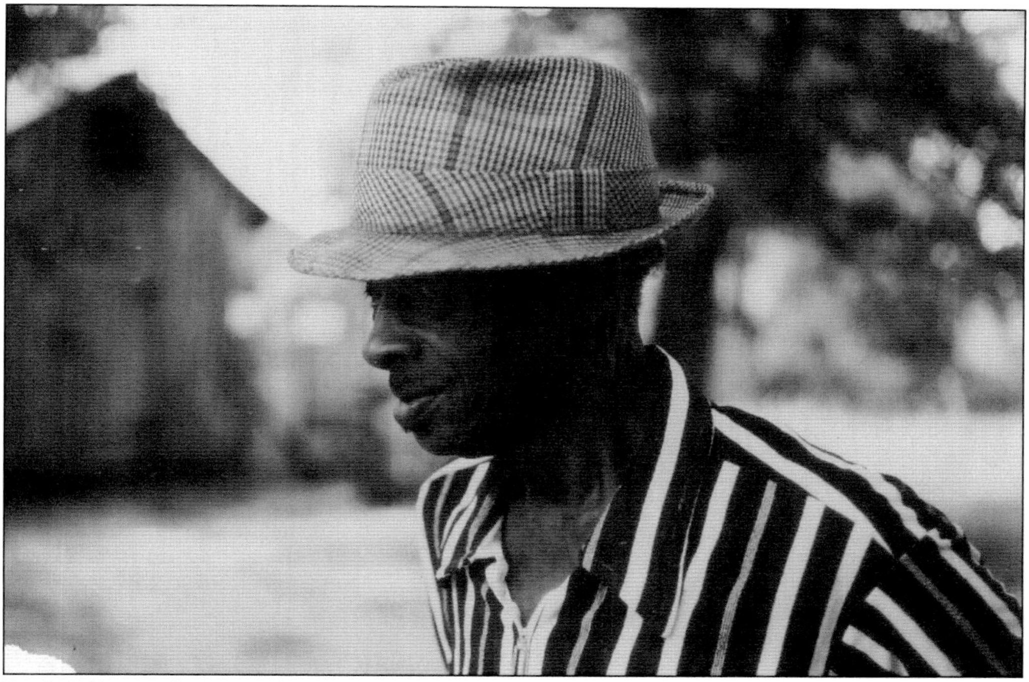

Fred William Alston was born in 1892. He was a World War I veteran and served in France. He returned to Hopkins after reaching the rank of sergeant first class. Fred and his wife, Eugenia, were early entrepreneurs who operated a variety store, a barbershop, and a gasoline pump in the village of Hopkins. (Rosa L. James Alston.)

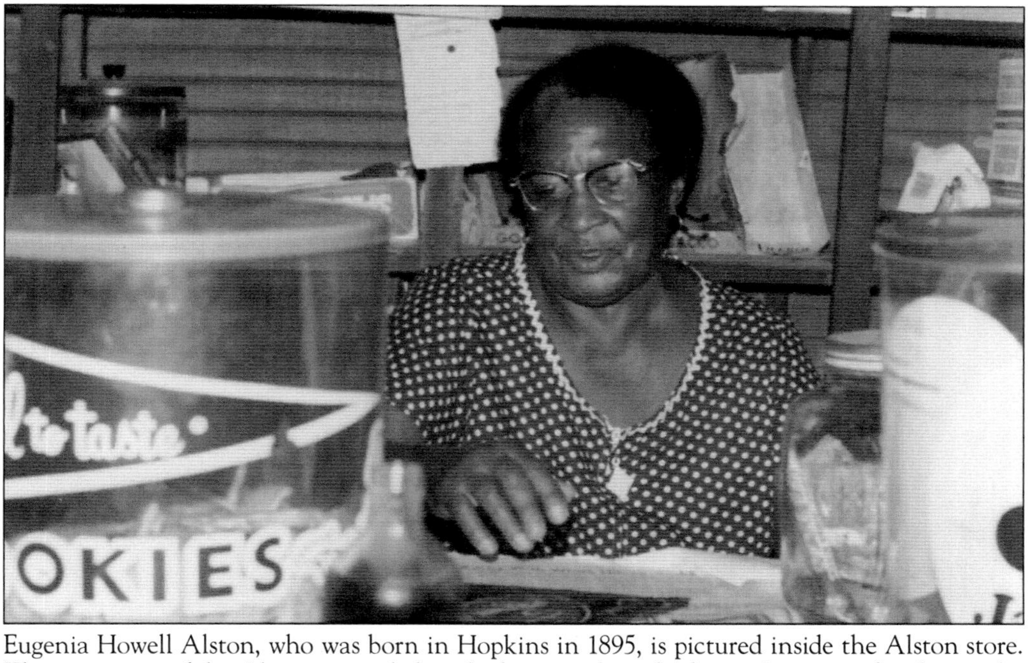

Eugenia Howell Alston, who was born in Hopkins in 1895, is pictured inside the Alston store. The generosity of the Alstons provided credit for a number of African American families in the community, and they also invested in real estate in the area. (Rosa L. James Alston.)

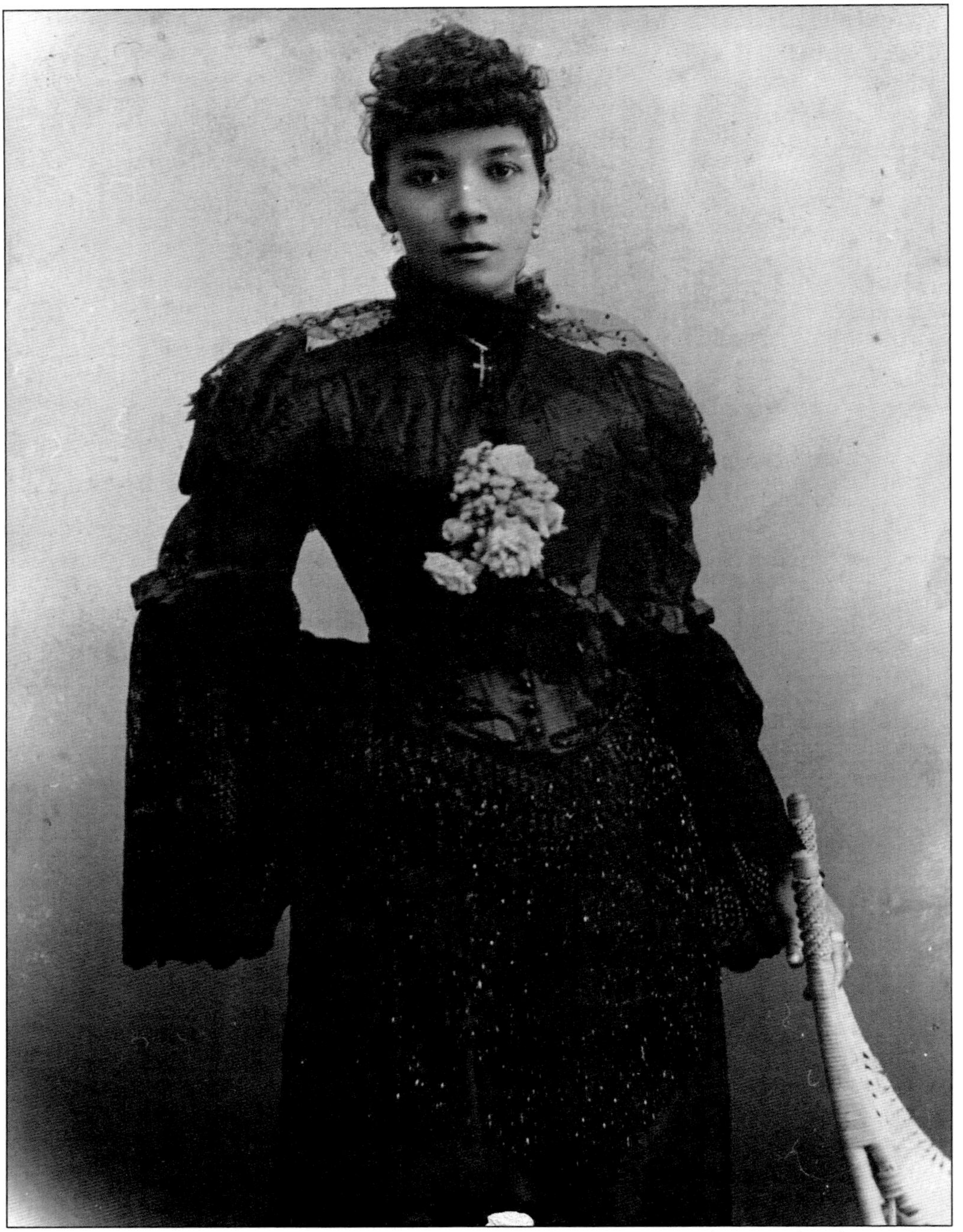

Pauline Bonner Howell was a student at Benedict College. Born in 1894, she moved to the Hopkins community when she married Charlie Howell. Their children were Alvin, Ruby, Ishmael, Charlie Jr., and Minnie. Several of the children became successful entrepreneurs, as were their parents. All were members of St. John Baptist Church. (Ruby Howell Robinson.)

Charlie Howell, son of Ishmael Howell, is pictured. Ishmael Howell, born in the year 1865, was employed by some of the wealthiest merchants in the Hopkins village, the Gorman brothers. They owned and operated most of the enterprises in the village, that included the cotton gin, gristmill, general store, and other businesses. Ishmael was considered an overseer or general manager. The Howell family owned large tracts of land where they farmed and established their own businesses. Several of their children became successful entrepreneurs as well. (Ruby Howell Robinson.)

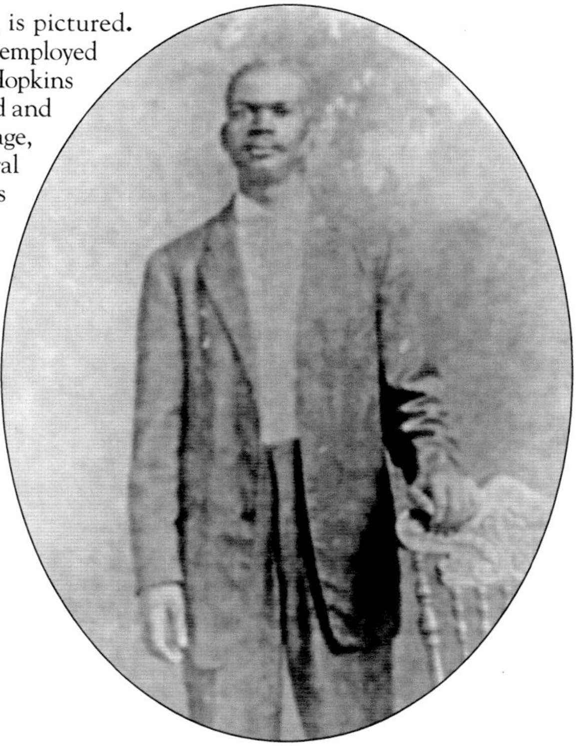

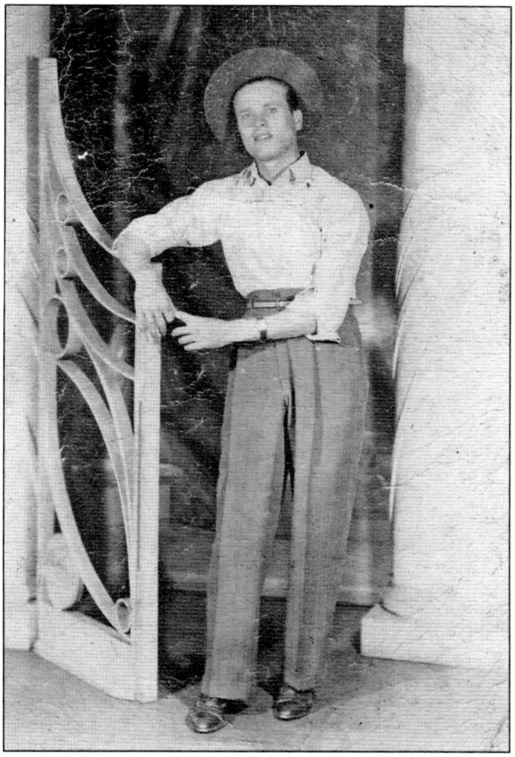

David Clarkson Sr. was born in 1921, the son of Zack Rice Clarkson and Wilhelmina Willis Clarkson. David worked at the family's cotton gin and sawmill; he was also a farmer. Fellow Booker T. Washington High School classmates remember him to be quite intellectual and fun-loving, and he was a masterful storyteller. David Sr. was married to Martha Ann Jones. His children are David Jr., Sharon, Mae Frances, and Dave. (David Clarkson Jr.)

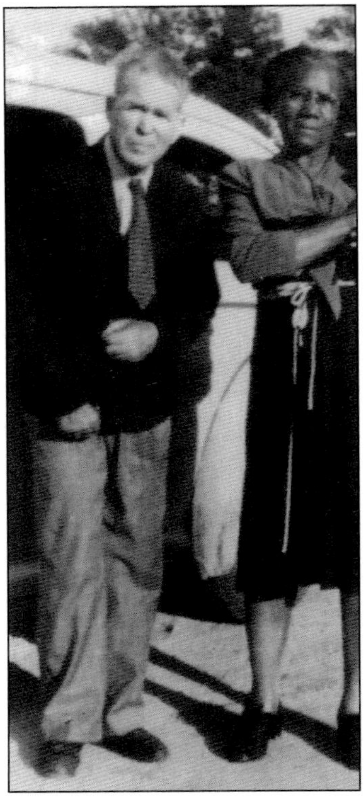

Eugene Cleveland Clarkson was the son of Polly Adams and Edward McGrady Clarkson. His father's lineage can be traced back to William Clarkson, who was born in England in 1760. Eugene was born in 1884 at the Meeting House plantation, where his mother had lived for most of her life. Meeting House was the plantation owned by Gracie Adams. Eugene was a prosperous farmer and a prominent businessman. (Caroline Clarkson Forney.)

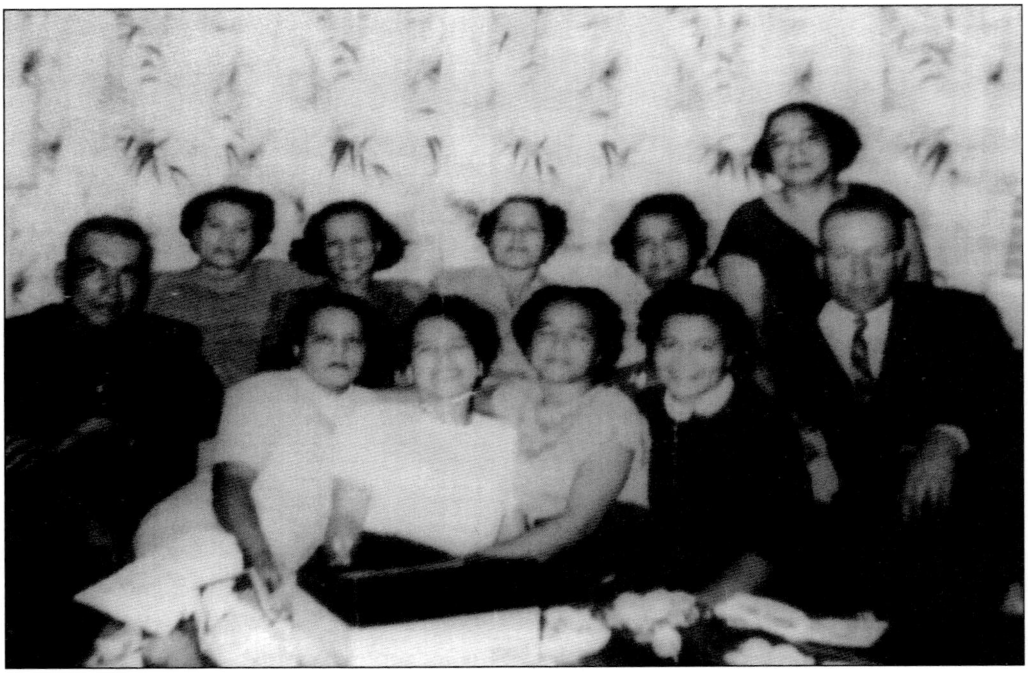

Eugene C. Clarkson married Hattie Prioleau, and to this union, 11 children were born: Polly, Moses, Eugene Wilbert, Rosa Bell, Leola, Francene, Mary Ethel, Marion Helen, Hattie, Wilhelmenia, and Emma Elzetta. (Caroline Clarkson Forney.)

The young Polly Clarkson, pictured here, was born in Hopkins in 1904. Her parents, Eugene and Hattie Prioleau Clarkson, established roots in the community and St. John Baptist Church. Polly graduated from Allen University and taught school for several years in Lower Richland County. Upon her marriage to Sanford Gibson, she moved to Philadelphia, where she operated a small, successful business. She was later married to Raleigh Brown and lived in Mays Landing, where she became involved in the welfare of the neglected. (Barber family collection.)

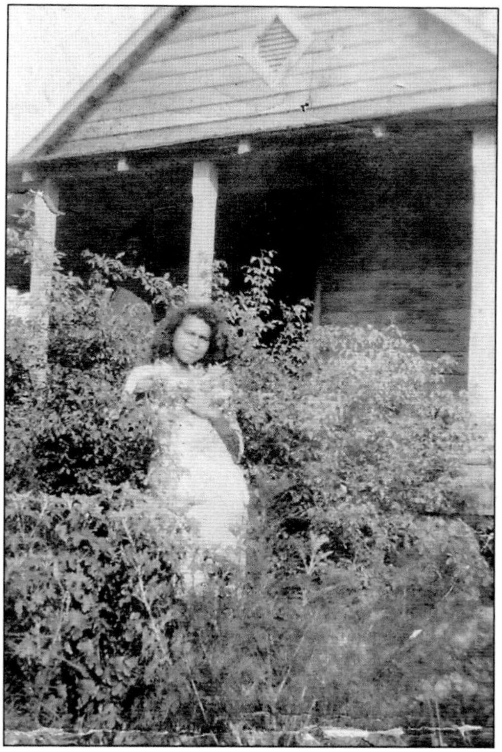

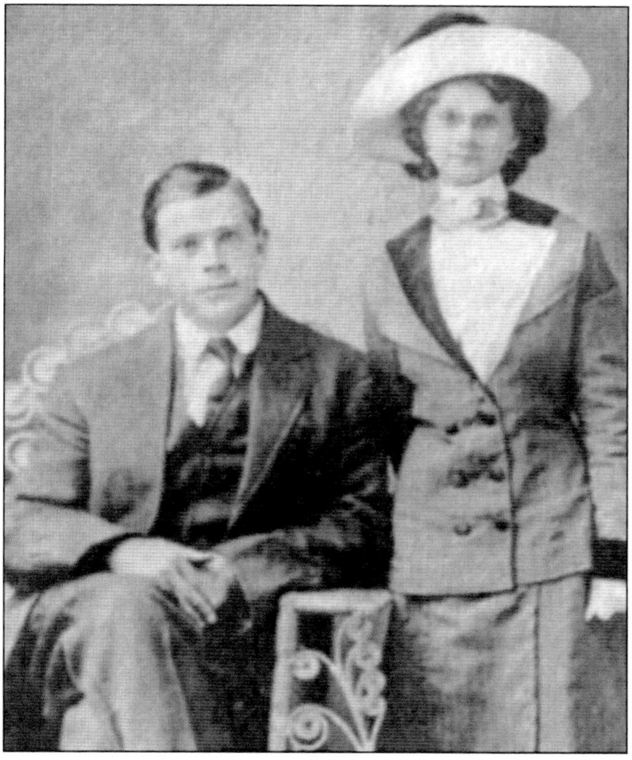

Zack C. Clarkson Sr. graduated from Benedict College in 1911 with a degree in elementary education. He constructed the first public school in Hopkins and operated the first cotton gin and sawmill in the area. He also taught school in Gadsden for 22 years. Before his death in 1961, he was honored by Clemson University for farm and home development and by the Richland County Conservation Commission. Their children were Zack Jr., Willis, David, Marian, Avery, Everette, and Eleanor. (Clarkson family collection.)

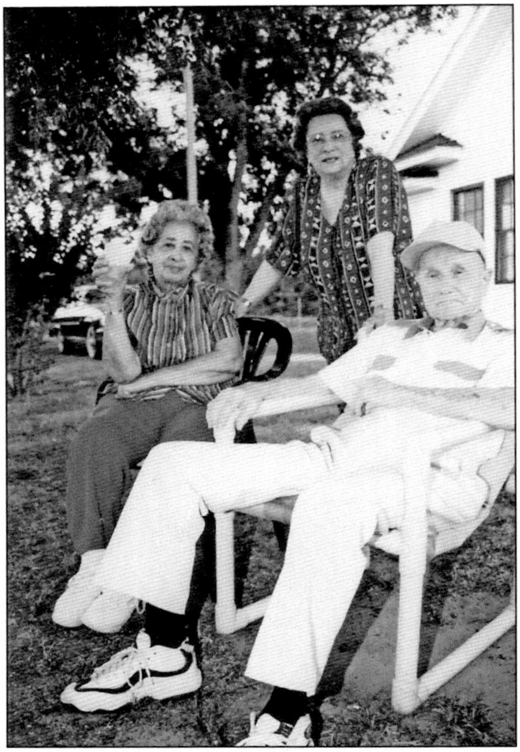

Zack Clarkson Jr. was the son of Zack and Wilhelmina Clarkson Sr. He was an activist, philanthropist, farmer, and partner in the family's cotton gin and sawmill. Zack married Rachel Scott from Eastover (seated left). Their children are Brenda, Zack III, Delores, and Tanya. Also pictured is his sister, Marian Clarkson Morgan; she married Dr. Clarence Morgan and lived in Columbia. Their children are Clarence (a doctor), Gail, and Dawne. (Caroline Clarkson Forney.)

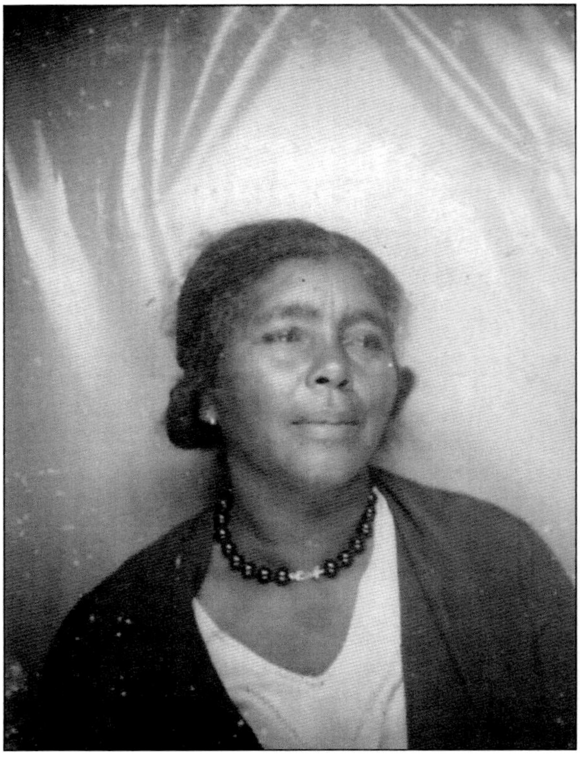

Leanna Floyd Clarkson was the mother of Henry Clarkson. She was possibly the daughter of Henry Floyd, who built a beautiful home in Hopkins in 1890. Leanna was known to entertain large parties for friends from Columbia who came to the homestead known as the O'Hanley Place. Her son, Henry, attended Benedict College until he entered the army and served in World War II. He completed his college education at Johnson C. Smith University, farmed, and later worked as a corrections officer until his retirement. (Barber family collection.)

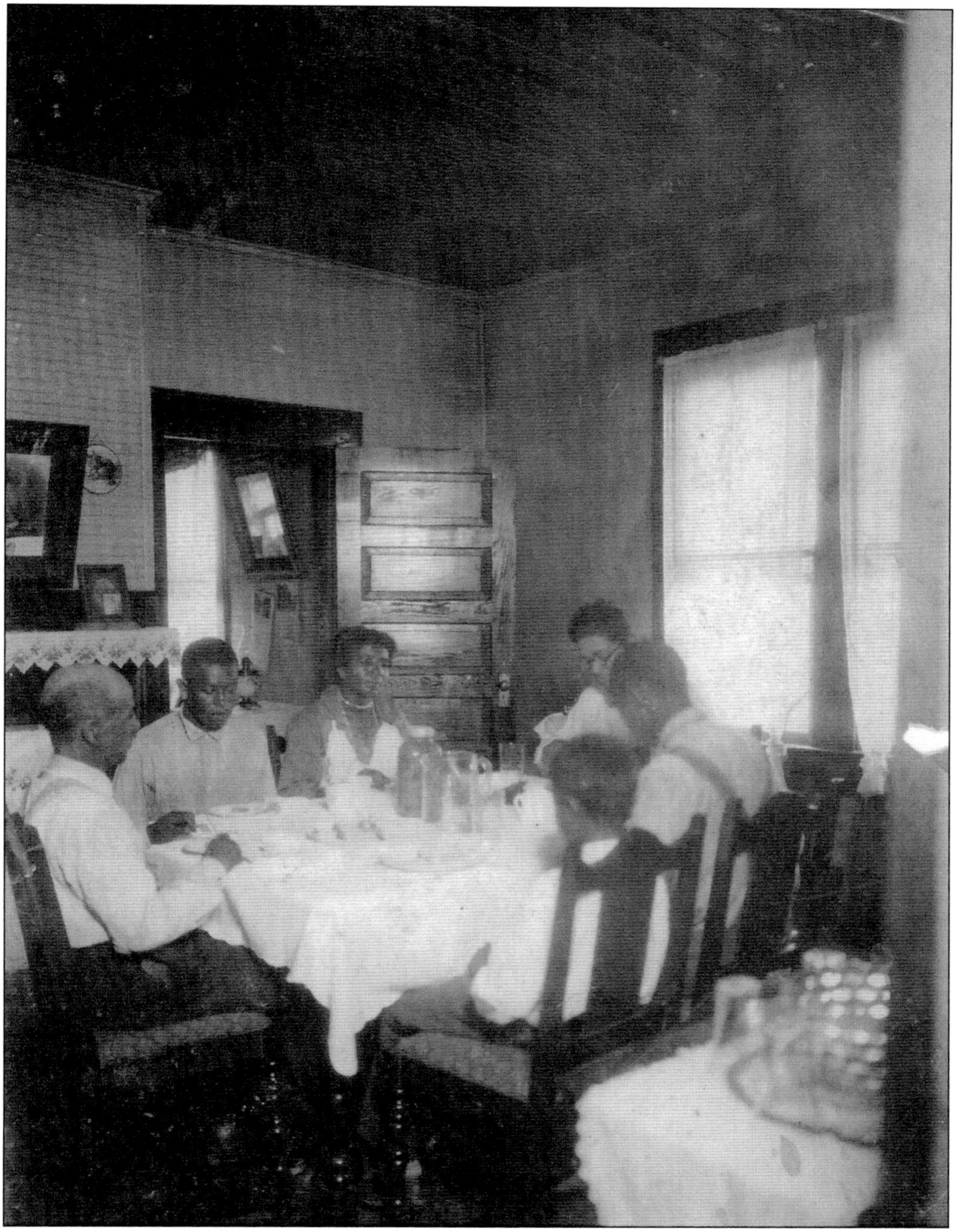

The Henry Clarkson family and Johnson Adams are pictured here in their home off Bluff Road. James Dessie Clarkson lived with his mother, Nan Burns, in the home of Dr. Hubert Clarkson in the village of Hopkins. When Dessie became of age, he married Leanna Floyd, the mother of Henry. George Floyd, a cashier for Victory Savings Bank in Columbia, also grew up in this home. (Jocelyn Clarkson.)

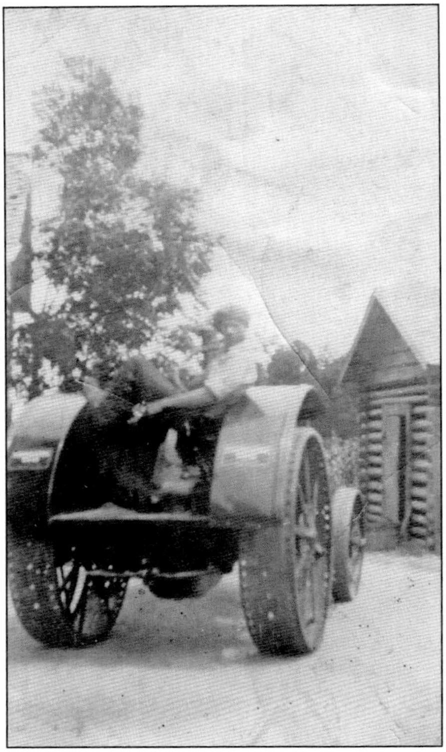

Willis Clarkson Sr. ran a thriving sawmill operation on Bluff Road. His brothers, Zack and David, operated the cotton gin that was located on the same property. He was known to be an astute businessman. The Clarkson brothers supplied lumber and materials to the majority of the area and were major employers of local residents at the time. They were members of Zion Benevolent Baptist Church. The children of Willis and wife Helen are Willis Jr., Helen, Marian, Joan, and Samuel. (Helen Clarkson Crawford and Samuel Clarkson.)

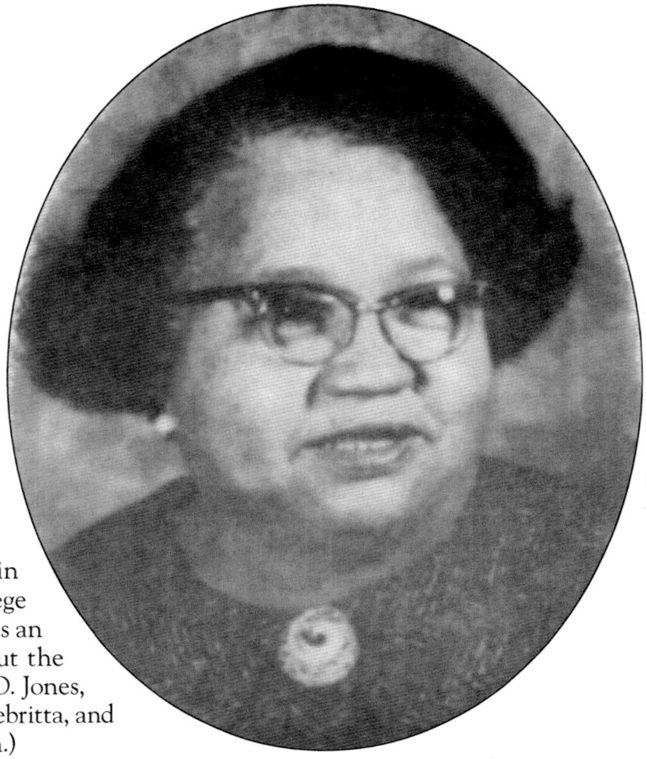

Rosa Bell Clarkson Jones was born in 1911. She attended Benedict College along with her sisters. She worked as an early interior decorator throughout the county. She was married to Willie D. Jones, and their children were Harvey, Fayebritta, and Frederick. (Barber family collection.)

Leola Clarkson Caison was born in Hopkins in 1913. Her parents were Eugene and Hattie Prioleau Clarkson. She graduated from Booker Washington High School and completed her degree at Benedict College in 1938. In 1939, she married Collier C. Caison and began teaching in area public schools. She and her husband began a drapery and upholstery business and built a reputation as premiere interior decorators. In 1979, Leola received the National Distinguished Alumni Award, later the Lula B. Gambrel Award, and was president of the Benedict College Senior Alumni Club in Columbia. (Barber family collection.)

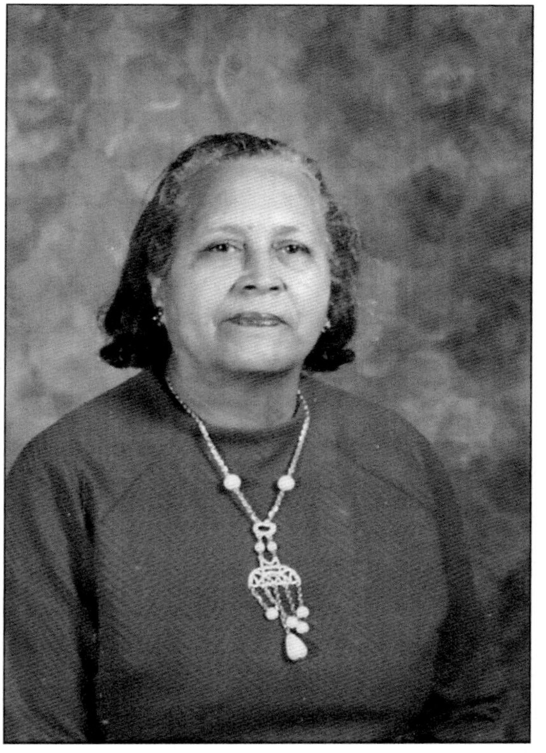

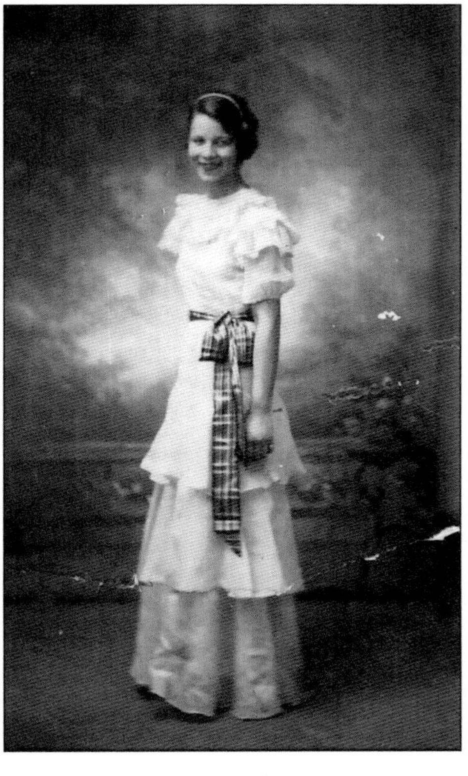

Rachel Prioleau Bailey was one of triplets born to William and Nellie Clarkson Prioleau. Along with her brother Joseph and her sister Rebecca, Rachel had 10 other siblings. She married Peter Bailey and lived in Philadelphia until 1984, when she returned to Columbia. She was well known and loved by many for her outstanding skills as a self-employed seamstress. (Barber family collection.)

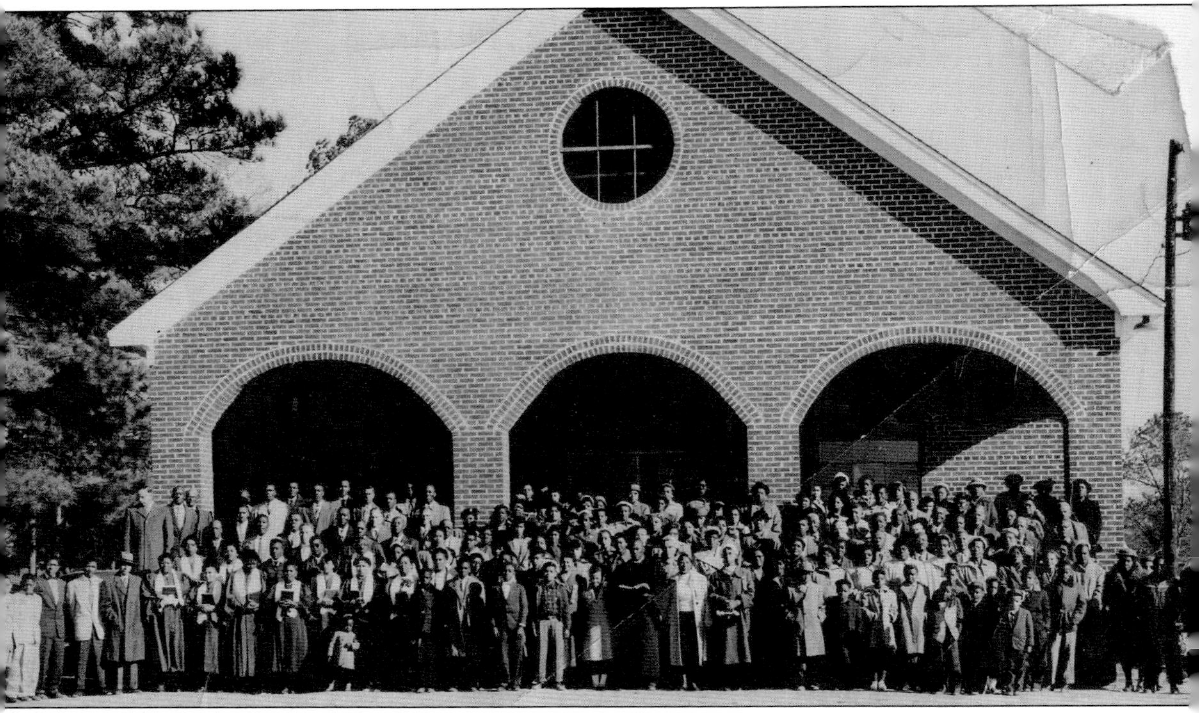

Zion Benevolent Baptist Church was organized 1870 in Weston, South Carolina. The first pastor of the church, Rev. Clem P. Davis, who was born in 1839, was one of the founding members. A wood-frame building was erected in 1901, and the first remodeling was completed in 1927 under Rev. J. W. Neal. The first deacons included Paul Sims, William Sims, Peter Brown, Robert Goodwin, Jack Cornish, Frank Jones, and Robert Jones. (Neal-Scott family collection.)

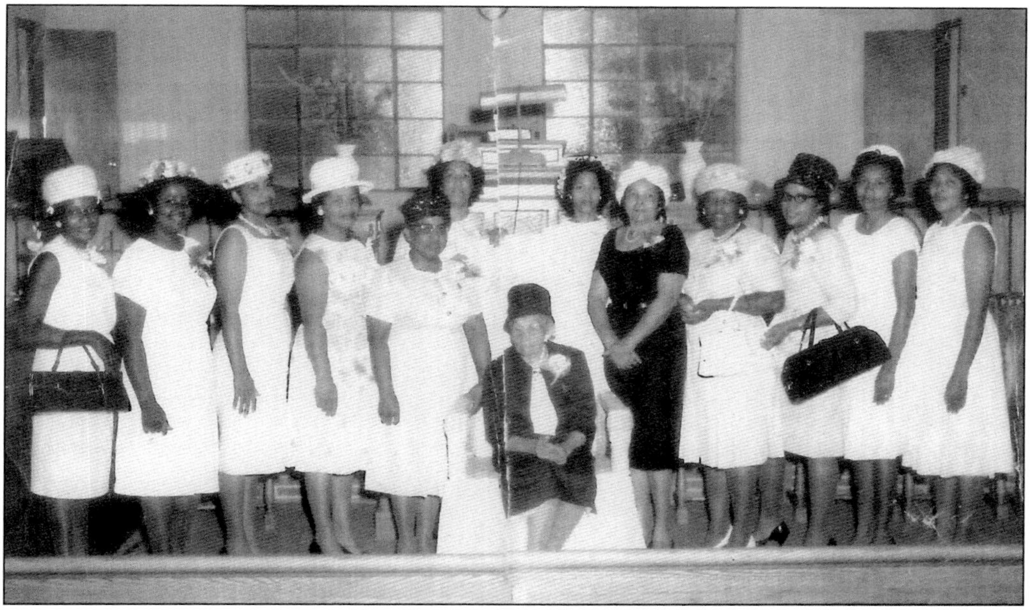

This photograph shows Rev. Jesse Neal's wife, Minnie Holley Neal, seated at center, being honored by Zion Benevolent Baptist Church's women's organization. From left to right are Louise Hill Goodson, Susie Mae Morris-Coles, Marthan Jones Clarkson, Mattie Gray Henry, Sarah Miller Neal, Mary Robinson Jones, Loristene Nips Robinson, Helen Taylor Clarkson, Julia Sims Dowdy, Rebecca Shiver Davis, Millie Goodson Goodwin, and Lillie Mae Adams. (Neal-Scott family collection.)

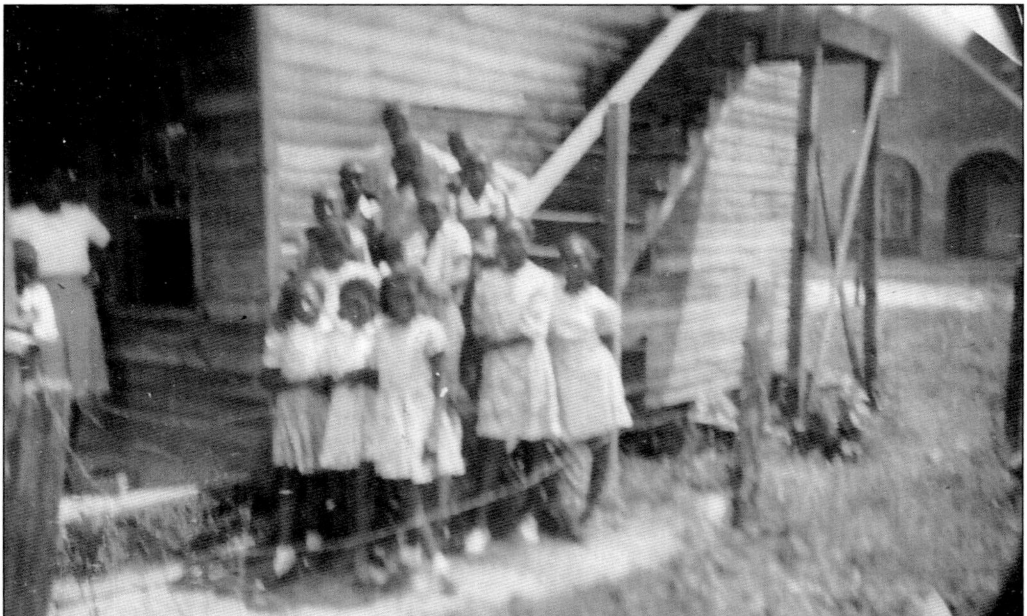

With almost every church building came a one- or two-room school for children of the recently freed slaves. Pictured is the early Zion Benevolent School; the church is in the background. (Neal-Scott family collection.)

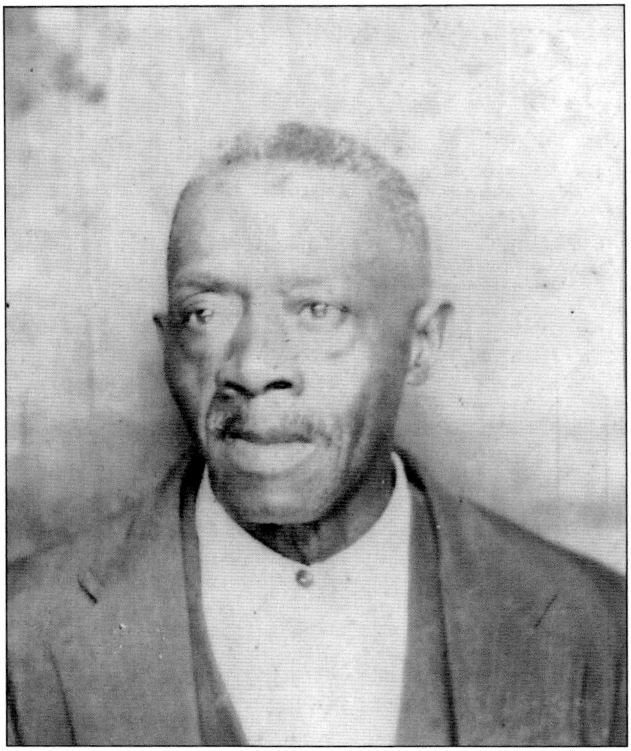

Rev. Louis Lowman, pictured here, was born in 1870 to Rev. William and Ellen Jones Lowman. The Lowmans were among the founding families of St. John Baptist Church. Louis became a choir leader at St. John and along with his brothers formed a singing group that was famous in Lower Richland. Louis' father, Rev. William Lowman, was elected to the South Carolina House of Representatives in 1874, during the Reconstruction era. (Barber family collection.)

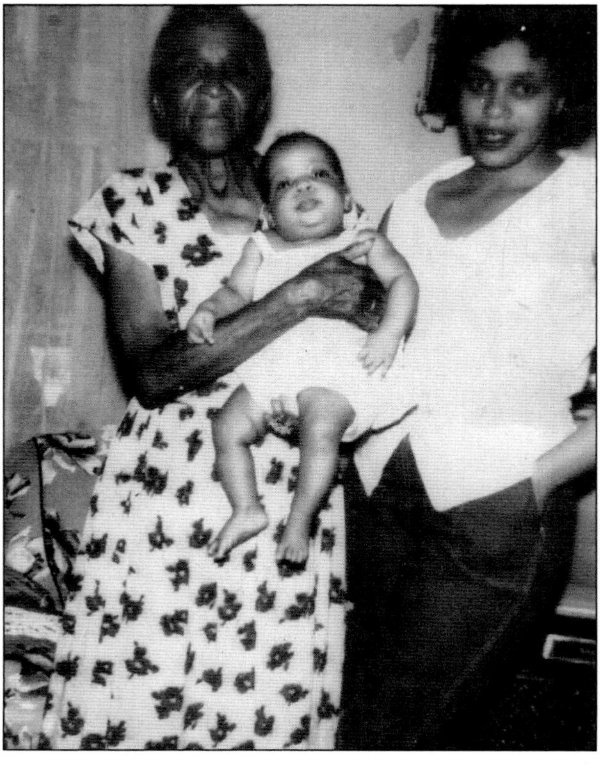

Eugenia Harris Lowman, pictured here on the left, married Rev. Louis Lowman in 1895. Louis became a preacher and pastored Pleasant Grove Baptist Church in Gadsden and Mount Olive Baptist Church in Kingville. They were the parents of Louis Jr., Corine, James, Levi, Joseph, Sam, Sarah, and Robert. (Joann Lowman Washington and E. Marie Jones.)

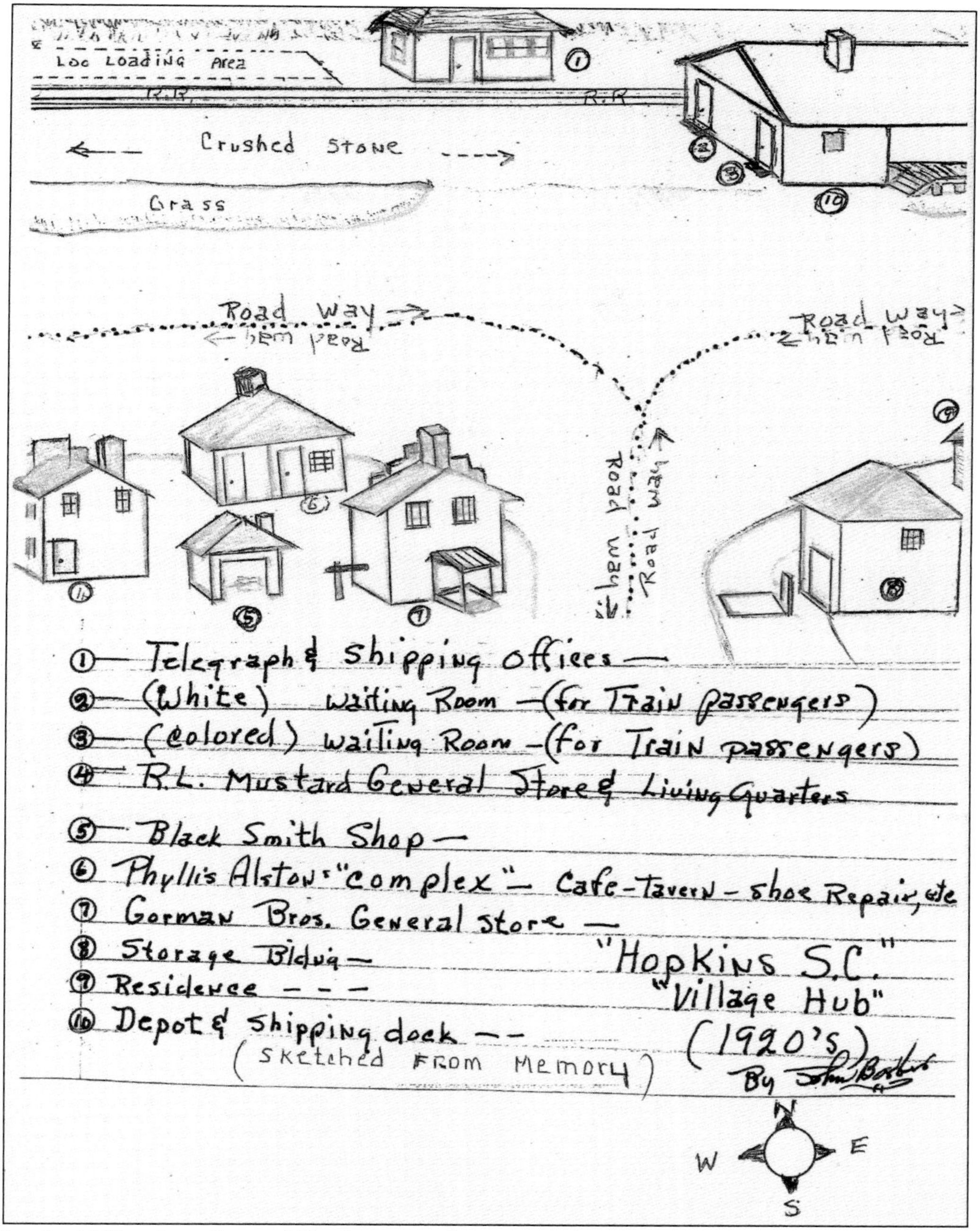

In the 1920s, the village of Hopkins was thriving, with general stores, gin mills, industries, residences, and a town hall. The drawing by John Barber Jr. shows the locations of businesses, residences, and the busy train depot. (John Barber Jr.)

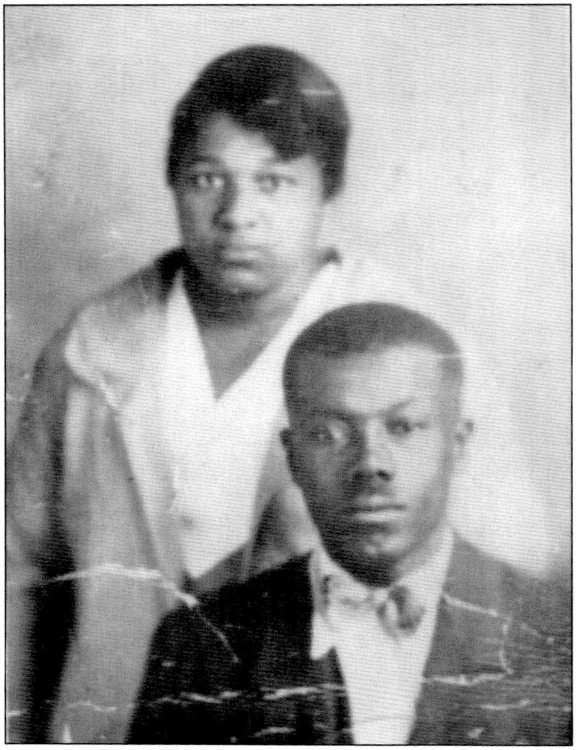

Isom "Mighty" Sims was a prosperous farmer and entrepreneur who operated a successful store on Bluff Road in the Hopkins community. The store was located near the Claytor School and across the road from the Clarkson gin and sawmill. He is pictured here with his first wife Lula Hopkins Sims. (Joann Lowman Washington and E. Marie Jones.)

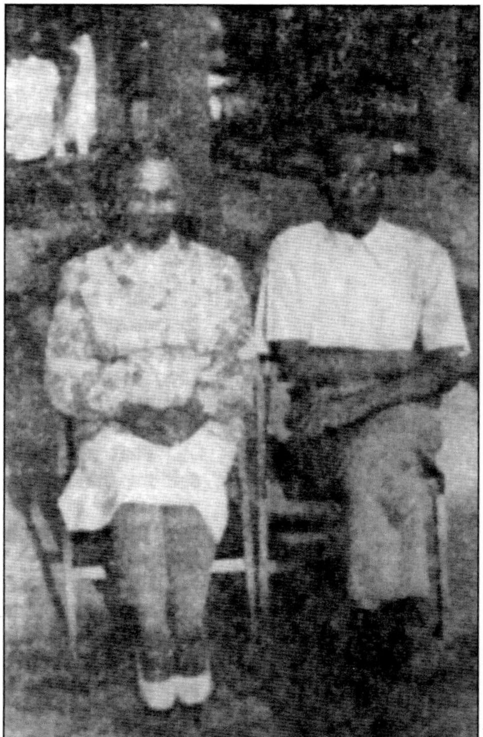

Abram Coles Sr. was born in 1895. He served in the army during World War I and later worked as a farm laborer for Dr. Hubert Claytor. He and his family were members of Zion Benevolent. They were parents of Williann, Ola, Burgest, Abram Jr., Barry, Etta, Octavia, Martha, Henry, and Mable. Their son, Abram Jr., was the one of Columbia's first African American fire station captains. (Neal-Scott family collection.)

Joseph McRant was born in Sandy Run, Calhoun County. In 1898, he graduated from Allen University, and he settled in the Hopkins community when he became principal of the Hopkins School. Professor McRant was trained as a cook while in the army; he eventually left the education profession to become a successful entrepreneur. He and his wife operated a variety store, a valet-pressing club, and a café in the village of Hopkins. The McRant Café was a popular location for drumshouts. The McRants' expertise in preparing food earned them a prominent place at the Negro State Fair, held in the Columbia Fairgrounds each year until desegregation. (Blanch McRant McFadden.)

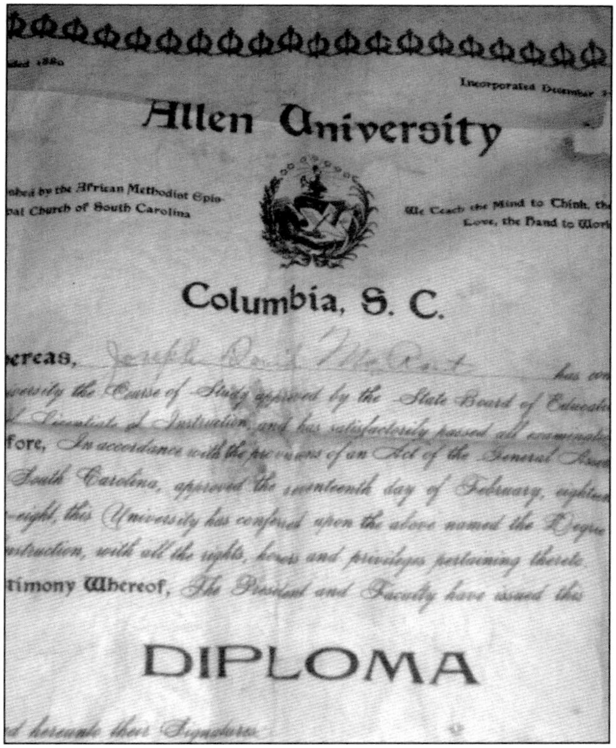

Incorporated December

Allen University

...by the African Methodist Epis-
...al Church of South Carolina

We Teach the Mind to Think, the
Love, the Hand to Work

Columbia, S. C.

...ereas, Joseph ... McRant has com...
...ersity the Course of Study approved by the State Board of Educa...
...Curriculum of Instruction, and has satisfactorily passed all examinati...
...fore, In accordance with the provisions of an Act of the General Asse...
South Carolina, approved the seventeenth day of February, eighte...
...eight, this University has conferred upon the above named the Degre...
...struction, with all the rights, honors and privileges pertaining thereto.
...timony Whereof, The President and Faculty have issued this

DIPLOMA

...d hereunto their Signatures

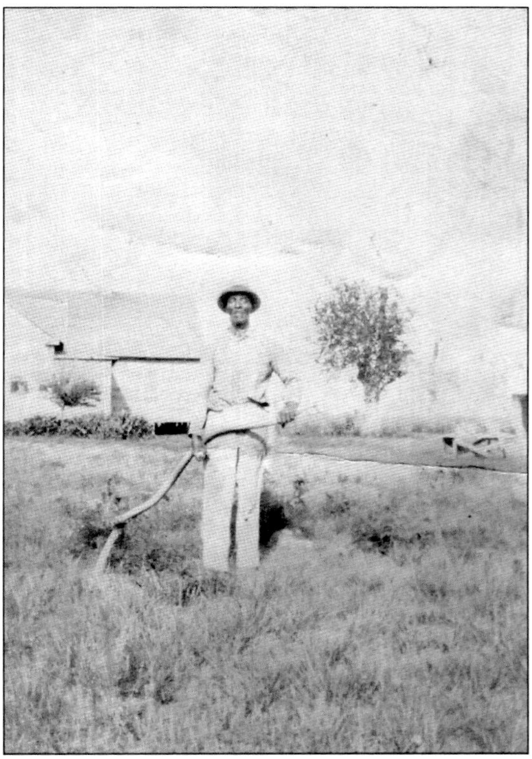

Jacob "Jake" Johnson was born in Newberry County in 1868. He was the son of John and Margaret Robinson Johnson. The family lived on the Old Field plantation, owned by the Hopkins family. Jacob became a master carpenter and farmer. He married Fannie Goodwin, and they became the parents of Pinky, Maggie, Frances, Harry, Nehemiah, Georgia Bell, Daniel, Willie, and Frank. (Blanch McRant McFadden.)

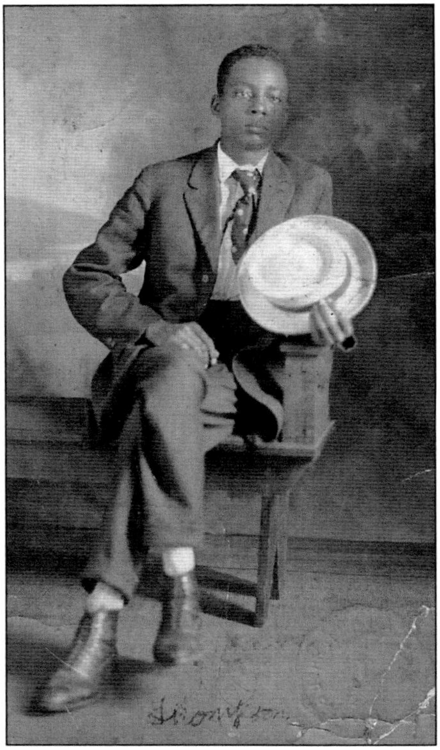

Herbert Thompson was the third spouse of Nellie Clarkson. He was the oldest son of Dennis Thompson, who had a large farm in the Horrell Hill area. The Tub Mill pond was located on the property. One of Herbert's sisters, known as Sugar, remained on the original homestead until her death in 2008. (Barber family collection.)

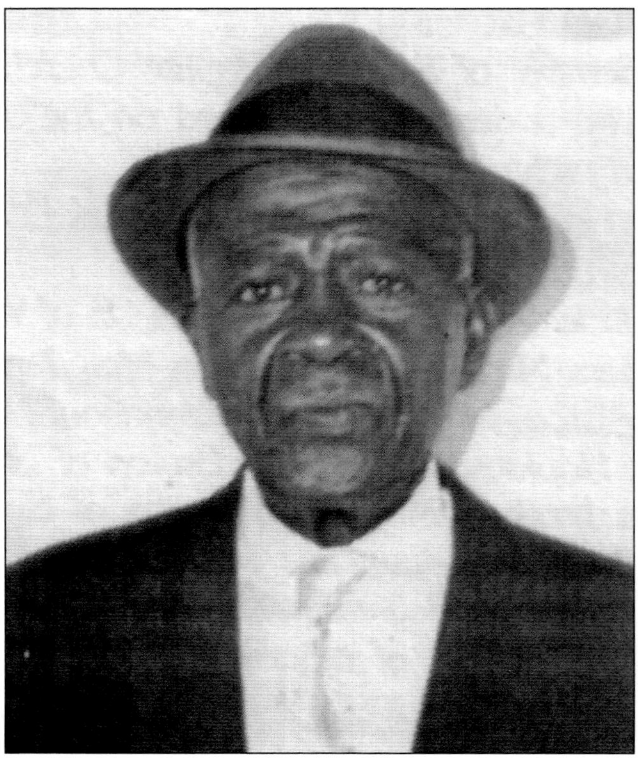

Charlie Evans was born in 1909 in Georgetown, South Carolina, but he moved to the Hopkins community at an early age to work for the railroad. He was married to Elise Jones, and their children were Lillie Mae, Janie Lee, Ernestine, Daisy Mae, Berneatha, Esther, Lucille, Charlie Jr., and Joseph. (Ernestine Alston.)

Mount Moriah Baptist Church was organized in 1872. Families of deacons and trustees L. Davis, P. Harris, S. Hopkins, M. Howell, J. Jones, R. W. Jones, F. McCoy, P. Sumter, and W. S. Sumter from New Light Beulah and Zion Benevolent selected the Bluff Road site next to the Congaree swamp. Rev. H. Golmand was the first pastor. The original cornerstone contains the spelling of "Mt. Maria" as the name. Westberry Neal is pastor emeritus. (Mount Moriah's current pastor, Rev. Dr. Blakely N. Scott.)

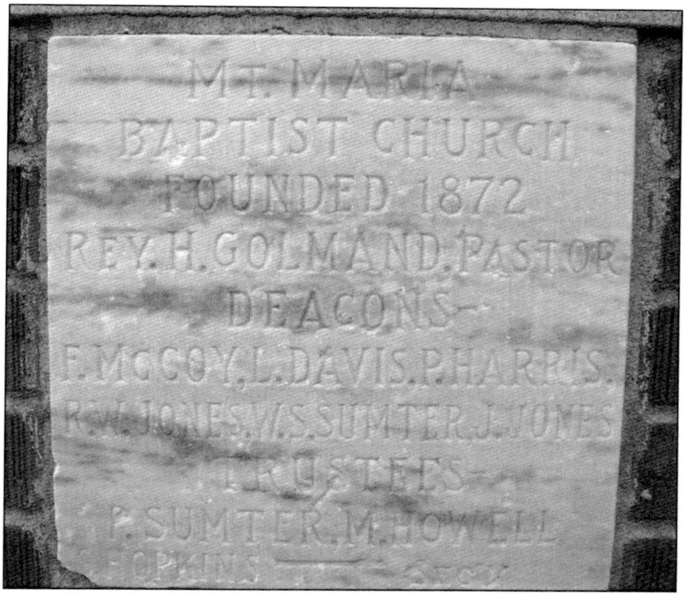

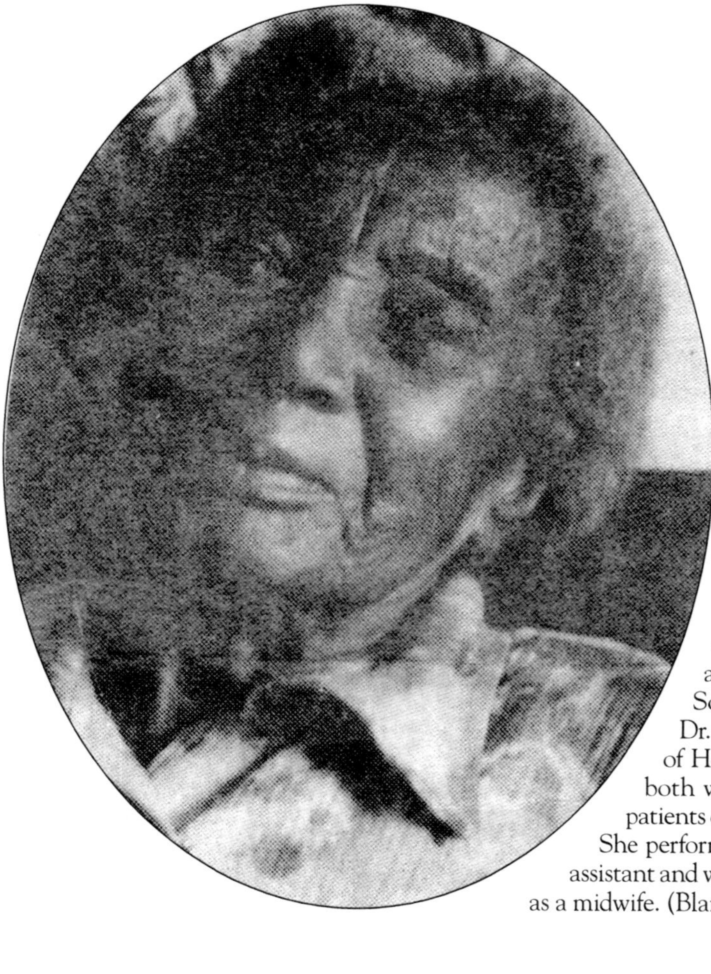

Mary Jane Carter was known as the nurse for the Hopkins community. After she completed her nurse training at Vorhees School in Denmark, South Carolina, she worked in Dr. Claytor's office near the village of Hopkins, and this office served both white and African American patients during the years of segregation. She performed the duties of a physician's assistant and worked from Dr. Claytor's office as a midwife. (Blanch McRant McFadden.)

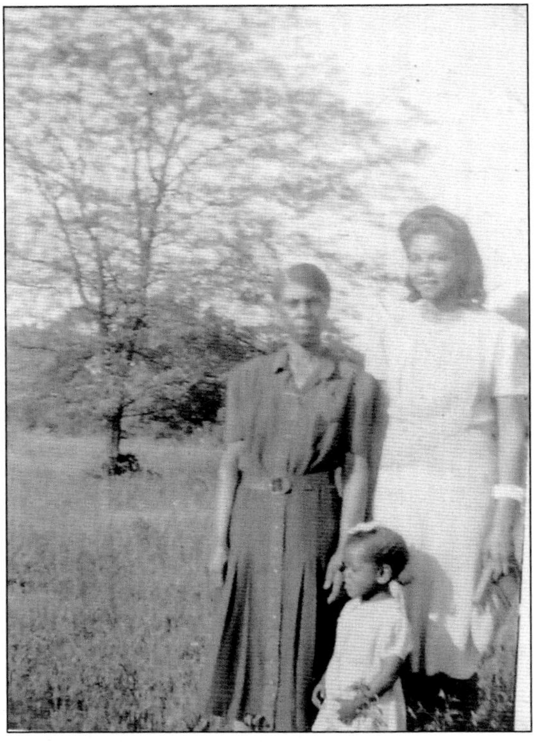

Mary Smith Newton was the daughter of Rev. and Mrs. Robert S. Smith of Manning, South Carolina. She moved to Lower Richland after marrying Peter Newton. Mary was the proprietor of one of the neighborhood stores in the Hopkins community. She was a member of St. John Baptist Church, where she served as president of the Daughters of Mission for 36 years. She also became a charter member of the Hopkins Parent-Teacher Association and a member of other civic and community organizations. (Barber family collection.)

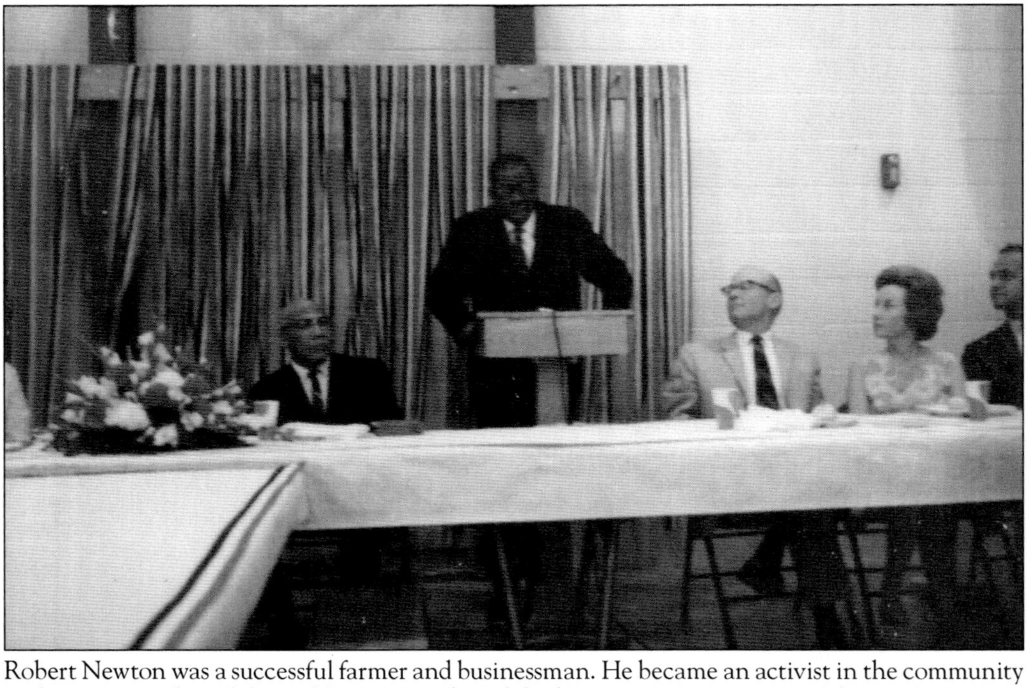

Robert Newton was a successful farmer and businessman. He became an activist in the community and a strong political force. He is remembered for his commitment to get African Americans registered to vote in the early 1960s. His grassroots efforts made it possible for the first park to be built in Hopkins. (Barber family collection.)

Jesse Newton was the son of Peter Newton and Mary Smith Newton. He was born in 1916 and educated in the Hopkins schools. He was enlisted in the navy for four years and later served in the army for 20 years. He returned home from his tours of duty and married Ethel Webber of Eastover. After the death of Ethel, he married Hattie Dwight of Hopkins. (Barber family collection.)

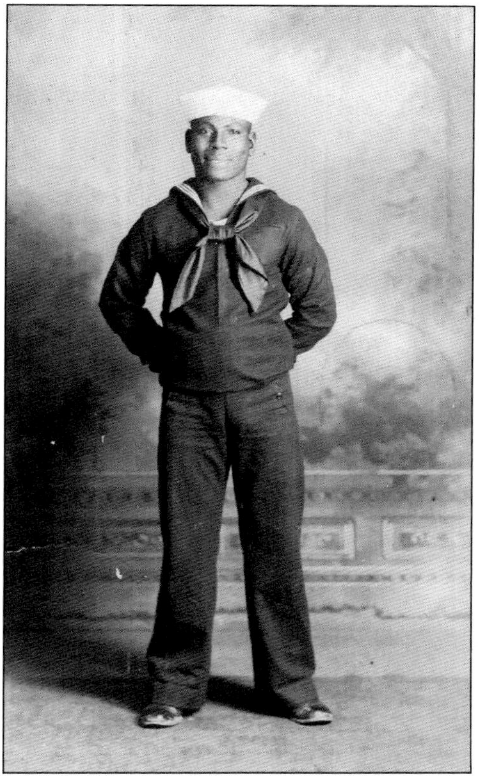

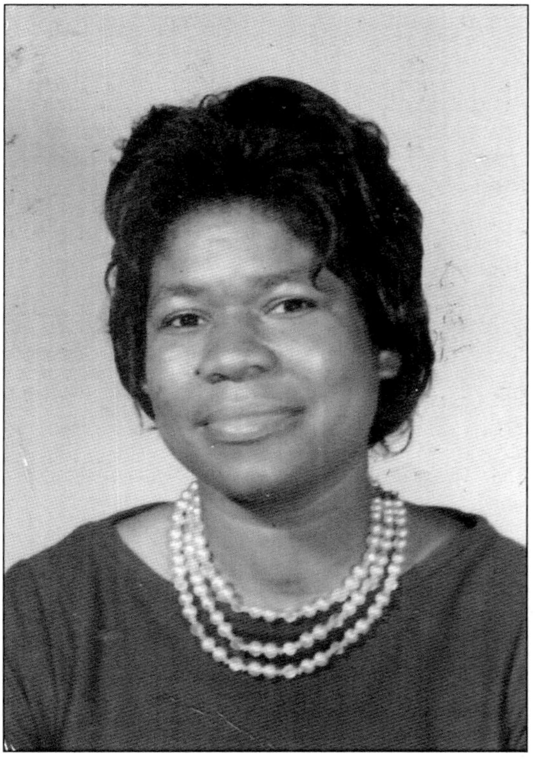

Hattie Newton Fruster was the daughter of Robert Newton and Vinnie Turnipseed Newton. She was educated in Richland County public schools, and she received a diploma from the Waverley School of Cosmetology in Columbia. During her adult life, she became actively involved in religious, educational, community, and political affairs. In the late 1950s and early 1960s, she participated in marches, demonstrations, and boycotts to end segregation in Richland County. Along with nine other Lower Richland residents, Hattie Fruster organized the first chapter of the NAACP in Lower Richland. (Barber family collection.)

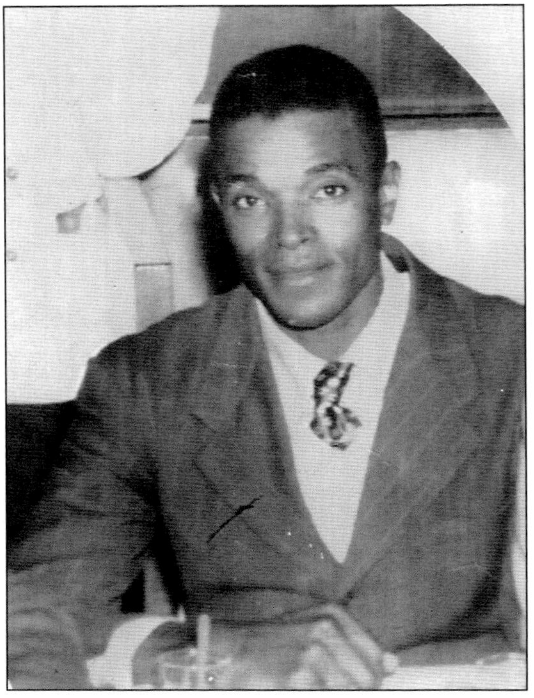

Alexander McRant was the son of Prof. Joseph McRant and Louisa Asmon McRant and reared by Martha Ann Howell McRant. He was educated in Richland County and later attended the Chicago Technical Institute Training School for Carpentry. McRant received a lifetime membership for completing 50 years of service with the Brotherhood of Carpenters and Joiners of America Local Union 1772. (Blanch McRant McFadden.)

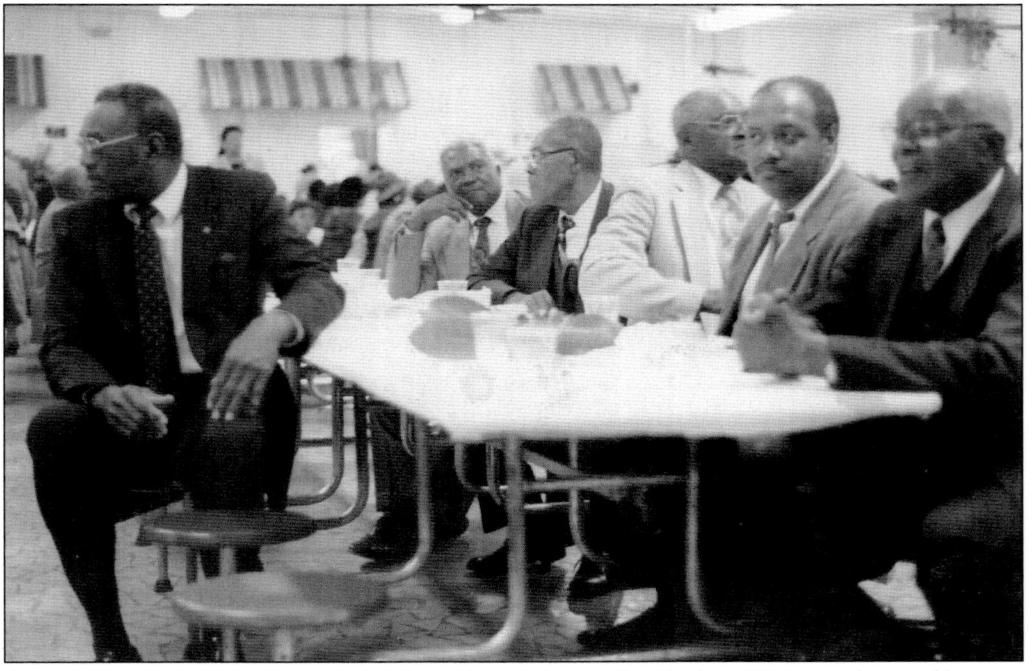

As a community leader, Alexander McRant (far right) served as Hopkins PTA president and became a member of the Richland County Democratic Party Committee. He was active in organizing registration drives and getting eligible voters to the polls. Alexander McRant was the first African American poll attendant for the Hopkins Precinct. He is shown here with other community leaders Ernest White, J. C. Woodard, and Robert Lowman. (Blanch McRant McFadden.)

Thaddeus (Tad) Goodson was born in Weston, South Carolina, in 1869, on the land owned by the family of *Tales of the Congaree* author Edward C. L. Adams. He is referenced in the book as being a sportsman, humorist, fatalist, and philosopher. Tad was Edward Adams's chauffeur, overseer, handyman, confidante, storyteller, and dedicatory subject of specific sections of the book. (Blanch McRant McFadden.)

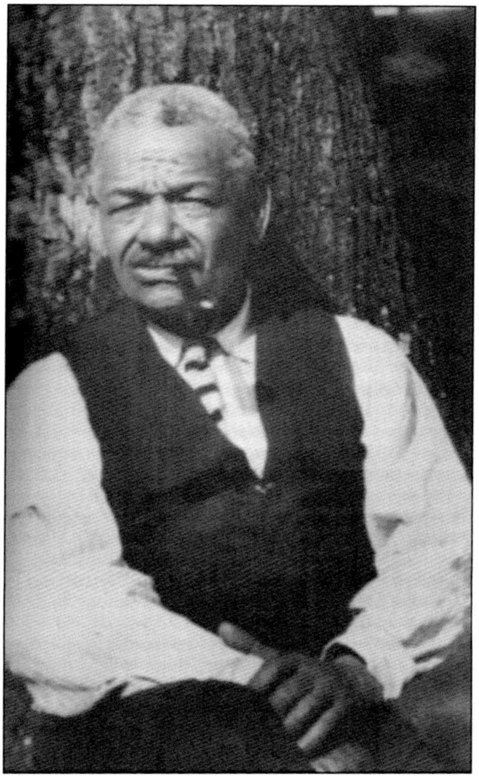

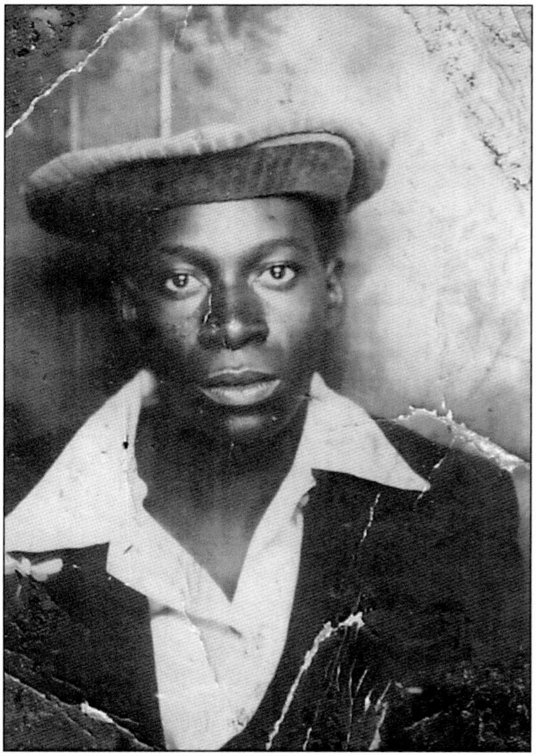

The Robert James family migrated to Hopkins with one of the large sawmill operations and settled. They lived near the Chappell property, on which they were sharecroppers for a time. Robert next became employed by a large farm operation. He later became a partner with London Brown drilling for water and installing what were known as pitcher pumps in homes. (Barber family collection.)

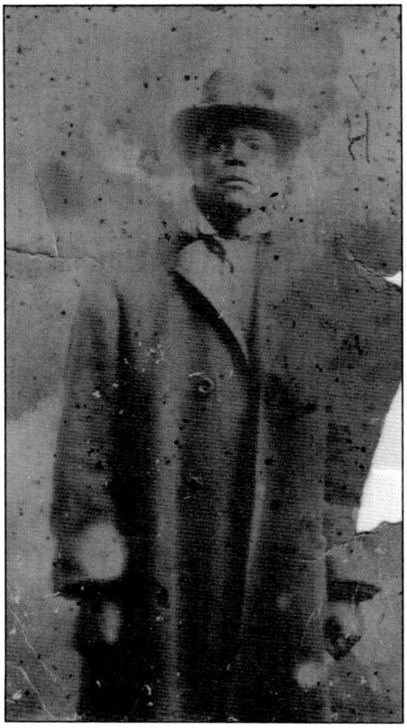

Frank Johnson was the son of Jacob Johnson and Fannie Goodwin Johnson. From his marriage to Margaret, his children were Newlyn, Glenmore, Elise, Frank, Martha, and Georgia Bell. His twin sister was Annie Frances. (Blanch McRant McFadden.)

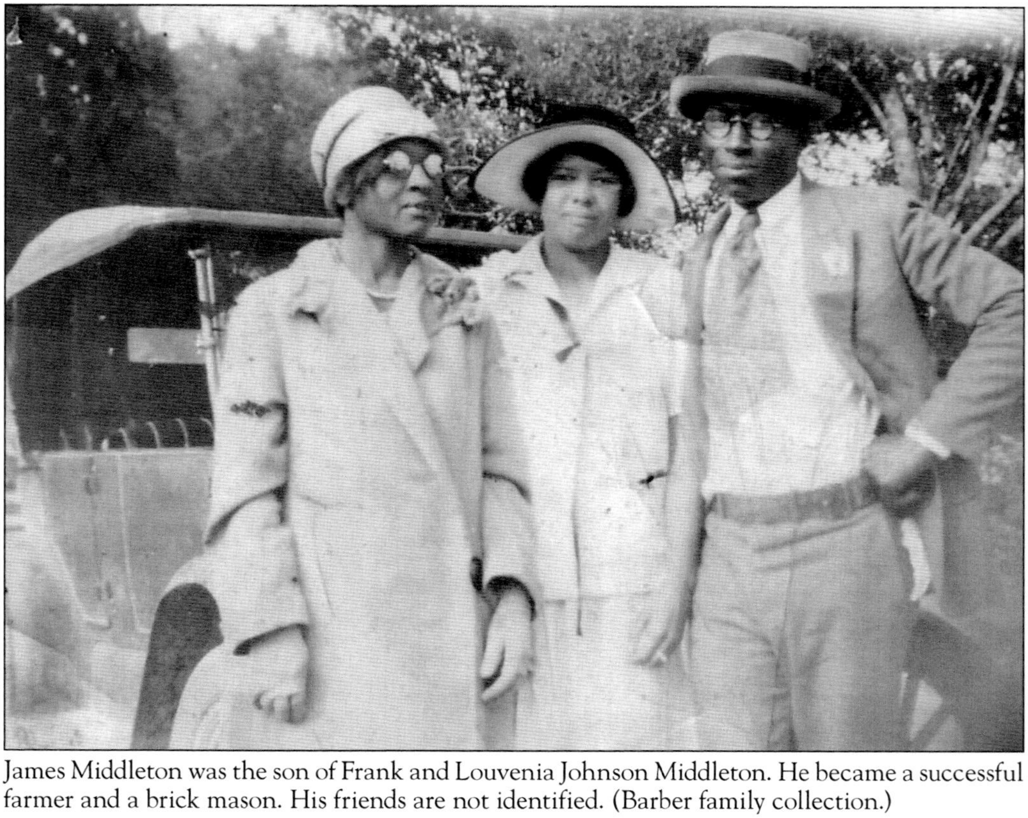

James Middleton was the son of Frank and Louvenia Johnson Middleton. He became a successful farmer and a brick mason. His friends are not identified. (Barber family collection.)

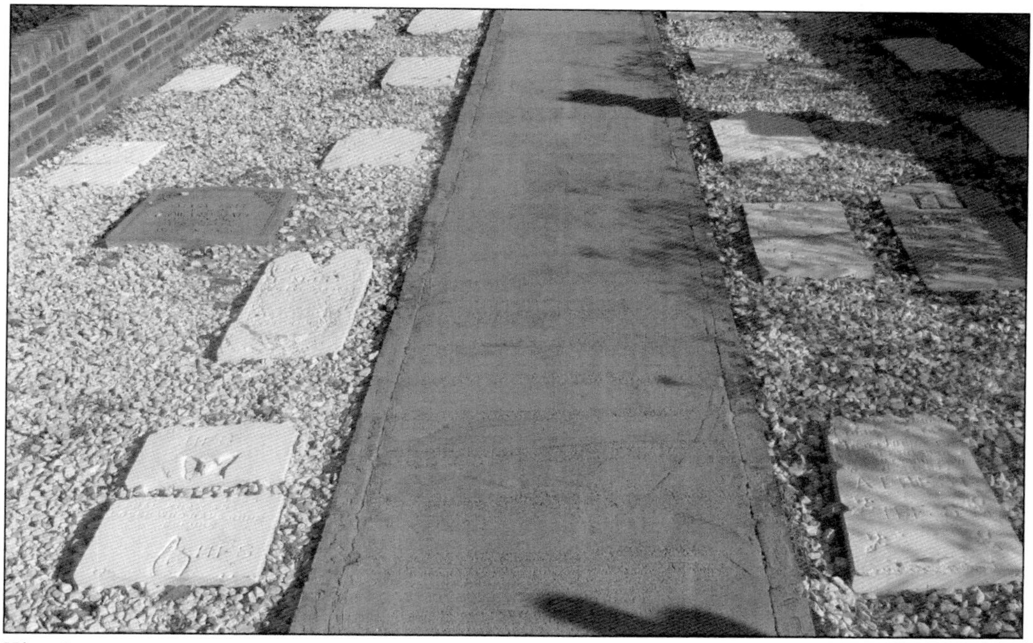

The Government Cemetery, also known as the Old Slave Graveyard, is located alongside Cabin Creek and dates back to 1870. The land was designated as a government graveyard for Negro soldiers, veterans, and their immediate families. After 1945, the graveyard was dismantled by a farmer, and over 30 headstones were tossed into the creek. The property was recovered and restored almost 50 years later, when C. W. Haynes and Company donated 2.09 acres to St. John Baptist Church on January 7, 1997. (Photograph by Deborah Scott Brooks.)

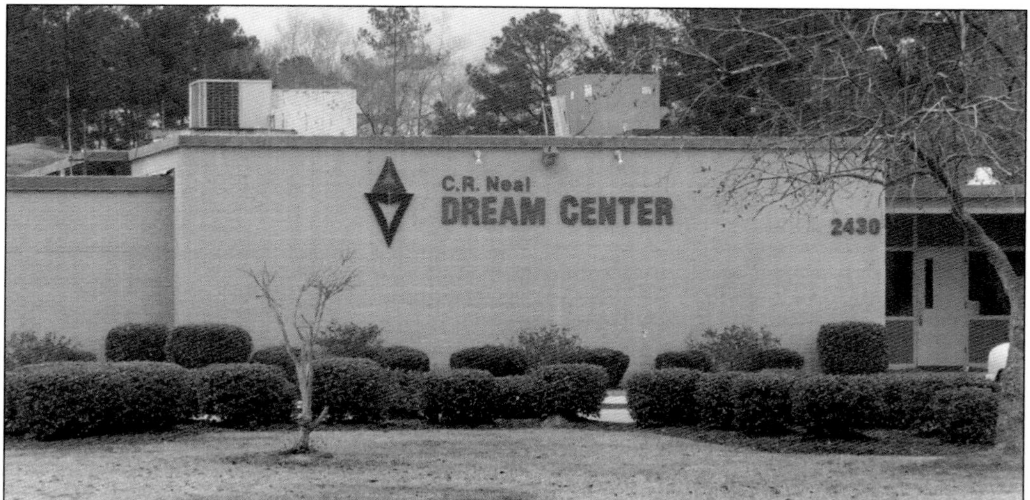

The C. R. Neal Dream Center was formerly the Atlas Road School and is now a community service center. Rev. Choatte R. Neal Sr. retired as a school administrator and principal from Richland Schools and was principal of Atlas Road Elementary School. He married Lavern Kohn Neal; their children are Green B., a retired medical doctor; Choatte Jr, a retired South Carolina state patrolman; Joseph H., a minister and South Carolina state representative; and Wilma, an entrepreneur. (Photograph by Deborah Scott Brooks.)

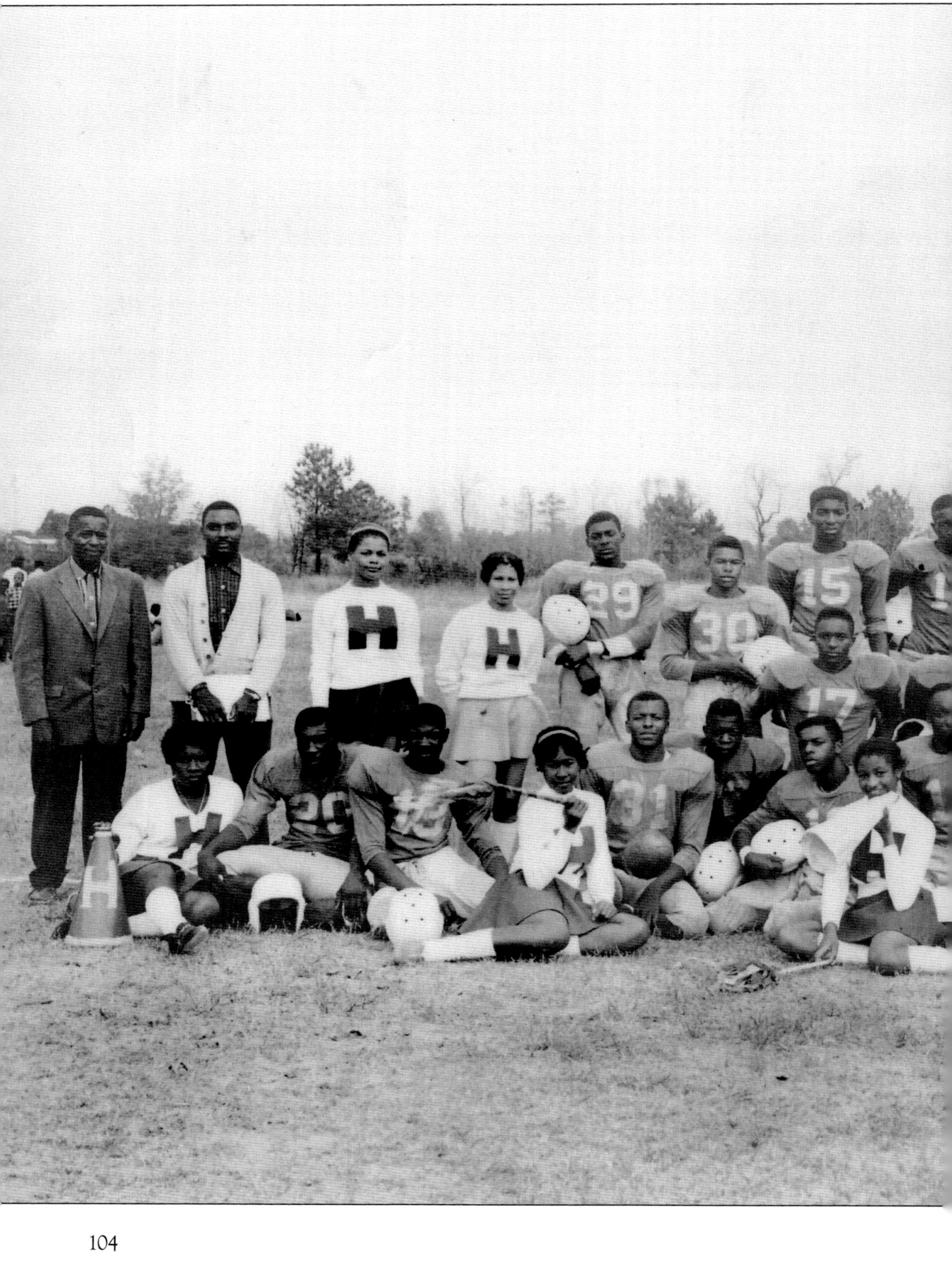

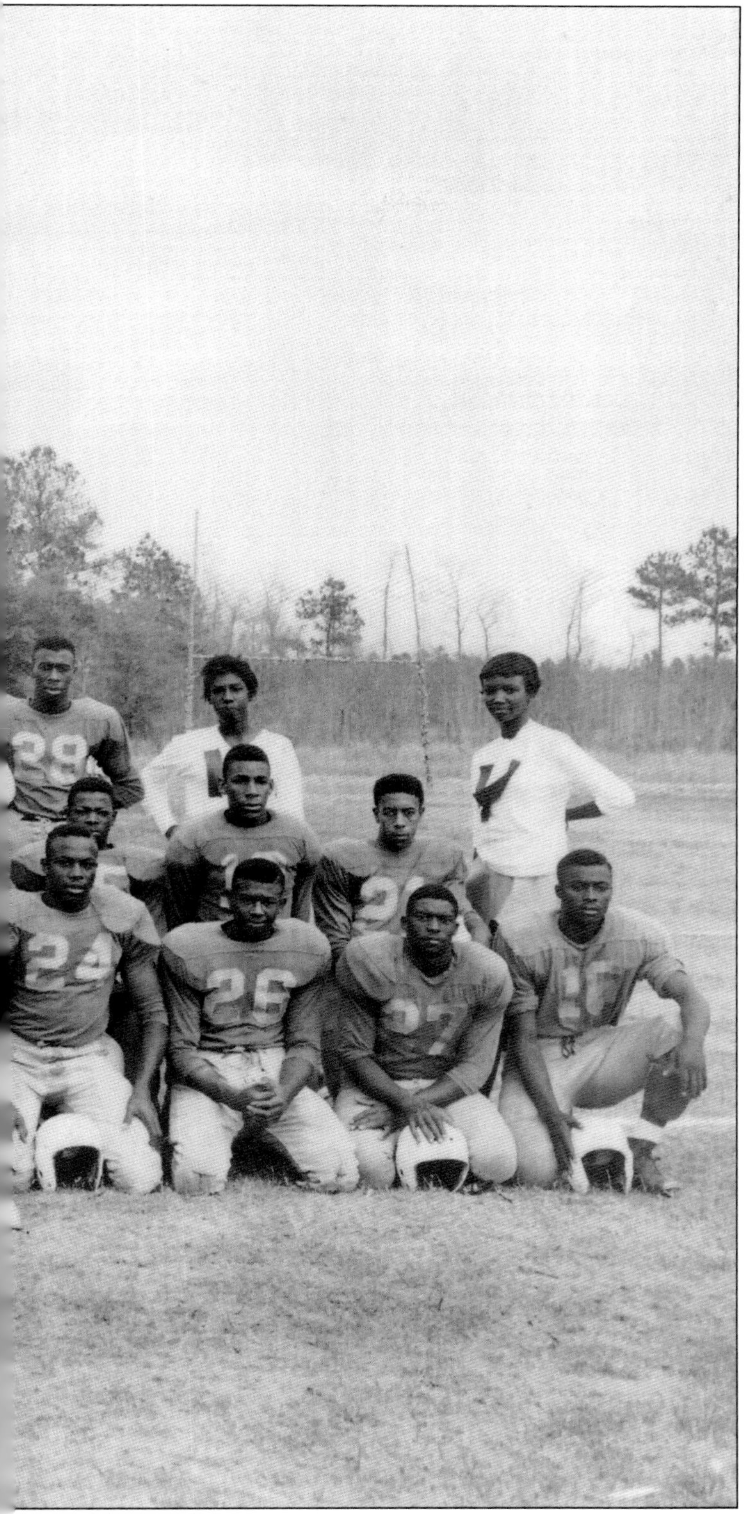

The Hopkins High School football team produced many talented athletes during these early years. Coaches Robert Pearson and Parnell Jones had the task of training players from all of the different communities in the area. Wearing jersey No. 15 in the center of this photograph is James Chandler, a scholar athlete who played for the Benedict College Tigers in Columbia after he graduated from high school. (Barber family collection.)

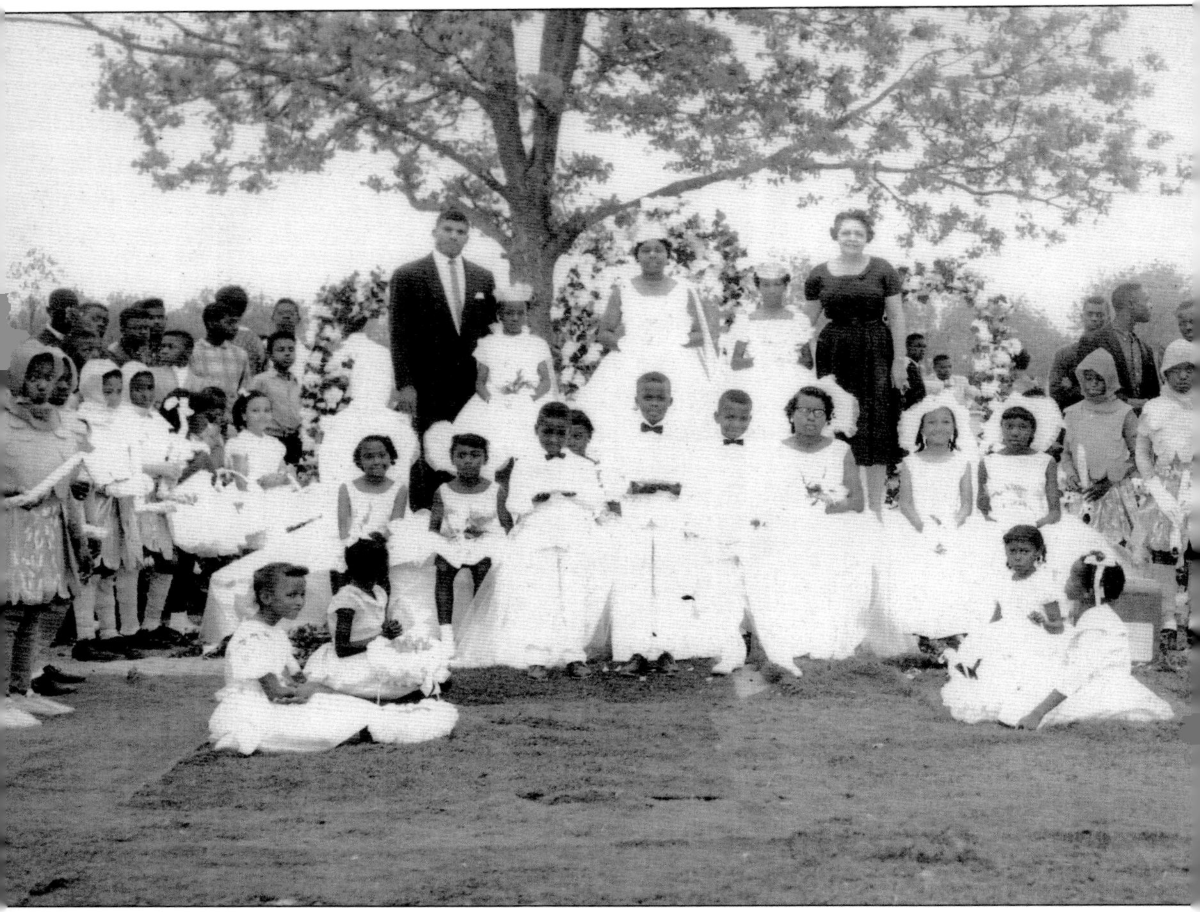

The annual Hopkins May Day pageant was a huge community event for parents and students. Joe E. Brown was assigned to Hopkins High School to fill the vacancy left by U. R. Barber in 1959. The campus was now complete with grades 1 through 12. Pictured with Principal Joe. E. Brown was the principal of the elementary school, Mrs. A. W. Franks. (Jocelyn Clarkson.)

Five

Eastover

The town of Eastover was created around 1870, when the Wilmington-Columbia-Augusta Railroad was built from Sumter to Columbia. Numerous freed African Americans were hired to build this railroad. The 1870 census listed over 25 African Americans who were employed as railroad hands. Incorporated in 1880, Eastover was credited with gradually displacing Kingville as the leading mercantile center in the Lower Richland region.

Mrs. Thomas B. Clarkson (Julia) and her daughter, Julia, organized a school for the slave children of the neighboring plantations in this part of Lower Richland. The location was in the yard of their Sandhills home off Garners Ferry Road. In 1871, an Episcopal chapel known as St. Thomas' Chapel was built on the same property by the Reverend Thomas B. Clarkson. Other schools for African Americans were built later as churches developed throughout the area. Schools and churches remained closely connected as families sought better opportunities for their children.

Zion was an early Gothic Revival church building with an impressive congregation from the Eastover community. The church was organized in 1845, and the third sanctuary was completed in 1911. The church was listed on the National Register of Historic Places in 1986. Shortly after that year, the church was destroyed by fire. All that remains are the arches.

The Goodwill plantation was developed around 1795 on the far east side of Lower Richland. The property borders the Wateree River in the Eastover community. The main house was constructed some time in the late 1800s. The canal irrigation system and mill pond, dug by slaves on the plantation, was one of the first in the state. The tenant house, carriage house, overseer's house, slave cabins, mill building, blacksmith shop, and lodge still remain. The Goodwill Baptist Church is located near this plantation site.

Zion Baptist Church, Daughter of Zion Baptist Church, St. Thomas Episcopal Church, and Antioch AME Zion were all strongholds and beacons of light in the Eastover area.

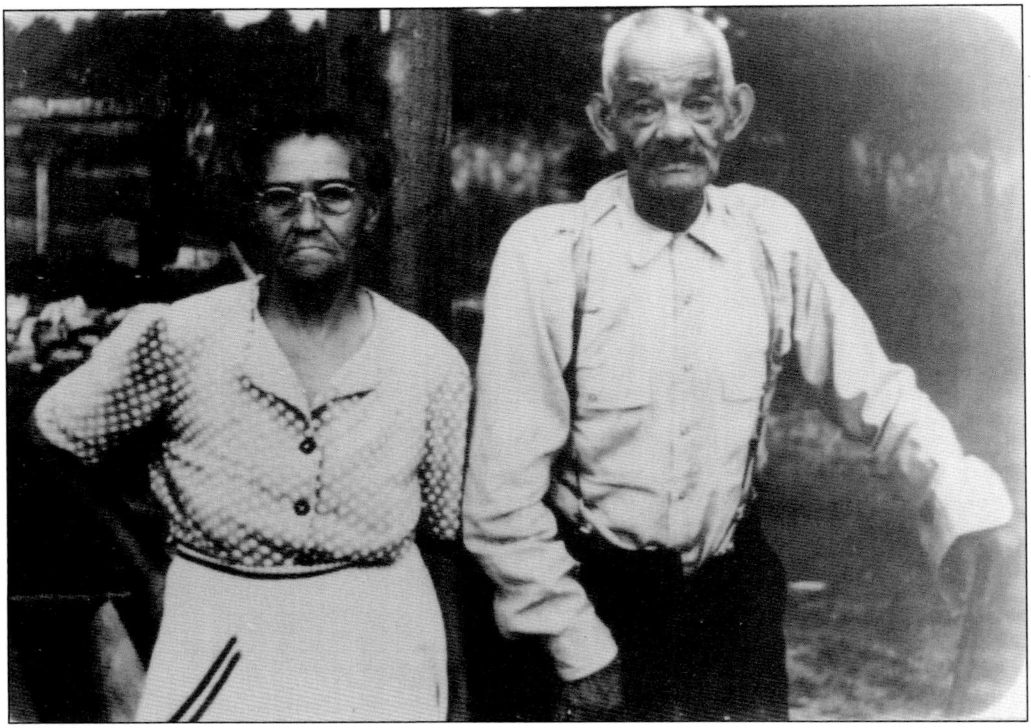

Jesse House is a descendant of plantation owner Jesse House, born in 1820 in Lower Richland. He was the son of Powell and Elizabeth House of Eastover. Pictured here, the younger Jesse was born in 1871. The House families lived on a large farm off Chain Gang Road. Many of the descendants of Jesse and Annie House still live in South Carolina and in various states. (Allen House.)

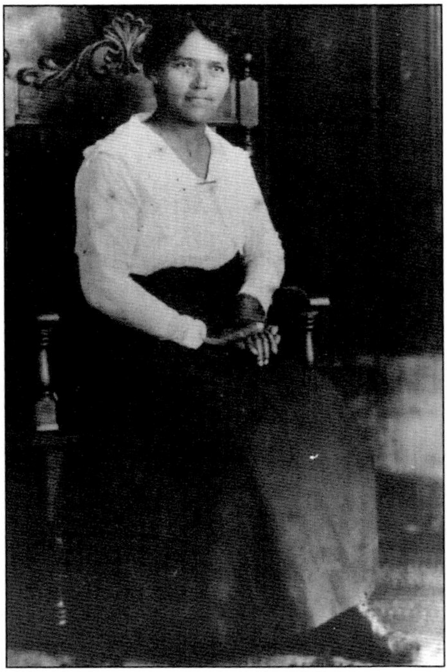

Annie House was born in 1870 and grew up in Eastover. She later married Jesse House. Their children were William "Bill" House, Lee, Louisa, Frank, John, Amy, and Elise. Jesse and Annie were members of Red Hill Baptist Church. Annie, a product of mixed parentage, worked alongside her husband on the farm in the Eastover area. (Allen House.)

Robert House was 1 of 10 children born to William House and Lillie Young House. William's grandfather Powell was one of two sons born to plantation owner Jesse House and Jane Boykin, a mulatto housekeeper from Camden. Powell's great-grandson Robert, who is pictured here, grew to be 6 feet 7 inches tall. Robert and his wife, Sarah Reese House, had one son, Allen Johnson House. (Allen House.)

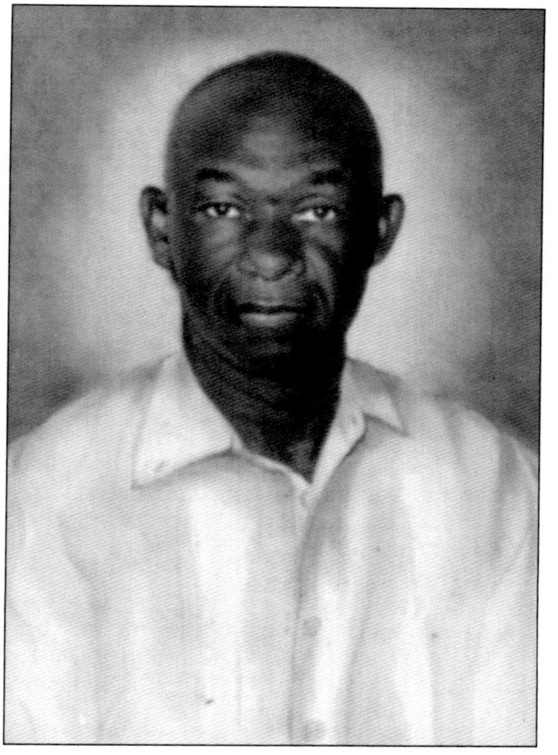

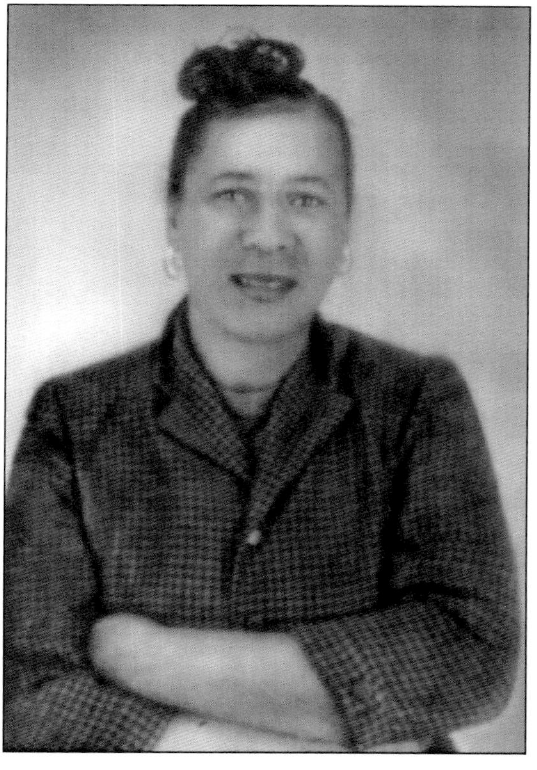

Sarah Reese was born in 1913. She was the daughter of Sampson and Lula Reese of Eastover. Her siblings were Jacob, Benjamin, Adel, Sampson, Edward, Josephine, Ruth, and Elizabeth. When Sarah became of age, she married Robert House, also of Eastover. They were members of Red Hill Baptist Church in Gadsden. (Allen House.)

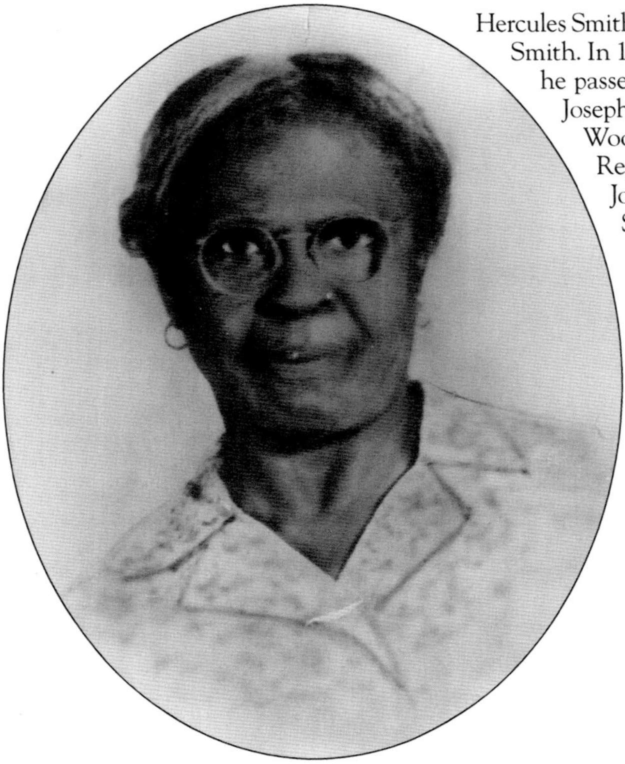

Hercules Smith Jr. was the son of Hercules and Mollie Smith. In 1891, as a student at Benedict Institute, he passed the exam to teach third grade. He, Joseph Sherman Collins, and Hampton W. Woodard represented Eastover in the 1895 Republican Constitutional Convention. Joseph Sherman Collins married Hercules Smith Jr.'s sister, Rinah. He operated a store and a cotton gin located on their 900-acre farm. Rinah is pictured here. (Billie Woodard.)

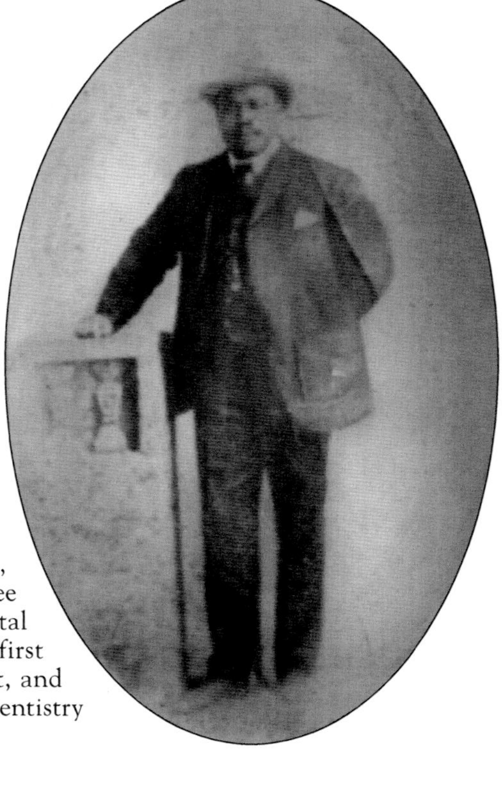

Joseph Sherman Collins became Eastover's first African American postmaster, and he also farmed corn, soybeans, rye, and barley. Joseph and Rinah Collins of Eastover had one son, Arthur Joseph, who was born in 1889. He earned a bachelor's degree from Claflin University and a doctorate of dental surgery from Howard University in 1913. His first dentist office was located at 1510 Main Street, and he worked on the family farm in between his dentistry appointments. (Billie Woodard.)

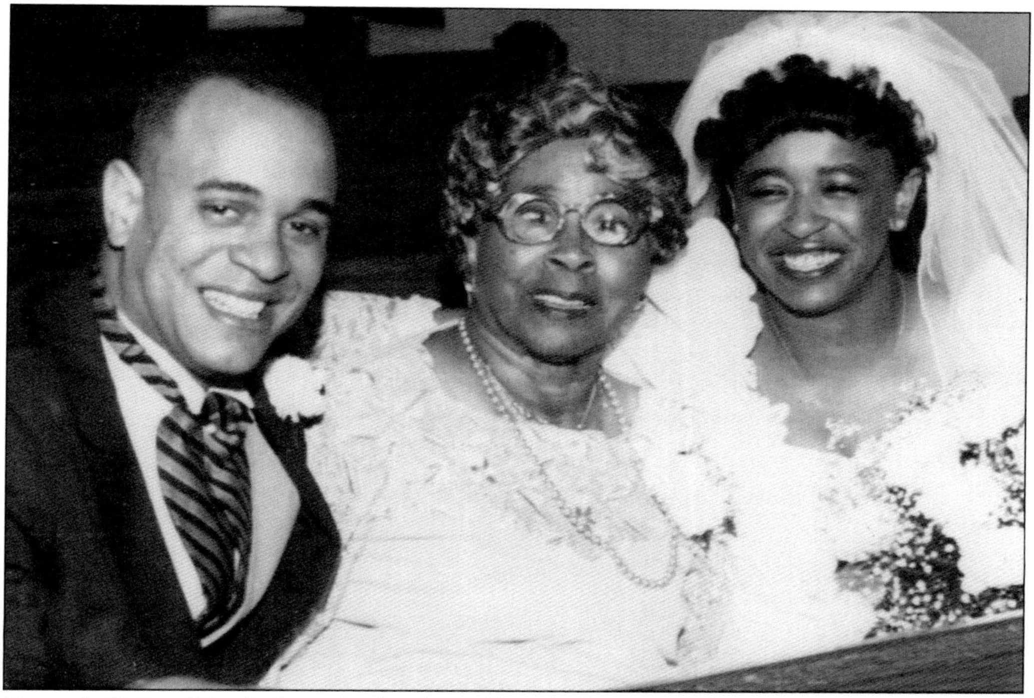

Gertrude Collins Woodard was the daughter of Joseph Sherman Collins and Rinah Smith Collins. She became a school teacher in Eastover. She married Hampton Woodard, and together they lived on a diversified 500-acre farm that included goats, cattle, pigs, and poultry. Her son Joseph Woodard inherited the farm, which became designated as a Century Farm by the South Carolina Department of Agriculture. (Billie Woodard.)

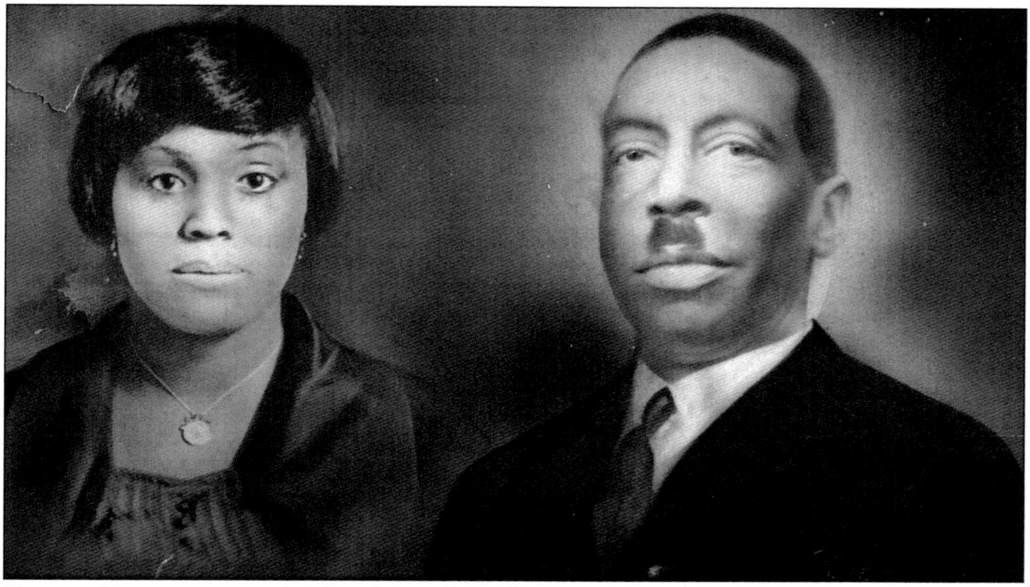

Katie Collins Scott was the daughter of Joseph and Rinah Collins. She attended schools in Richland County and completed the requirements in college to become a teacher. Katie married Lindsey Scott and taught in the Webber School until her retirement. (Billie Woodard.)

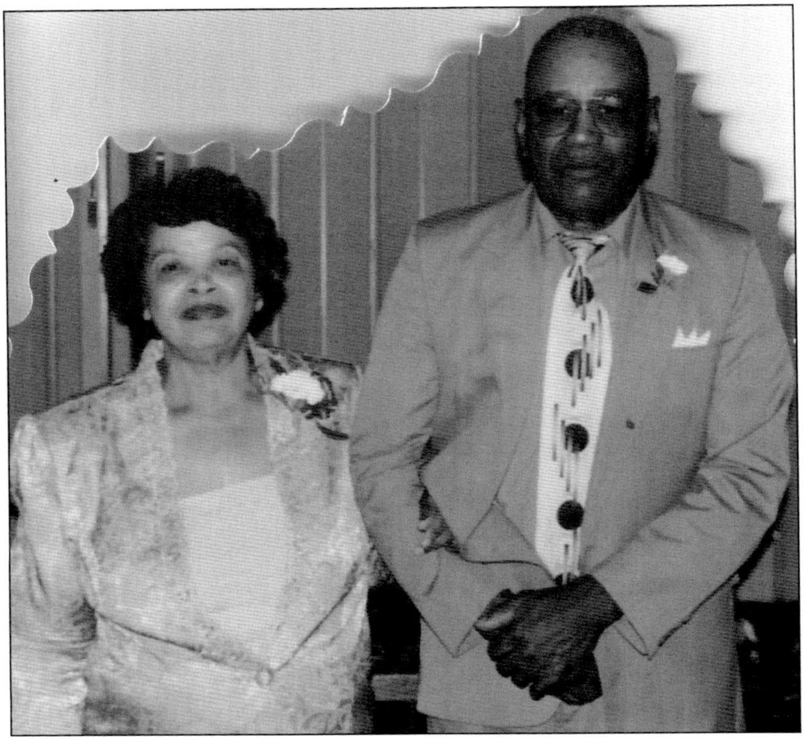

Joseph C. Woodard, son of Hampton Woodard and Gertrude C. Woodard, was born in 1931. He met his wife, Billie, after a tour of duty in the army. She was a student at Allen University. They became teachers in the Eastover and Hopkins Schools while maintaining the farm that had been in the Collins family for over 120 years. (Billie Woodard.)

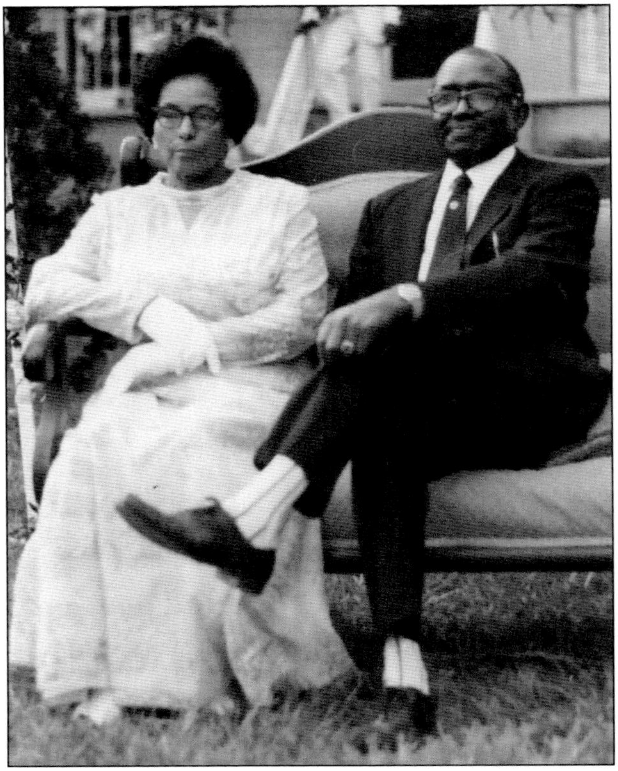

Rev. Isaac Bartley Butler became the pastor of the Daughter of Zion Baptist Church in Eastover while he was teaching at the Texas School in nearby Lugoff. It was here that he met and married Emma Angeline Harris. He began preaching in 1934 and served three other churches: Siloam Baptist Church in Congaree, Pleasant Grove Baptist Church in Gadsden, and St. Mark Baptist Church in Columbia. Reverend Butler served as the educational, agricultural, and religious leader in the development of his community. (Mary B. Walker.)

Emma Angeline Harris Butler was one of the state's most outstanding educators and community leaders. She was the daughter of Sam and Alice Harris of Eastover. After she graduated from Benedict College, she taught at Gum Springs School and later at Crossroads Elementary School for 41 years. She provided the inspiration for Emma Butler Tents, an organization that helps to feed the hungry, cares for the sick and aged, and provides scholarships for students. (Mary B. Walker.)

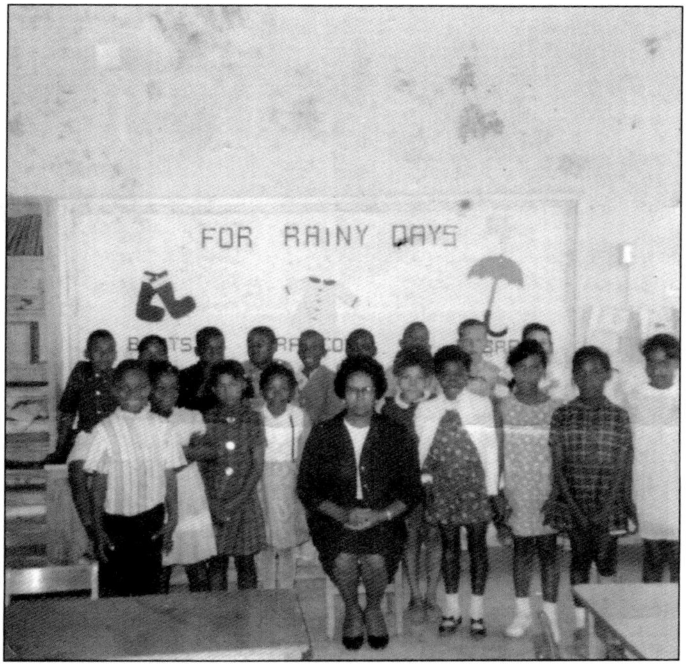

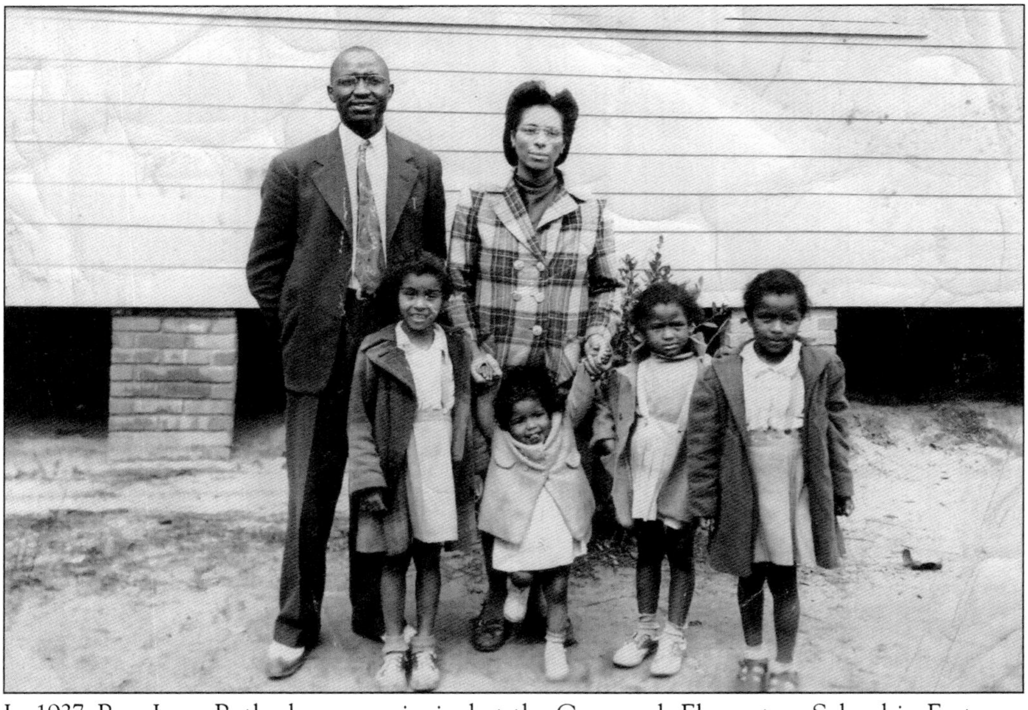

In 1937, Rev. Isaac Butler became principal at the Crossroads Elementary School in Eastover. Reverend Butler was also active in community activities, including the Farm Bureau of South Carolina, 4-H Clubs, adult education programs, improving race relations, and early registration campaigns for black voters in the South, in addition to preaching the gospel for over 60 years. (Mary B. Walker.)

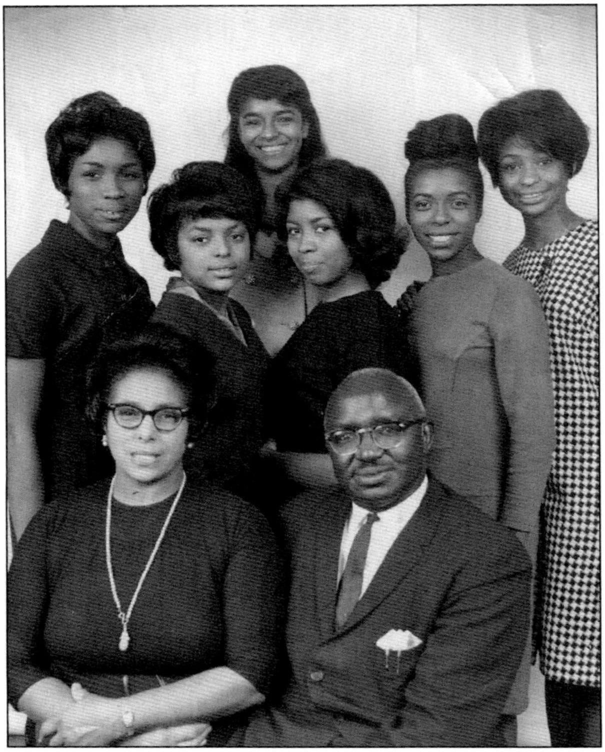

Angeline Butler (third row, center) was one of six daughters of Rev. Isaac and Emma Butler. She entered Fisk University, where she was immersed in music and the civil rights movement. The beginning of her national exposure to show business came in 1962. She performed on the NBC *Bell Telephone Hour*, CBS *Camera Three*, Johnny Carson's *Tonight Show*, the *Dick Cavett Show*, the *Steve Allen Show*, and other variety shows. She worked with Duke Ellington in the Sacred Music Concerts during the early 1970s. After receiving a master of arts degree in ethnomusicology, she became one of the founders of the Martin Luther King Jr. Museum at Crenshaw High School in Los Angeles. (Mary B. Walker.)

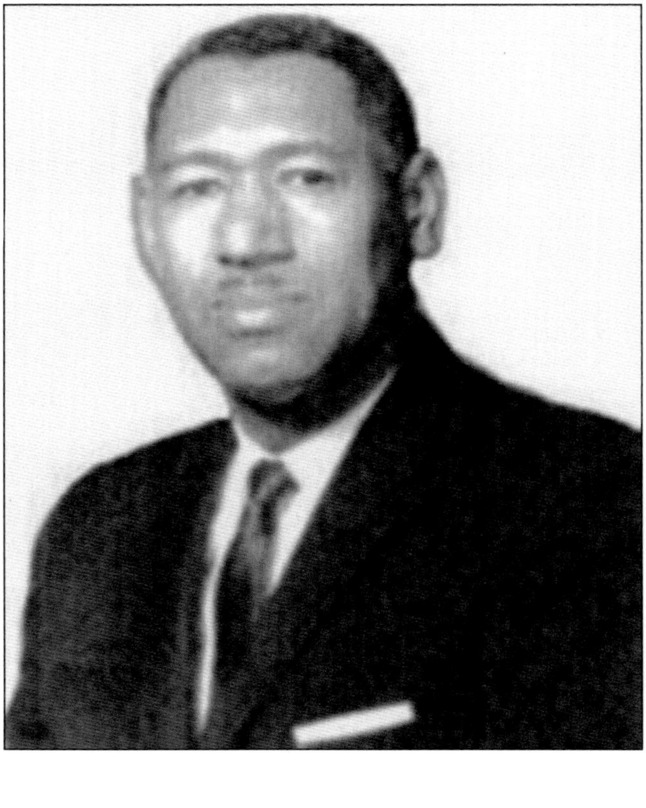

Lewis C. Dowdy, a native of Eastover, became the first chancellor of North Carolina A&T University in 1972. He was inaugurated the sixth president of North Carolina A&T in 1964. In 1951, Dowdy joined the faculty as instructor of education and director of student teaching. Lewis C. Dowdy graduated from Allen University with his bachelor of arts degree, received his master of arts degree from Indiana University, and earned his doctorate of education degree from Indiana University. (Allen Dowdy.)

Mayor Lewis N. Scott (1938–1995) was born and educated in Eastover. In 1972, he became the first African American elected to the office of mayor in a Richland County municipality. He served a total of six terms as mayor. During his first term in office, he created the annual Eastover Parade and Festival for his beloved hometown. (Neal-Scott family collection.)

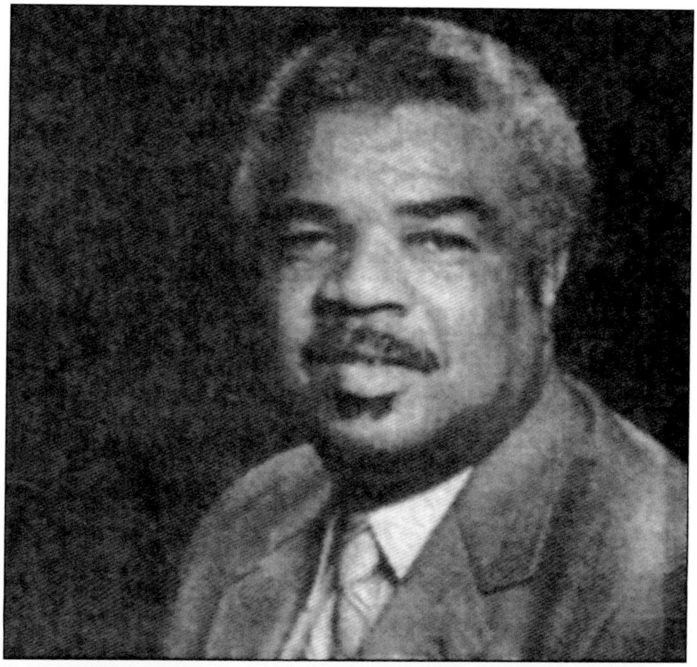

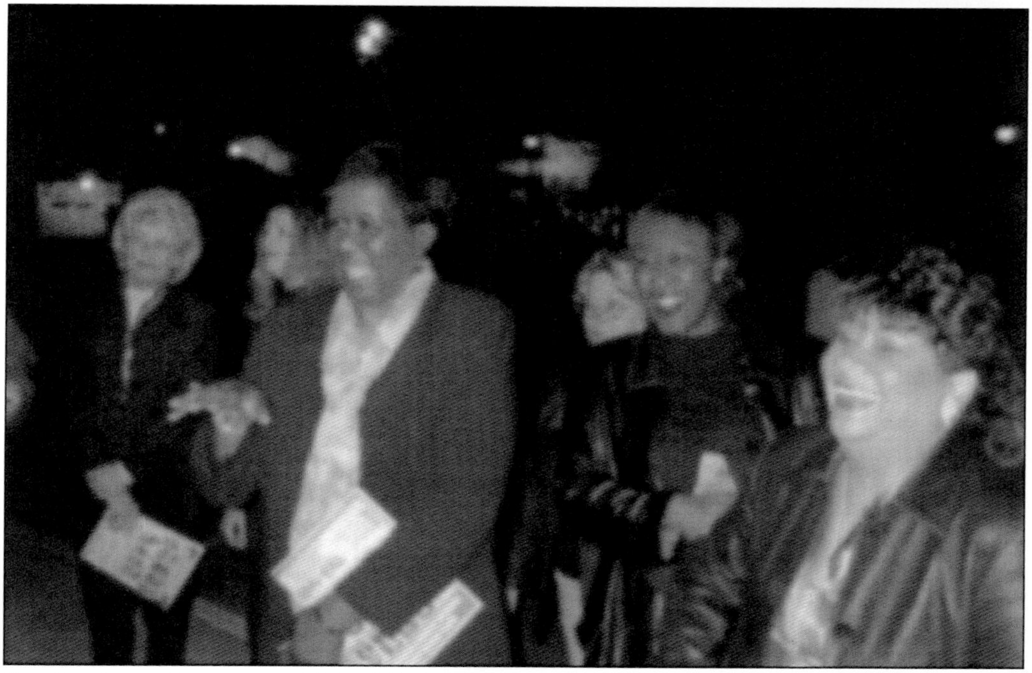

Bernice Green Scott was the 7th of 11 children on a family farm in Lower Richland. Scott began her career in public service as an assistant to the court administrator, county ombudsman, records clerk in the county treasurer's office, tax collector, and an assistant to the clerk of council for Richland County. These work experiences combined to propel her into the role of the first African American elected to the council under the single-member district plan in 1988. She later became the first African American to chair Richland County Council. (Bernice G. Scott.)

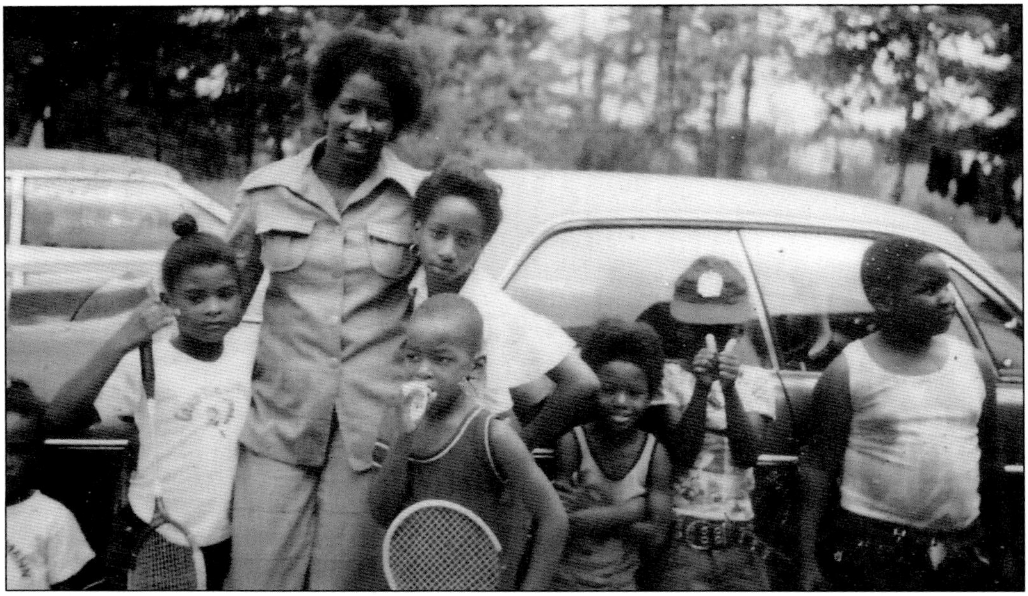

A concurrent resolution was adopted in January 2009 commending Bernice Scott for her many contributions to her community and for her untiring efforts to establish good government at the local level. Some of her civic contributions include being a member of the Central Midlands Regional Planning Council; vice chairman of the transportation committee; member of the Richland County Administration and Finance Committees; member of the Soil and Water Conservation Board; and chairman of the board of directors for the Richland Community Health Care Association. (Bernice G. Scott.)

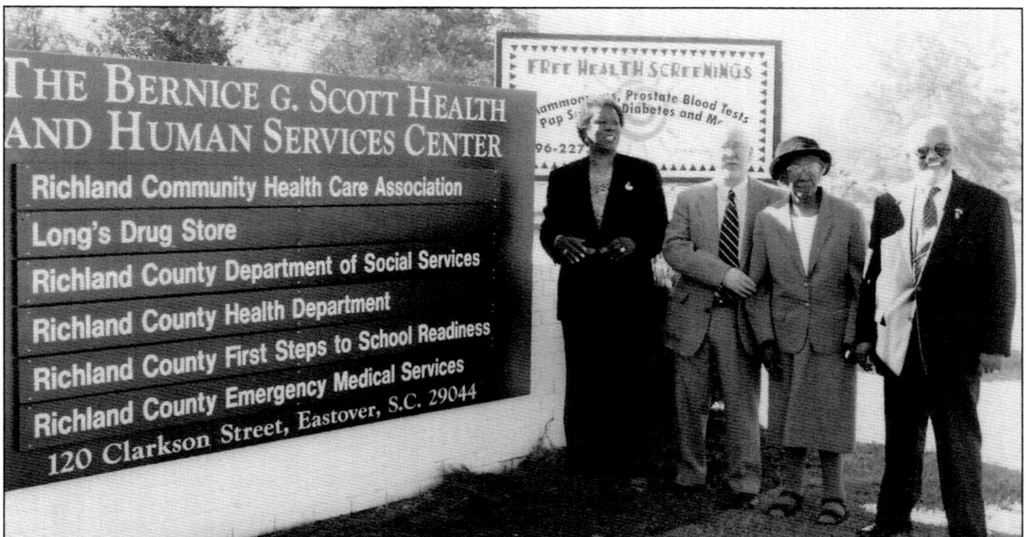

The Lower Richland Health Center, located in the city of Eastover, was renamed in honor of Bernice Green Scott in 2004. She was instrumental in keeping the health center open in this section of Lower Richland. She has also worked tirelessly to implement the master drainage plan in Gadsden and Eastover; to obtain sewer service in the communities of Arthurtown, Little Camden, and Taylors; and to obtain fire protection in the rural areas of the county. (Bernice G. Scott.)

Jacob Stroyer published his autobiography in 1885 with details about his family and their lives in South Carolina on the plantation of Col. M. R. Singleton, now known as the Kensington Mansion. His father was born in Sierra Leone, Africa, and sold into slavery. After the emancipation, many of his family members remained in Lower Richland. Joseph Stroy, a direct descendant, became a barber and was elected Hopkins magistrate. (Barber family collection.)

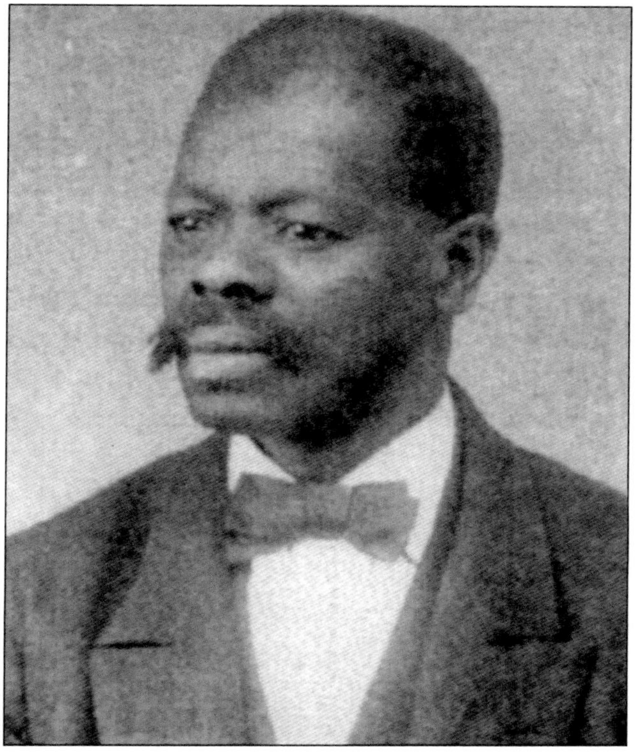

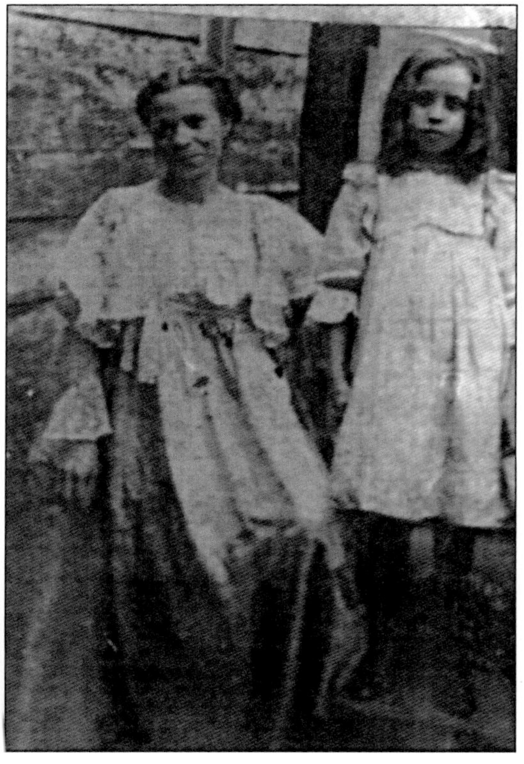

Carrie Sims was born in 1878 to James and Martha Green Sims, ex-slaves from the Elm Savannah plantation. She lived across from Joel R. Adams's Gadsden plantation and worked there. Carrie bore four children by the plantation owner's nephew, Jim Uriah Adams; they were Martha, Theresa, Harry, and Jason. There is controversial lore that she was poisoned because of that interracial relationship; Carrie died days after her last child's birth. (*Almost Forgotten* by Brenda Clarkson Turpeau.)

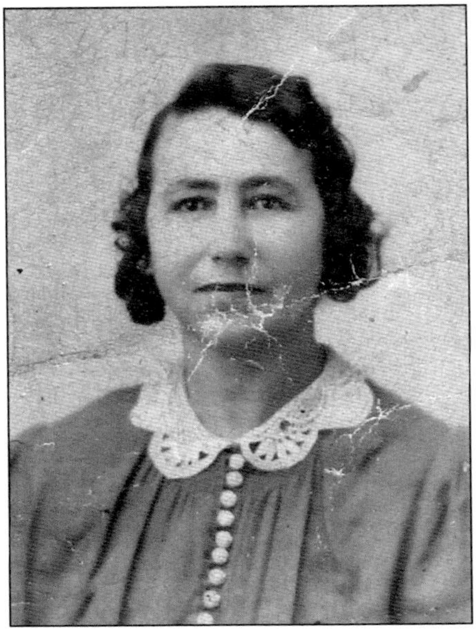

Martha Adams Scott was born in 1901 to Carrie Sims and Jim U. Adams, a Gadsden plantation owner family member. She was orphaned at the age of nine and often told family members of how she climbed on a wooden box to prepare her dying mother's last meal on a cast iron stove. Martha and her siblings then lived with her paternal aunt and uncle, Sarah and Samuel Williams. (Neal-Scott family collection.)

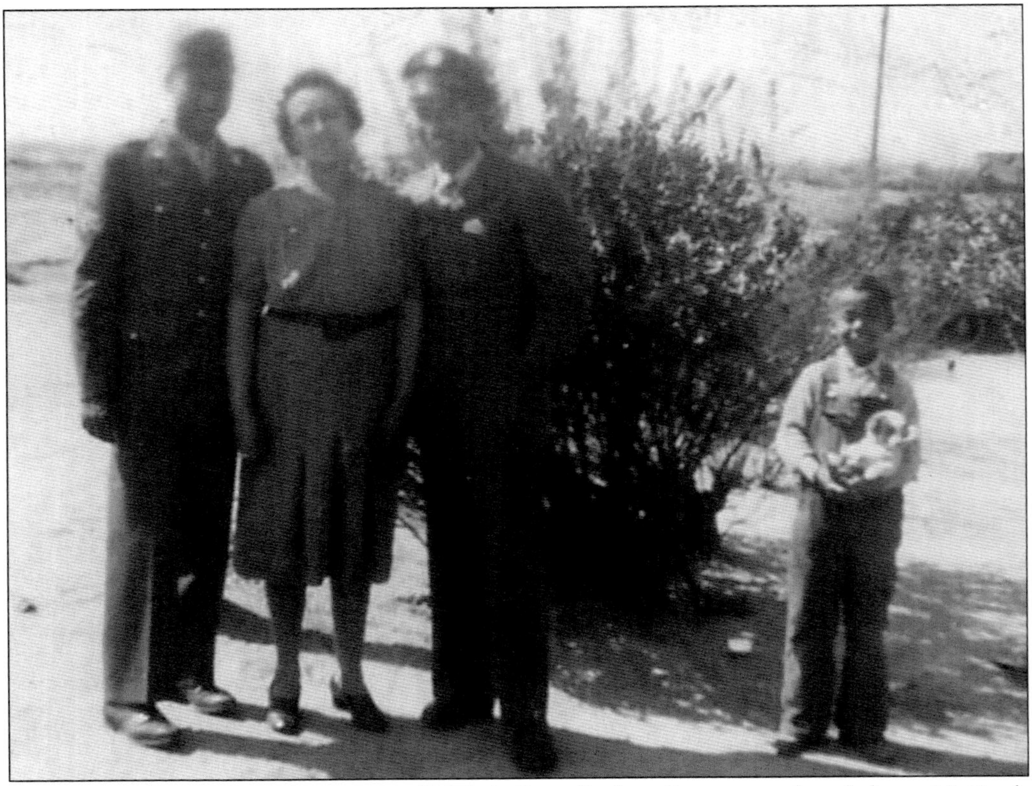

At 18 years old, Martha Adams married Blakely Scott Sr. from Eastover and settled on a McCords Ferry Road farm, which was deeded to them by Blakely's father, Benjamin. Their 15 children were Blakely Jr., Sarah, James, Rachel, Robert, Susie, Alma, Walter, Johnnetta, Myrtle, Harry, Ulysses, Herman, Timothy, and Anthony. This photograph shows Martha with sons Blakely Jr. and Walter, who both were in the military, and young Anthony. (Neal-Scott family collection.)

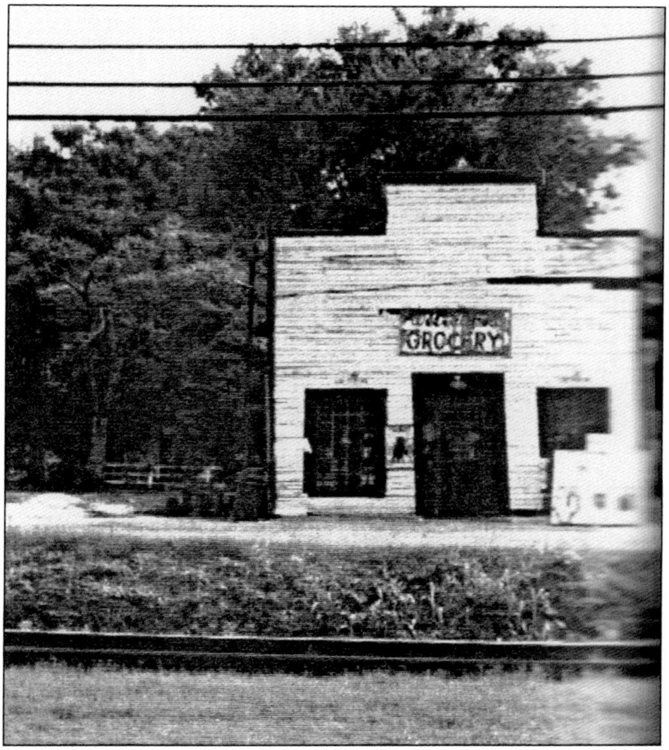

Benjamin Scott was born in 1866 and was the son of Stephen and Viney Garvin Scott, Whitehall plantation ex-slaves. Ben married Dorcas Weston in 1892. He was a Mount Zion Baptist founding member and deacon and known for "raising" the spiritual, "All that Come with A Sweet Good Will." This photograph is of Main Street butcher shop, general store, and upstairs weekend dance hall owned by Benjamin and son Jeff. Dancing admission was 25¢. (*Almost Forgotten* by Brenda Clarkson Turpeau.)

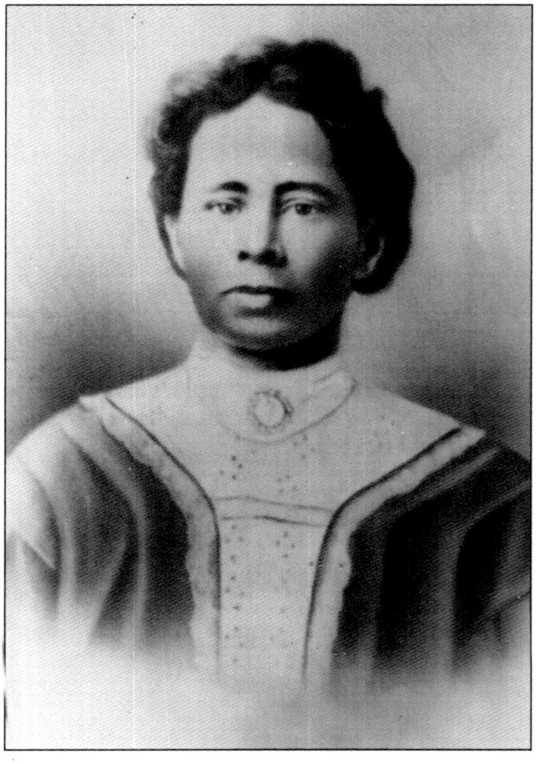

Dorcas Weston Scott was born around 1878. At that time, she had a sister who was a year older named Reter and a baby brother named George. Her parents were Edward and Julia Weston, both born in 1857 and who both were slaves on a Congaree plantation. Dorcas married Benjamin Scott in 1892; they owned a farm off McCords Ferry Road and had 11 children. (Neal-Scott family collection.)

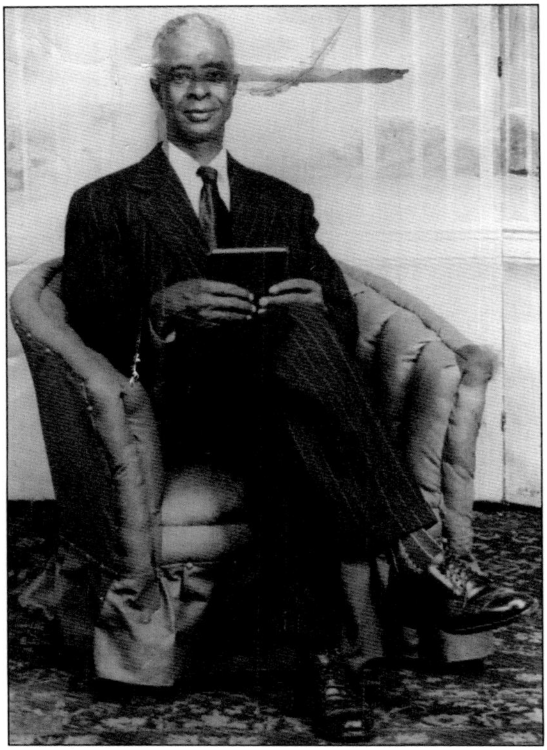

Blakely Scott Sr., born in 1896, was a son of Benjamin and Dorcas Weston Scott. His World War I army registration card shows he was a 21-year-old, unmarried laborer on his father Ben's farm. At age 23, Blakely married 18-year-old Martha Adams; they had 15 children. He acquired more land over time and operated a large and generally a self-sufficient farm. Blakely Sr. died in 1957. (Neal-Scott family collection.)

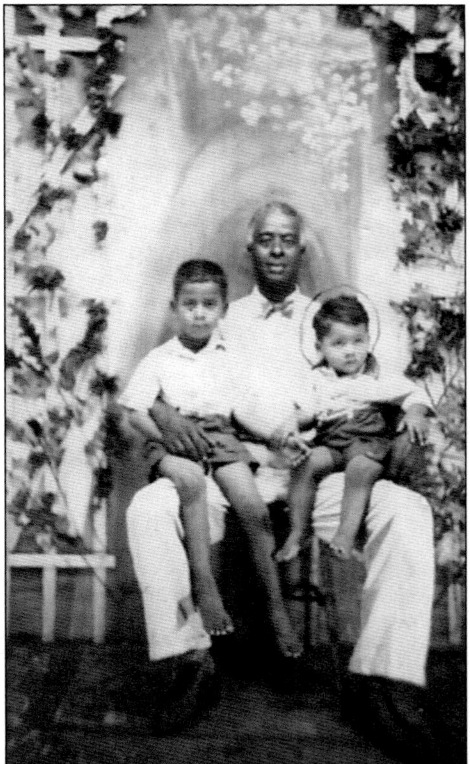

Blakely Scott Sr. is pictured with sons Anthony and Timothy. At one time, Blakely Sr. drove the school bus. One story, told by Julius Murray, recounts how Blakely Sr., who only received a fourth-grade education in a one-room school, made sure he had something to eat each morning; once provided him with a glove for playing baseball; and encouraged neighborhood children to take advantage of their opportunity for schooling. (Neal-Scott family collection.)

Deacon Blakely Scott Jr., born in 1920, was Blakely and Martha Adams Scott's first child. At age 15, he left Eastover and completed Booker Washington High School. He was a Mount Zion Baptist member and later became a deacon at Columbia's First Nazareth. He was a Democratic Convention delegate, an elections poll worker, and PTA president. He married Lillie Neal from Hopkins; they had three children: Blakely III (a reverend doctor), Deborah, and Detra. (Neal-Scott family collection.)

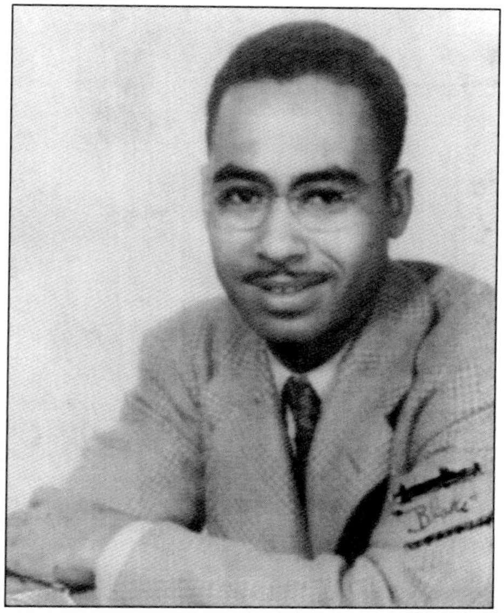

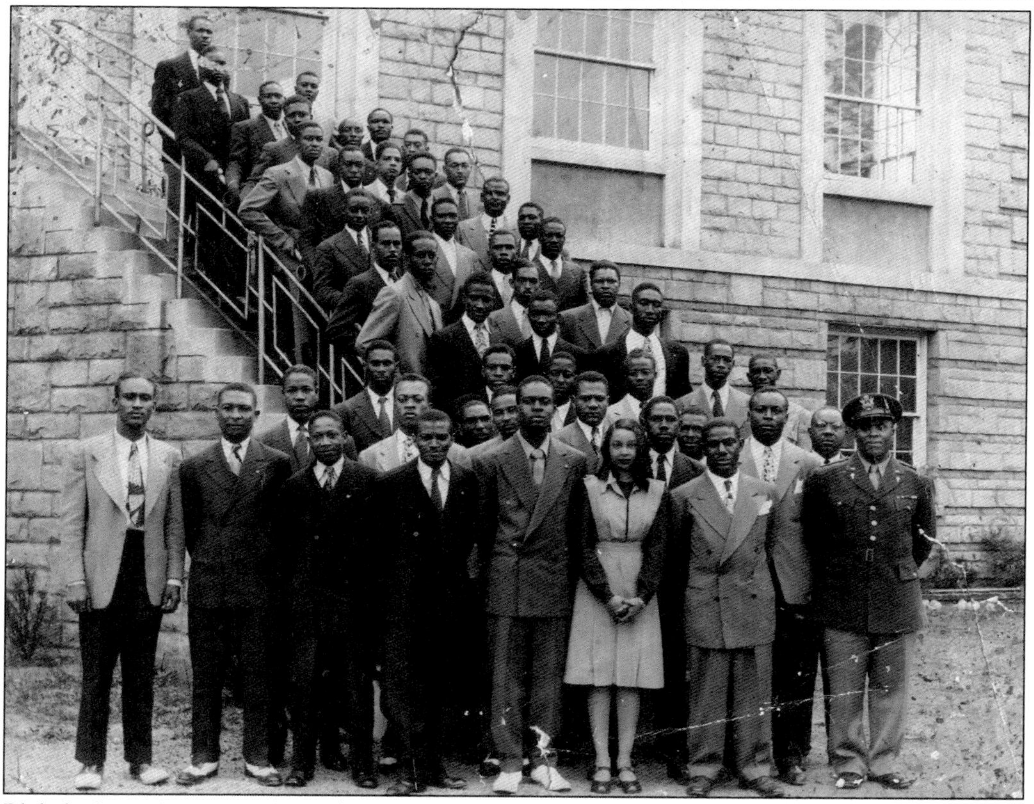

Blakely Scott Jr. returned to complete Allen University after serving in the U.S. Army during World War II. He obtained his degree in 1946 and is pictured among the graduates standing on the steps of the Joseph Simon Flipper Library, one of several campus buildings listed on the National Register of Historic Places. Blakely Jr. began his career in Eastover as St. Phillip's principal and teacher and eventually retired from the postal service in 1977. (Neal-Scott family collection.)

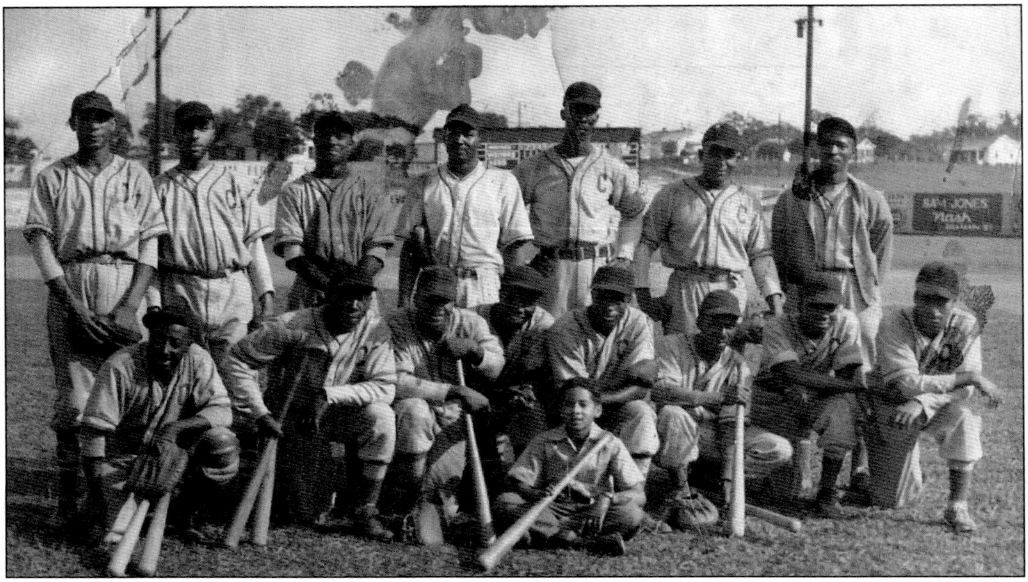

Blakely Scott Jr. was a prolific pitcher known as "Lefty" and played semi-professional baseball for the Columbia Red Caps/All Stars, an African American baseball team. Despite the racial climate, Blakely Jr. was offered a contract with the Cincinnati Reds, and he explained that he declined for the sake of maintaining his family's stability. As a little league baseball coach, Blakely Jr. influenced the lives of many young men of the Edgewood community. (Neal-Scott family collection.)

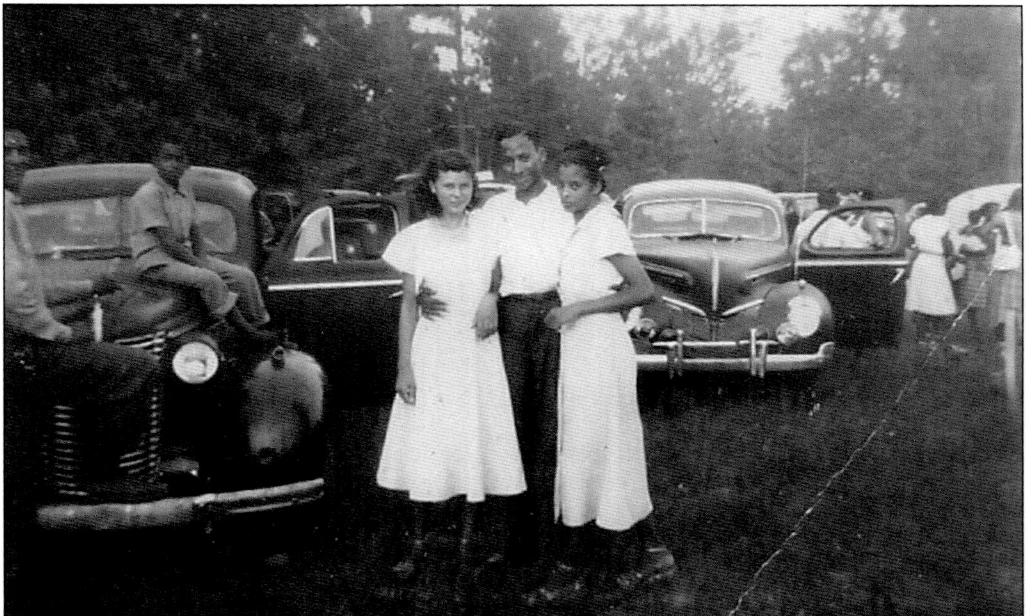

Three children of Blakely Sr. and Martha Adams Scott are pictured. They are Ulysses (sitting on car), James (center), and Susie (right). Susie married Lawrence Merriweather and moved to New Jersey. Ulysses also moved to New Jersey and became a partner in Scott's barbershop and a minister. James married Holly Simons of Eastover, moved to Columbia, and retired from Fort Jackson. Others are unidentified friends. (Neal-Scott family collection.)

Pictured is Joshua DeVeaux's tombstone. It is located at St. Phillip AME Church. Joshua was born into slavery in 1831, died at the age 92 in 1923, and was one of Jim and Tina's children. After emancipation, DeVeaux children Caleb and Ephraim assumed the Neal plantation owner's name, migrated, and purchased land. Six siblings kept the DeVeaux name. Tina and sons Joshua and Peter purchased Hickory Hill plantation parcels. (Photograph by Deborah Scott Brooks.)

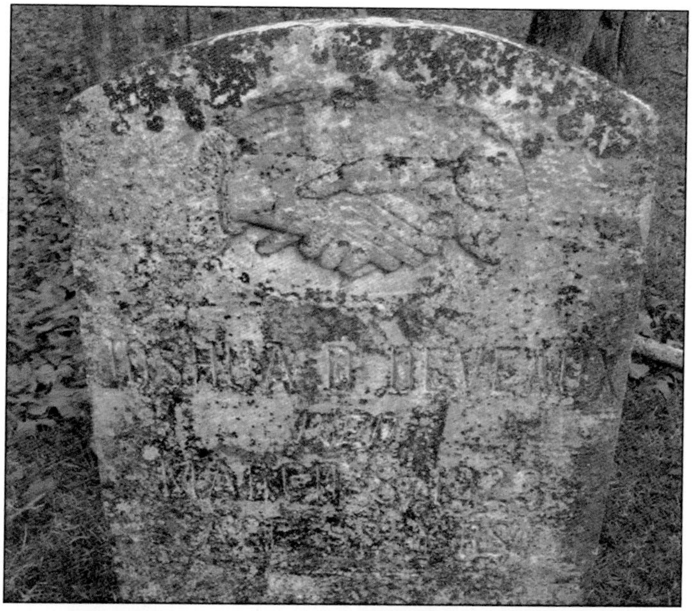

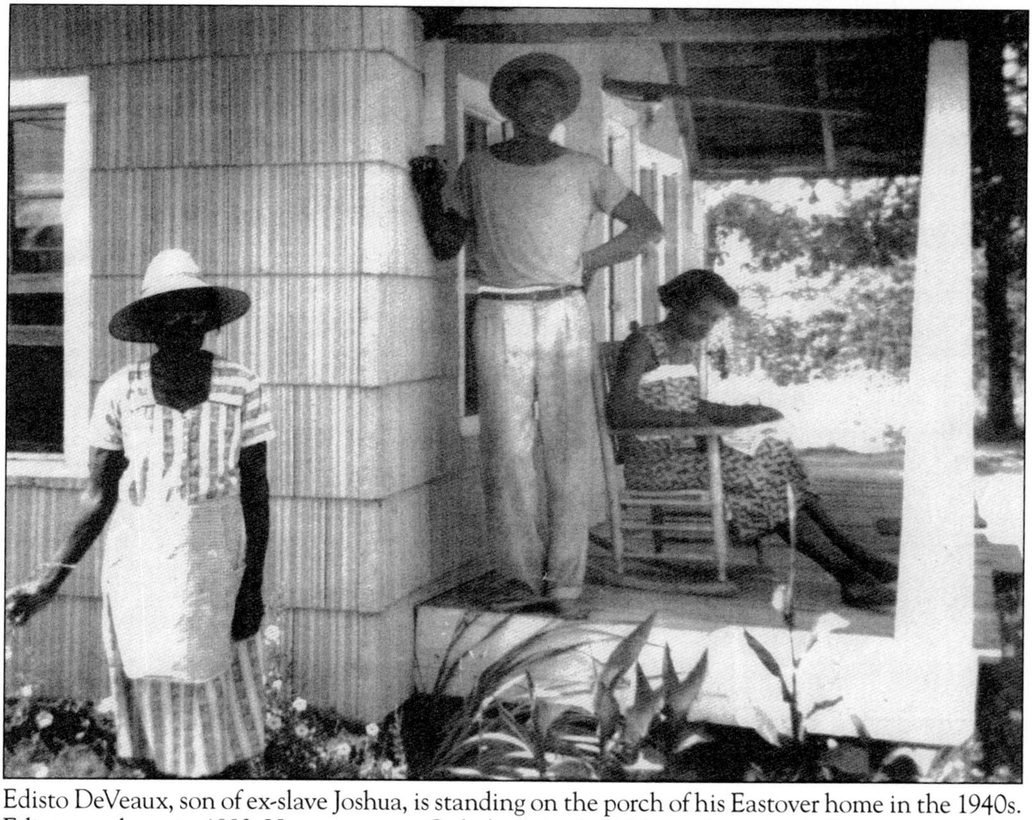

Edisto DeVeaux, son of ex-slave Joshua, is standing on the porch of his Eastover home in the 1940s. Edisto was born in 1893. His spouse was Ophelia Pringle DeVeaux (standing). Also pictured is an unidentified daughter. Many DeVeaux family members still reside on the original land and are employed in diverse occupations, including farming. (Alton DeVeaux.)

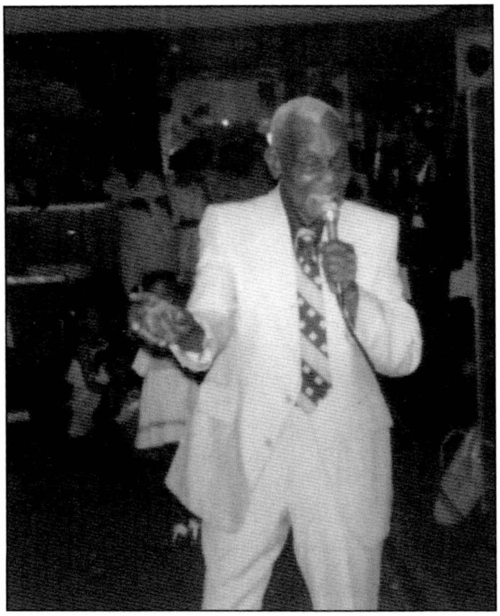

Ephraim DeVeaux was born in 1880. He was the son of ex-slave Joshua DeVeaux and was named for his uncle Ephraim Neal. He was an active member of the NAACP and St. Phillip's AME Church until his death at 107 years old. The DeVeaux family is traced back to Jim and Tina, who were slaves transported from Virginia. They were settled on John Neale's plantation in Kingville. (Neal-Scott family collection.)

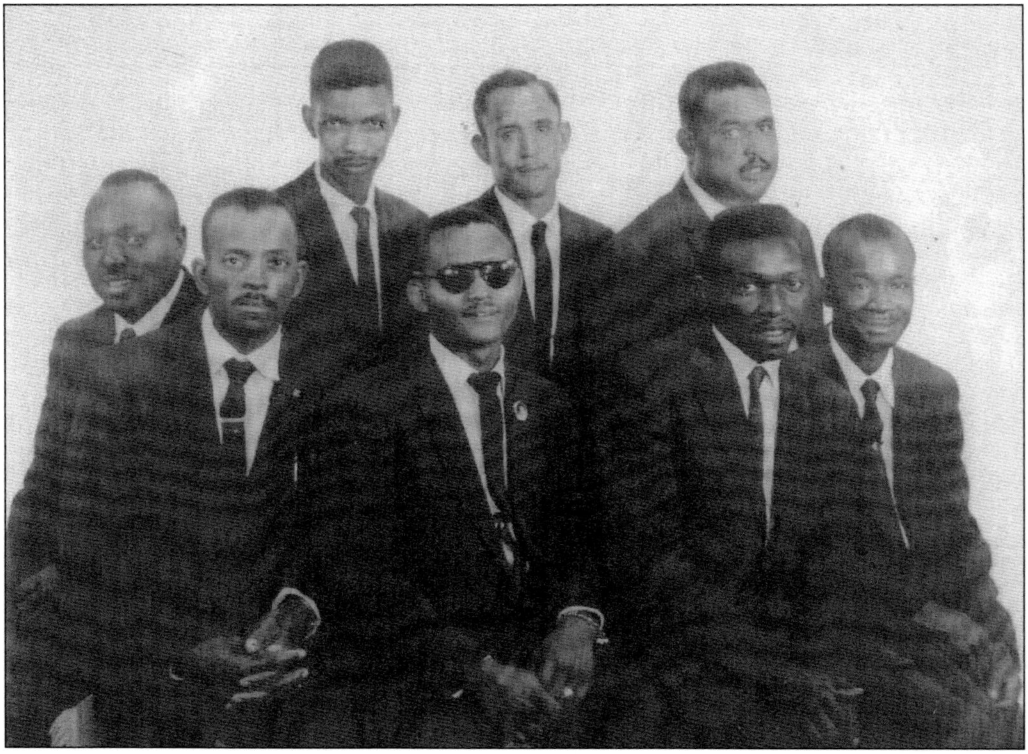

The Carolina Gospel Singers of Eastover were organized in the early 1950s. Along with the Rising Stars, this group performed at churches in Richland, Sumter, and Kershaw Counties. Their talent and popularity led to several gospel recordings. From left to right are (first row) Thomas Gunter Sr., Willie Kelly, Jessie Gilmore, David Cohens Sr., and Colie Miller Sr; (second row) John Sims, Willie Wilson, and Richard Simons. (Thomas Gunter Jr.)

Lottie Simons, born in 1896, was the daughter of Ozier and Julia Taylor McBeth. She was married to Rev. Gaddie Lee Simons Jr. and was the mother of 10 children and 3 stepchildren. She became a licensed midwife in the early 1950s and was widely known as the "Doctor of Hope." In her community, she was a founder of the Helping Hands Club and a charter member of the Eastern Stars of Lower Richland. In 1978, she was recognized by the governor as South Carolina Senior Citizen of the Year. (Zack and Levola Taylor.)

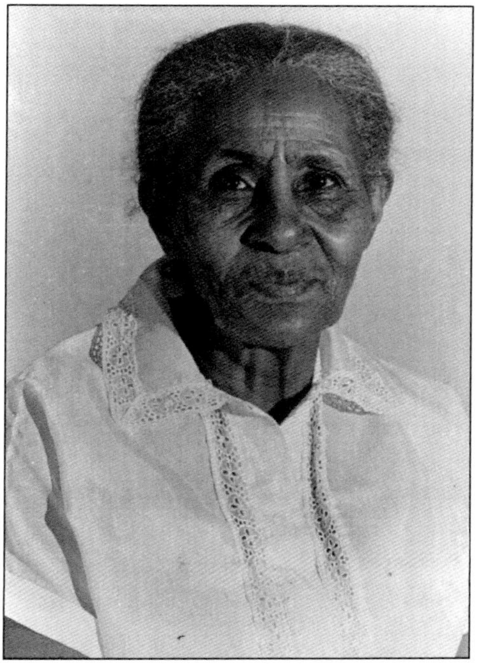

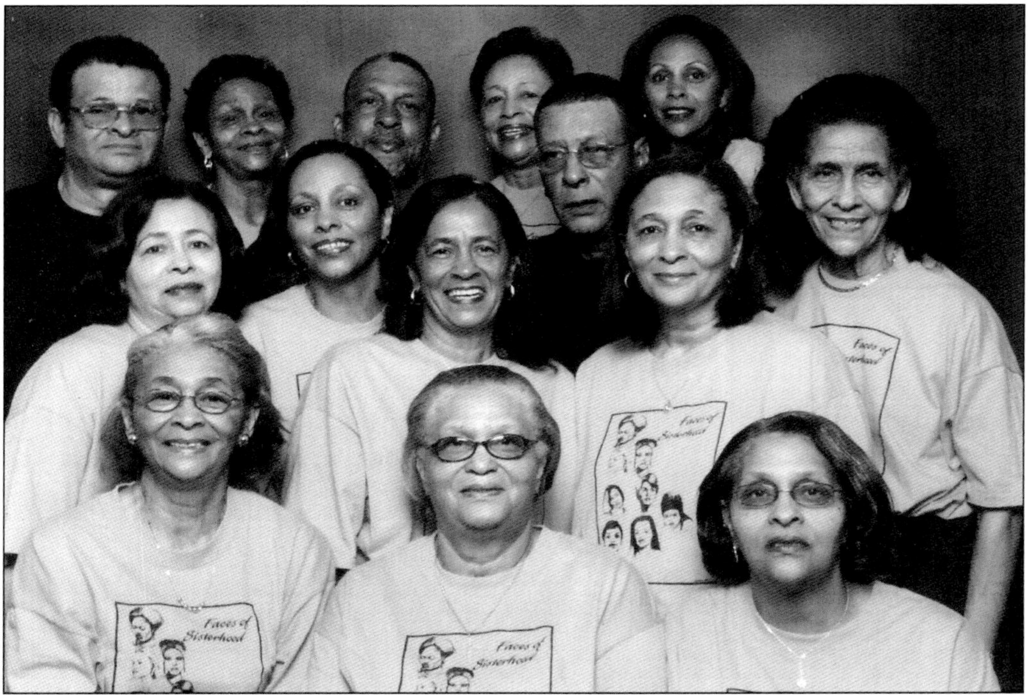

Constinee Simons Jr. was a civil service employee and skilled carpenter. He was a board member of the Crossroad Community Center, District 5 Community Development Committee, and Crossroad Masonic Lodge. The children of Constinee and Christobel Chavis Simons are Constinee Jr., Donald, Curtis, Holly, Juanita, Mary, Gracie, Barbara, Paulette, Glenda, Levola, Catherine, Deborah, Carolyn, and Brenda. (Zack and Levola Taylor.)

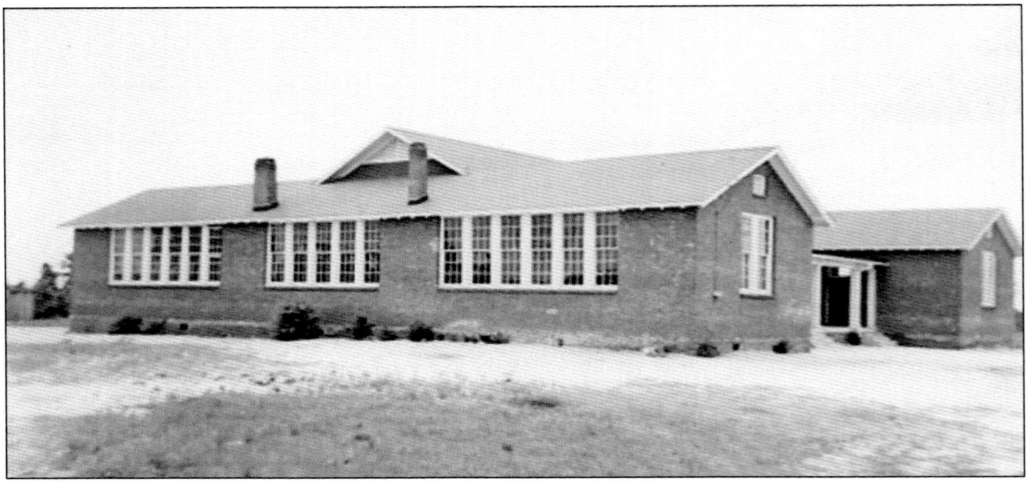

Webber School was founded in 1907 and built on land donated by brothers William and Paul Webber Sr. Mamie Webber was the first principal. Paul Webber Sr. was a farmer and businessman, owning a large hotel across from the state capitol in Columbia. Paul Jr. taught economics at South Carolina State College, served with the South Carolina Governor's Office, and married Clemmie Embly, who became a South Carolina Mother of the Year. (Barber family collection.)

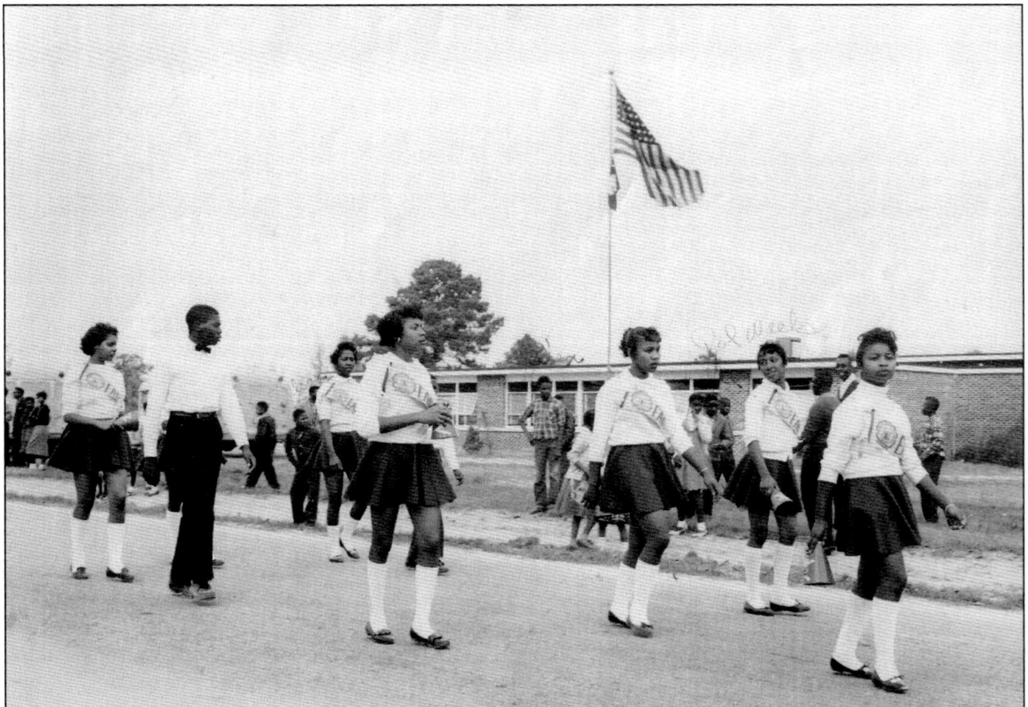

Webber High School students were always invited to participate in the annual Hopkins High School homecoming parade on Clarkson Road in Hopkins. Elaborate preparations were made to decorate floats and feature cheerleaders and homecoming queens. Some early teachers were Frank Adams, Margaret Anderson, a Mr. Bracey, a Mrs. Brandenburg, Eva Cheeseboro, a Mrs. Fitzpatrick, Ed Hall, Joseph Jackson, a Mr. Nelson, Margaret Patterson, and Carolyn Trezvant. (Barber family collection.)

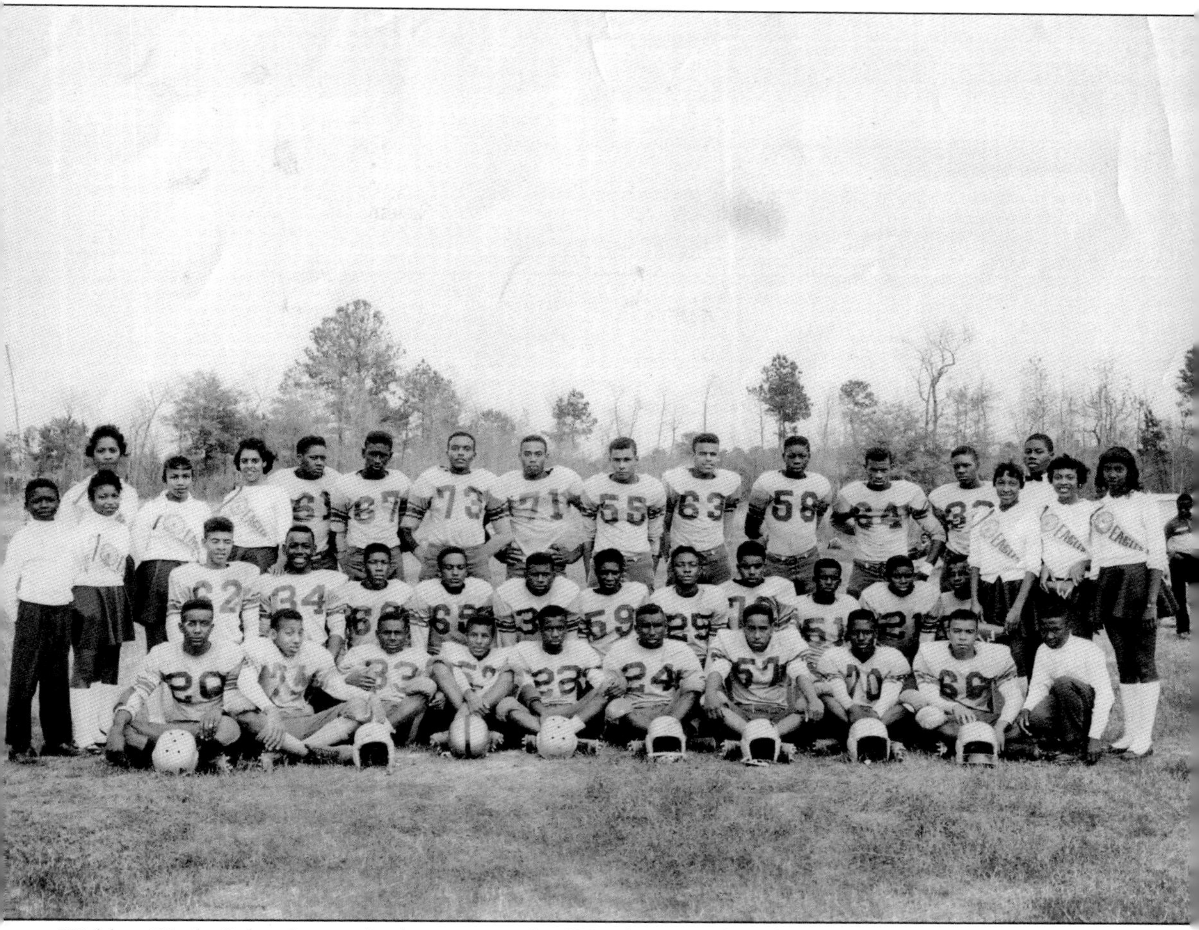

Webber High School was the biggest rival of Hopkins High School in any athletic event. Homecoming games drew hundreds of supporters from each school. Webber burned in 1929, and classes were held at Mount Zion Church until the new and larger school was completed. (Barber family collection.)

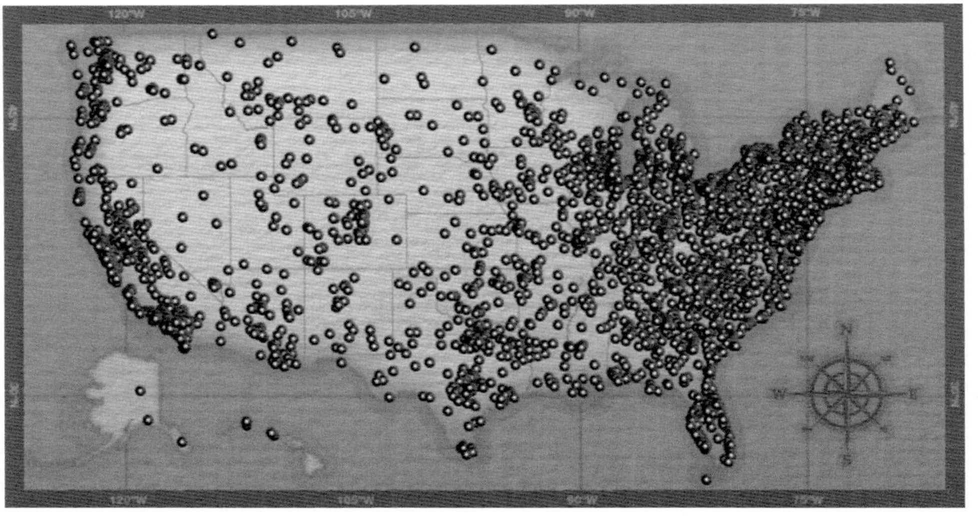